The Way We Argue Now

The Way We Argue Now

A STUDY IN THE CULTURES OF THEORY

Amanda Anderson

PRINCETON UNIVERSITY PRESS

PRINCETON AND OXFORD

Copyright © 2006 by Princeton University Press

Published by Princeton University Press, 41 William Street, Princeton, New Jersey 08540

In the United Kingdom: Princeton University Press, 3 Market Place, Woodstock, Oxfordshire OX20 1SY

Library of Congress Cataloging-in-Publication Data

Anderson, Amanda, 1960–
    The way we argue now : a study in the cultures of theory / Amanda Anderson.
      p.   cm.
    Includes bibliographical references and index.
    ISBN-13: 978-0-691-11403-3 (alk. paper)—ISBN-13: 978-0-691-11404-0
(pbk. : alk. paper)
      ISBN-10: 0-691-11403-X (alk. paper)—ISBN-10: 0-691-11404-8 (pbk. : alk. paper)
      1. Theory (Philosophy).   2. Reasoning.   3. Discussion.   4. Debates and debating.
I. Title.

  B842.A53 2006
  140—dc22   2005048814

British Library Cataloging-in-Publication Data is available

This book has been composed in Sabon

Printed on acid-free paper. ∞

pup.princeton.edu

Printed in the United States of America

10 9 8 7 6 5 4 3 2 1

For Allen

Contents

Acknowledgments

MANY FRIENDS AND COLLEAGUES have read and responded to the essays contained in this book, or to talks related to them. I wish especially to thank James Eli Adams, Michael Bérubé, James Buzard, Sharon Cameron, Jerry Christensen, Bill Connolly, Jonathan Culler, Rita Felski, Frances Ferguson, John Guillory, Webb Keane, George Levine, Jonathan Loesberg, Janet Lyon, Carine Mardorossian, Walter Michaels, Andrew Miller, Richard Moran, Jeff Nunokawa, Davide Panagia, Adela Pinch, Bruce Robbins, Harry Shaw, Michael Szalay, David Thomas, Irene Tucker, and Joseph Valente. I also want to thank the students in my two graduate seminars on ethos and argument at Hopkins; they embraced the topic when it was at its earliest stages of development and helped me to advance my thinking in crucial ways.

The final portions of the book were drafted during a fellowship year at the Center for the Critical Analysis of Contemporary Culture at Rutgers University. I thank especially George Levine and Carolyn Williams for hosting a terrific year of seminars and lectures. I received acute readings of my work-in-progress by the other fellows; I thank Ed Hartmann in particular for his formal reply to my pieces. At Princeton University Press, I was fortunate in having excellent editorial guidance, and I want to thank both Mary Murrell and Hanne Winarsky. I also thank audiences at the following universities and venues: the School for Criticism and Theory at Cornell University, the English Institute at Harvard University, the University of Michigan, Princeton University, the University of Chicago, Rutgers University, the University of California-Irvine, and Northwestern University.

My family continues to provide a base of support that is both deep and wide. I thank Sara Anderson, Philip and Patricia Anderson, Helen Anderson, Howard Goodfriend, Warren and Alice Hance, and Chris and Lindsay Kosnik. I also thank my wonderful children, Jackson and Emily, for being so vividly and so assuredly themselves. As for my husband, Allen, to whom this book is dedicated, there is simply no one with whom I would rather argue, which is to say, live.

Chapter 1 originally appeared as "Debatable Performances: Restaging Contentious Feminisms," *Social Text* 54 (1998): 1–24. Copyright 1998, Duke University Press. Used by permission of the publisher. Chapter 2 originally appeared as "The Temptations of Aggrandized Agency: Feminist Histories and the Horizon of Modernity," *Victorian Studies* 43:1 (2000) 43–65. Used by permission of Indiana University Press. Chapter 3 originally appeared as "Cosmopolitanism, Universalism, and the Divided Legacies of Modernity," in Pheng Cheah and Bruce Robbins, eds., *Cosmopolitics: Thinking and Feeling Beyond the Nation* (Minneapolis: University of Minnesota Press, 1998), 265–89. Copyright 1998, University of Minnesota Press. Used by permission of the publisher. Chapter 4 originally appeared as "Universalism, Realism, and the Science of the Human," *Diacritics* 29:2 (1999): 3–17. Used by permission of Johns Hopkins University Press. Chapter 5 originally appeared as "Pragmatism and Character," *Critical Inquiry* 29:2 (2003): 282–301. Copyright 2003, University of Chicago Press. Used by permission of the publisher. Chapter 6 originally appeared as "Argument and Ethos," in Jane Gallop, ed., *Polemic: Critical or Uncritical* (New York: Routledge, 2005). Used by permission of the publisher.

The Way We Argue Now

THE WAY WE ARGUE NOW is at once diagnostic and revisionist, polemical and utopian. Through close analyses of contemporary academic debates, this collection of essays examines the governing assumptions and styles of argumentation that characterize what is broadly known as "theory" across several humanities and social science disciplines. The turn to theory dates back to the 1960s and is associated with several interrelated schools of thought, among them poststructuralism, postmodernism, deconstruction, psychoanalysis, Marxism, feminism, postcolonialism, and queer theory. These schools have profoundly influenced disciplinary methodologies and self-conceptions, and in this book I will pay especial attention to the form such influence has taken in literary studies, cultural studies, and political theory. In exploring scholarly formations and controversies associated with these approaches, this book assesses debates internal to academic culture and hopes to advance a better understanding of theory as a contested and not a unified field, one that moreover is developing in ways that recent assessments of the field, most strikingly those that have announced theory's demise, have failed to capture.[1]

At the same time, however, the book engages in an internal critique of certain tendencies within the field of theory. These essays repeatedly draw attention to the underdeveloped and often incoherent evaluative stance of contemporary theory, its inability to clearly avow the norms and values underlying its own critical programs. In particular, I contest the prevalent skepticism about the possibility or desirability of achieving reflective distance on one's social or cultural positioning. As a result of poststructuralism's insistence on the forms of finitude—linguistic, psychological, and cultural—that limit individual agency, and multiculturalism's insistence on the primacy of ascribed group identity and its accompanying perspectives, the concept of critical distance has been seriously discredited, even as it necessarily informs many of the very accounts that announce its

Habermas

---

[1] I have in mind especially Terry Eagleton's *After Theory* (New York: Basic Books, 2004), as well as the flurry of confirming reviews and write-ups it received, including one entitled, "Cultural Theorists, Start Your Epitaphs," *New York Times*, January 3, 2004. Eagleton claims not only that the era associated with names like Jacques Derrida and Roland Barthes is long past, but that what is needed is a turn to questions of morality, love, religion, death, and suffering. I will be arguing, contra Eagleton and his gleeful admirers, that theory has already to a significant extent made this turn internally. Eagleton's argument is premised on a highly selective understanding of cultural theory.

bankruptcy. The alliance between the poststructuralist critique of reason and the form of sociological reductionism that governs the politics of identity threatens to undermine the vitality of both academic and political debate insofar as it becomes impossible to explore shared forms of rationality. Given these conditions, in fact, this book might well have been called "The Way We Fail to Argue Now."[2]

To counter the tendencies of both poststructuralism and identity politics, I advance a renewed assessment of the work of philosopher Jürgen Habermas, whose interrelated theories of communicative action, discourse ethics, and democratic proceduralism have provoked continued and often dismissive critique from theorists in the fields of literary studies, cultural studies, and political theory. The book is in no way an uncritical embrace of Habermas's theory, however. Rather, it offers a renewed assessment of the notions of critical distance and procedural democracy in light of the arguments that have been waged against them. In part I do this by giving airtime to those debates in which Habermas and like-minded critics have engaged poststructuralism. But I also try to give Habermas a new hearing by showing the ways in which his theories promote an understanding of reflective distance as an achieved and lived practice, one with an intimate bearing on questions of ethos and character. Typically dismissed as impersonal, abstract, and arid, rational discourse of the kind associated with the neo-Kantianism of Habermas and his followers is often employed as a contrast to valorized ideals of embodied identities, feelings and passions, ethics and politics—in short, all the values that are seen to imbue theoretical practice with existential meaningfulness and moral force. This very opposition, which has effectively structured many influential academic debates, involves a serious misreading and reduction of the rationalist tradition, which at its most compelling seeks precisely to understand communicative reason and the aspiration to critical distance as an embedded practice, as an ongoing achievement rather than a fantasmatic imposition. This aspiration, moreover, also characterizes collective forms of liberal politics, including the practices and procedures that constitute the democratic tradition and are so vital to its ongoing health and stability.

More generally, and throughout the book, I draw out the practical

<hr />

[2] For a related critique, see Walter Benn Michaels, *The Shape of the Signifier* (Princeton: Princeton University Press, 2004). Michaels argues that with the "end of history" and the replacement of ideology with identity, we no longer disagree about anything because only identities, and not beliefs, matter, and because identity is taken to determine how we view the world. I share Michaels's concern with the demise of disagreement and the problem of relativism, but I wage my critique from a different vantage point and ultimately seek to reintroduce dimensions of ethos, and stances toward identity, into a renewed conception of argument.

imagination of theories in order to contest the assumption that theory is overly abstract, irrelevant, or elitist and to draw attention to an all but ubiquitous pull, even in theories from very different and even antagonistic traditions, toward questions of embodiment and enactment—questions of practice, that is. With varying degrees of explicitness and self-awareness, I argue, contemporary theories present themselves as ways of living, as practical philosophies with both individualist and collective aspirations. Indeed, many recent theoretical projects join in a desire to correct for, or answer to, the overly abstract elements of earlier forms of theory. This movement manifests itself in various and not entirely commensurate ways; within literary studies, to take a central example, it appears in a keen attention to the social position of writers, readers, and characters, an increasing focus on the sensibility or location of the critic or theorist, and a concern with the ethics of reading and criticism more broadly. It is my contention that these developments reflect a persistent existential movement toward thicker characterological conceptions of theoretical postures and stances, though it is rarely put in these terms. Indeed, the interest in characterological enactment often operates below the radar, or with only half-lit awareness. One symptom of the underdeveloped yet nonetheless insistent nature of this aspect of contemporary theory is the fact that the term "*ethos*," which reflects a general interest in the ethical texture of theory's project, appears regularly across recent work in literature and political theory.[3]

I am interested in exploring this turn toward the existential dimensions of theory, claiming it as a kind of dialectical advance, and using it to reconsider our understanding of those forms of political theory—rationalism and proceduralism—that have been framed as most ethos-deficient. But the story is somewhat more complicated and internally contested than this brief summary might lead one to expect. These complexities have largely to do with a point I raised at the outset: namely, that highly constrained sociological forms have governed the analysis of subjectivity and personal experience in literary and cultural studies after poststructuralism. In the late 1980s, an interest in first-person perspectives and in the lived experiences of diverse social groups emerged among critics who felt that the high altitudes at which theory operated failed to capture the density and meaningfulness of individual and collective life. There were a series of famous "confessional writings" by critics, which

---

[3] Ethos and character are internally related terms, as I discuss in chapter 6. The former is more focused on the ambient social conditions and norms that guide practice, the latter on the inculcation—and reflective cultivation—of values in the form of habits, dispositions, styles. Ethos includes a collective dimension as well as an individual one, while character is primarily individualist.

often opposed themselves to theoretical approaches.[4] Within theory it-self, there was also an increasing attention to subjective effects and en-actment, and a subsequent tendency to focus the lens on the middle dis-tance and the close up, to relinquish the panoramas and the aerial views. Thus, not only did a new subjectivism emerge in opposition to theory, it also began to affect theory itself as an internal pressure. The most telling example here would be the dramatic late turn in the work of Michel Fou-cault, which set aside the far-reaching examinination of modern power and modern institutions to explore the "care of the self" within antiquity and, to a lesser degree, within modernity, as well. While Foucault's previ-ous work had been interested in the forms of subjectivity engendered by modern disciplinary power, the later Foucault was interested in the manner in which individuals understood, conducted, and therefore in some sense owned, their moral, social, and physical lives.[5]

What should be noted about much of this work on the individual subject, however, is that it gave preeminence to sociological or group identity—variously defined by the categories of class, race, ethnicity, na-tionality, gender, and sexuality. One of the recurrent themes of this book is that a narrow understanding of selfhood and practice results from an overemphasis on sociological, ascribed, or group identity. Intellectual practices over the past several decades have been profoundly enriched and advanced through analysis of the ways that identity categories shape bodies of knowledge, cultural life, and relations of power. But it is also the case that contemporary forms of sociological and cultural reduction-ism limit how critics and theorists imagine the relation between intellec-tual and ethicopolitical life.[6] The conviction that identity is fundamentally

[4] For both analysis and examples of confessional criticism see H. Aram Veeser, ed., Con-fessions of the Critics (New York: Routledge, 1996).

[5] Foucault's "turn" is located between volumes 1 and 2 of The History of Sexuality. Vol-ume 1 is seen as closer in method and theory to Discipline and Punish, and governed by a conception of modern disciplinary power's constitution of subjects. Volumes 2 and 3, in shifting to the classical period, examine individual everyday practices in the realms of ethics and sexuality. See Michel Foucault, Discipline and Punish: The Birth of the Prison, trans. Alan Sheridan (New York: Vintage, 1977); The History of Sexuality: An Introduction, vol. 1, trans. Robert Hurley (New York: Random House, 1978); The History of Sexuality: The Use of Pleasure, vol. 2, trans. Robert Hurley (New York: Vintage, 1985); The History of Sexuality: The Care of the Self, vol. 3, trans. Robert Hurley (New York: Vintage, 1986).

[6] Of course, there are also sociological accounts of what I am calling "sociological re-ductionism." The locus classicus is Daniel Bell's The Cultural Contradictions of Capitalism (New York: Basic Books, 1978). For further discussions of the sociological and political conditions promoting identity politics, see Wendy Brown, States of Injury: Power and Freedom in Late Modernity (Princeton: Princeton University Press, 1995); Nancy Fraser, Justice Interruptus: Critical Reflections on the Post-Socialist Condition (New York: Rout-ledge, 1997); Seyla Benhabib, "The Liberal Imagination and the Four Dogmas of Multicul-turalism," Yale Journal of Criticism 12, no. 2 (1999): 401–13.

status-based, pregiven in some fundamental way by the groups or categories that make up the sociological map, constrains the resources of
practical and ethical discourses in key ways.[7] This discursive poverty is
evidenced by the two ethicopolitical options that often seem to be on offer: on the one hand, there is a strong theoretical tradition, deriving from
poststructuralism and queer theory, that advocates the subversion of identity by any means possible—the denaturalization of what are nonetheless
inescapably imposed identities by means of parody, irony, or resignification.[8] On the other hand, by those more interested in the virtues of mosaic
diversity and more convinced of the importance of socialized belonging,
there is a quasi-communitarian commitment to the notion that forms of
cultural affiliation must be acknowledged, defended, or cushioned, particularly from what is seen as the evacuating force of liberal or rational
agendas.[9]

The "politics of identity" (to suggest something less reified and discredited than "identity politics") is a theoretically and practically significant dimension of contemporary historical and sociological life. It is not my aim
or desire to somehow argue it out of existence (as though that were possible). But limitations ensue when the politics of identity is imagined to cover
all available intellectual and ethicopolitical space. The privileging of only
those forms of critique that are associated with the postmodern modes of
irony and negative freedom, moreover, results in a widespread and deleteri-
ous rejection of the resources of the Kantian and liberal traditions. I question the assumptions fueling this recurrent bias and advance a defense of
critical reason, discourse ethics, and those political forms and institutions
that seek reflectively to realize liberal and democratic principles.

From a somewhat different but equally important angle, I explore how
contemporary theory is already pursuing a less constrained understanding

[7] A clarification is in order here about the use of the term "sociological." Many theorists
whom I mean to include under such a description would refuse the idea that their understandings of identity can be adequately described by this term—this would be especially
true of critics for whom psychoanalysis is a fundamentally informing paradigm. But insofar as such critics subscribe to a notion of the symbolic, which is discursive but also fundamentally coterminous with the cultural and the social order, and insofar as sexual identities
are distributed within this order and are crucially determinative of individual experience,
then they are still operating by means of what I here designate as a sociological map, even
if they call it something else, such as the symbolic order, the heterosexual matrix, or the
heteronormative regime. The key element at play in such theories is the assumption that
identity means, above all, categorical or group identity, and that self-understanding and individual enactment play themselves out primarily in relation to this identity.

[8] The most influential instance of such an approach can be found in Judith Butler, *Gender Trouble: Feminism and the Subversion of Identity* (New York: Routledge, 1989).

[9] See James Tully, *Strange Multiplicity: Constitutionalism in an Age of Diversity* (Cambridge: Cambridge University Press, 1995).

of first-person experience (singular and plural), one which finds expression in ways that consistently exceed the sociological grid. This is evident in what many have hailed as a general turn to ethics, but it is also evident in recent forms of theory for which, as I have already suggested, a kind of cultivated ethos or characterological stance seems central, if not fully theorized. Among these, and of central interest in the essays collected here, I would count the later Foucault, cosmopolitanism, and, most provocatively, proceduralist ethics and politics (with its emphasis on sincerity and civility). A less reflective but symptomatically interesting version of this attentiveness to ethos appears in contemporary pragmatism, which I take up in order to underscore the constrained ways in which nonsociological understandings of identity make their presence felt in practical philosophies of the present. The book concludes by resituating the concepts of ethos and character within an analysis of proceduralist theory and liberal institutions, both as a way of answering to some of the most pointed critiques of reason and liberalism's purported impersonality, and as a way of introducing the notion of a "culture of argument," by which I mean the discursive practices and habits that underpin the unfinished project of modernity and the evolving institutions of liberal democracies.

I should perhaps clarify what I mean by "nonsociological." In advocating a fuller incorporation of understandings of character and ethos into our theories and practices, I mean to suggest that individuals and collectivities can and do cultivate habits, dispositions, and attitudes that can in no simple way be attributed to any easily identifiable and limiting sociological determination. Of course it is always the case that conceptions of virtue and character bear the marks of their historical and cultural locations, and that individuals and collectivities are necessarily faced with discrete fields of action. But that does not mean that character and ethos are always class or culture-bound in some limiting way, nor does it mean that forms of character always bespeak a determination by forces of power, or alternately, an ideological denial of such determination. The French sociologist Pierre Bourdieu's theories have promoted the view that manners, habits, and characterological identifications are not only social in origin, but also work to establish forms of distinction that articulate hierarchies of power.[10] Bourdieu, like Foucault, has provided immensely valuable tools for the understanding of power within everyday life. But it is by no means clear to me that the characterological dimensions of normative ethical and political theories (be they personal, political, or institutional virtues), or of course those theories themselves, are so susceptible to sociological reduction.

---

[10] Pierre Bourdieu, *Distinction: A Social Critique of the Judgement of Taste*, trans. Richard Nice (Cambridge, Mass.: Harvard University Press, 1984).

The essays collected here were written over several years—both du
and after the completion of an earlier book, *The Powers of Distance:
Cosmopolitanism and the Cultivation of Detachment*.[11] It may be useful
to situate this project in relation to that book, which in many ways provides historical context for the present study. Focusing on intellectual
and aesthetic practices in nineteenth-century Britain, *The Powers of Distance* argues that nineteenth-century writers gave ethical depth and justification to modern intellectual postures precisely by insisting that they
profoundly affected character. In demonstrable ways, the postures of distancing that characterized scientific objectivity, omniscient realism, and
aesthetic disinterestedness were construed by nineteenth-century thinkers
as integrally linked to the moral fate of the practitioner. For example,
scientific writers sought to project an ideal of "moralized objectivity," to
borrow the term used by historian of science Lorraine Daston, while
writers such as Matthew Arnold and John Stuart Mill fundamentally
integrated ideals of exemplary character into their conceptions, respec-
tively, of disinterestedness and epistemological advance.[12] There were
also instances of character-damaging theoretical postures that contrasted
sharply with character-enhancing practices: for example, Charles Dickens was haunted by the idea that the cultivation of a systems-view of the
social world—one that analyzed relations of hierarchy and power—was
both necessary to the project of realism and potentially highly harmful
to individuals, whose critical practices might reify into habits of suspicion
that would thwart the bonds of affection that underwrite ideals of family
and community.

Uniting these disparate nineteenth-century views is a commitment to
the notion that intellectual and aesthetic postures are always also lived
practices. As such they allow and even invite the same kinds of ethical assessments that individuals routinely bring to their personal, social, and
political lives. Recent scholarly trends have tended to treat ideals of critical detachment as illusory, elitist, and dangerous, invested in unattainable
perspectives and disregarding of embodied existence and the experience
of differently situated, and differently enfranchised, social groups. Such
assumptions fail to capture the keenly reflective and vexed relation that
many thinkers, both historical and contemporary, have had toward the
personal side of what have been precipitously judged to be impersonal
(objective, disinterested, scientific, detached) practices. They also fail to

[11] Amanda Anderson, *The Powers of Distance: Cosmopolitanism and the Cultivation of
Detachment* (Princeton: Princeton University Press, 2001).

[12] See Lorraine Daston, "The Moral Economy of Science," *Osiris* 10 (1995): 3–24; Lorraine Daston and Peter Galison, "The Image of Objectivity," *Representations* 40 (1992):
81–128; and Lorraine Daston, "Objectivity and the Escape from Perspective," *Social Studies of Science* 22 (1922): 597–618.

recognize not only that intellectual and political forms of detachment—such as liberalism, aestheticism, cosmopolitanism, and proceduralism—emerge historically but also that they can become embedded and habitual in ways that might seem unlikely at the time of their emergence.

The approach that I adopt shares the spirit of two influential trends in contemporary theory, although it can also be usefully distinguished from them: these are, roughly speaking, the turn to ethics and the turn to affect (or feeling). As Lawrence Buell argues, the new interest in ethics has been influenced from a number of directions, including the emphasis on "care of the self" in the later work of Foucault, claims for an ethics of deconstruction in the work of Jacques Derrida and J. Hillis Miller, and arguments for a more traditional and specifically literary ethics in writings by Wayne Booth and Martha Nussbaum.[13] The distinctive work of Emmanuel Levinas, which departs from deconstruction in its insistence on the priority of ethics to epistemology, has also exerted considerable force with its assertion of the primacy of the relation to the other.[14] All of these theoretical currents (and crosscurrents) are pertinent to any renewed interest in ethos in contemporary theory, and the essays here have been broadly influenced by this larger context (there is extended treatment of both Nussbaum and Foucault). But I depart from many of the assumptions and approaches that characterize this more general terrain, primarily through an emphasis on reflective reason. While some notion of cultivated practice could certainly be said to inform the ethics advanced by all these writers, I favor an approach that lays stress on the capacity of reflective reason, through which the subject acknowledges and advances valued practices (whose value accrues from both the goals being pursued and the means by which habitual orientations toward such goals can be fostered). The assumptions here are at once Kantian, in their insistence on critical capacity and self-authorization, and Aristotelian, in their interest in self-cultivation and character. Such assumptions are not entirely at odds with the work of the later Foucault, and they are compatible with the reading-based ideals of Nussbaum and Booth. But

[13] Lawrence Buell, "What We Talk About When We Talk About Ethics," in Marjorie Garber, Beatrice Hanssen, and Rebecca L. Walkowitz, eds., *The Turn to Ethics* (New York: Routledge, 2000), 1–13. See also Michel Foucault, *Ethics: Subjectivity and Truth*, ed. Paul Rabinow (New York: New Press, 1994); Jacques Derrida, *Cosmopolitanism and Forgiveness* (New York: Routledge, 2001); J. Hillis Miller, *The Ethics of Reading: Kant, de Man, Eliot, Trollope, James, and Benjamin* (New York: Columbia University Press, 1987); Wayne C. Booth, *The Company We Keep: An Ethics of Fiction* (Berkeley: University of California Press, 1988); Martha C. Nussbaum, *Love's Knowledge: Essays on Philosophy and Literature* (New York: Oxford University Press, 1990).

[14] For a helpful discussion of ethics in Derrida and Levinas, see Simon Critchley, *The Ethics of Deconstruction* (Edinburgh: Edinburgh University Press, 2000).

the strong interest I have in the "character" of various theories—the ways in which the practices they advocate get imagined in distinctly characterological terms—lends my approach a certain distinctiveness. Moreover, there is outright divergence from the approach to ethics in Levinas, with its stress on the ethical subject as receptive patient rather than self-cultivating agent, and in Derrida, who invokes a similarly displaced subject and dwells overwhelmingly on the shared condition of semiotic undecidability or openness. The deconstructionist emphasis on acknowledging the radical conditions of undecidability surrounding any decision resides at some distance from the agent-centered ideas of character and self-cultivation I am developing here.

Recent attention to affect might also be seen as related to the approach that I adopt here, especially insofar as work focused on the category of affect has often claimed significance precisely for its attention to lived experience and for its attempt to add experiential or existential depth to theoretical approaches. There are a wide range of writings in literary, cultural, and political theory that either demand that affect should be integrated into what is typically defined against it—reason, thought, analysis—or claim that affect can bring theory or politics alive. In *The Radical Aesthetic*, for example, Isobel Armstrong argues for a developed analytic of emotion as a key feature of a renewed understanding of the aesthetic and its political possibilities: the underlying assumption is that modern thought has had a particularly impoverished understanding of emotion. Armstrong explicitly associates emotion with the category of life.[15] Similarly, recent work by Eve Kosofsky Sedgwick has shown that specific affects might be said to typically characterize or accompany specific forms of theory.[16] The work in this area is highly varied, but it does tend to share an assumption that affect has the potential to enrich, correct, or even displace theory. By connecting theoretical postures to living practices, social relations, and psychological experience, this work is provocative in the same way that I hope an emphasis on characterology and ethos will be found provocative.

However, just as Aristotle thought it necessary to distinguish logos, pathos, and ethos from one another, I, too, will argue for the analytical distinctiveness and value of ethos as over and against pathos (affect). More importantly, I will suggest that contemporary theory would do well to use ethos to disrupt the conceptual dynamic frequently set into play by opposing pathos to logos. One central problem in elevating affect as the most significant answer or counterforce to theory's perceived

---

[15] Isobel Armstrong, *The Radical Aesthetic* (Oxford: Blackwell, 2001).

[16] See especially Eve Kosofsky Sedgwick, "Paranoid Reading and Reparative Reading; or, You're So Paranoid You Probably Think This Introduction is About You," in Sedgwick, ed., *Novel Gazing: Queer Readings in Fiction* (Durham: Duke University Press, 1997), 1–37.

abstractness is that it allows one to skirt the question of critical reflection. Since affect is typically presented in somatic and noncognitive terms, it often serves as a safe solution within a critical climate that has become suspicious not only of the perceived impersonality of abstractness, but also of the forms of rationality that many of the abstract theories themselves denounce. While the spectrum of work on affect is rich and closely allied to the topos of ethos that I will pursue here, it is also symptomatic of a larger inability to conceptualize the characterological imagination of theory itself and to address how practitioners might reflectively realize, promote, and ultimately even render habitual those postures that best encompass its intellectual and ethicopolitical values.

One particularly symptomatic example of the turn toward affect as an answer to the perceived abstraction and bluntness of theory can be found in Charles Altieri's *Postmodernisms Now*.[17] In his book, Altieri distinguishes between "what is living and what is dead" in postmodernism. As theory, Altieri contends, postmodernism is largely and deservedly dead. But in its imaginative aesthetic incarnations—in other words, as art— postmodernism is living. In Altieri's view, it is only through the aesthetic— conceived as particularistic, existential, and nongeneralizable—that postmodernism can exorcise the demon of theoretical fetishism. And interestingly, Altieri consistently singles out affect as the vivifying force, and primary indexical sign, of aesthetic life.

Altieri usefully identifies a number of constraints in the postmodern theoretical imagination, and he is particularly impatient with the reductive hermeneutic imposed by overattention to identity politics. But it is also the case that he aims to create a sharp demarcation whereby theoretical abstraction simply fails to capture the more authentic enactments of artistic expression. Such a demarcation denies to theory the possibilities that he locates in the arts, whose aim is "not to offer theoretical solutions but to envision imaginative stances for living within and finessing and even building upon what we cannot resolve" (15). *The Way We Argue Now* insists that such stances already inhabit theory—with greater and lesser degrees of explicitness—and that arguments like Altieri's distort and stereotype theory, thereby foreclosing an appreciation of the extent to which theory itself grapples with the issue of living enactment. And to the extent that theory values the reflective life, its own understandings of individual and collective practice are more comprehensively recognized if we can show how they project not only affective dimensions, but also ethical ones.

---

[17] Charles Altieri, *Postmodernisms Now: Essays on Contemporaneity in the Arts* (State College: Pennsylvania State University Press, 1998). Page-number references will be made parenthetically in the text.

In any event, to point this out is not to erase the distinction between art and theory but rather to acknowledge what might be called, in an extension of the characterological interest, the novelistic imagination of particular theories. If, as I argue in one of the essays here, ethics always precedes epistemology insofar as the question "how should I live" precedes the determinations of any epistemological project, then theory cannot coherently cut itself off from life in the first place. There are certainly more and less abstract, more and less vividly practical, theoretical systems—and there are many, many different forms of theory, not all of which imagine their own ethos in ways that I find productive, tenable, or interesting. But what this book consistently refuses is the tendency to dismiss the resources of theory through reference to negative terms such as "abstractness," "thinness," or "aridity."

The situation that I aim to describe is complicated by the fact that ethos itself has emerged as a somewhat localized term of art over the past couple of decades, one that is often specifically set against critical reason. Indeed, as I argue in chapter 6, the influential late stage of the Habermas-Foucault debate in both Britain and America, a debate that made itself particularly felt in the fields of literary and political theory, was structured by an assumption that Foucauldian ethos was fundamentally opposed to the investment in argument that animated Habermas's democratic proceduralism as well as his discourse ethics. More generally, to the extent that "ethos" has appeared as a valorized term in contemporary theory, it designates a somewhat mystified ideal of enactment that defines itself against the explicitness and perceived normalizing force of reason. To take simply one example from the realm of poststructuralist political theory, I will cite from Chantal Mouffe's insistence on the limitations of the Habermasian approach and her offering up of a notion of "democratic ethos" as a more viable and attractive alternative.

It is necessary to realize that it is not by offering sophisticated rational arguments nor by making context-transcendent truth claims about the superiority of liberal democracy that democratic values can be fostered. The creation of democratic forms of individuality is a question of *identification* with democratic values and this is a complex process that takes place through a diversity of practices, discourses, and language games. . . . Liberal democratic principles can only be defended in a contextualist manner, as being constitutive of our form of life, and we should not try to ground our commitment to them on something supposedly safer. To secure allegiance and adhesion to those principles what is needed is the creation of a democratic *ethos*. It has to do with the mobilization of passions and sentiments, the multiplication of practices, institutions, and

language games that provide the condition of possibility for democratic subjects and democratic forms of willing.[18]

This series of statements forwards the idea that political principles and values can only be defended and promoted if they are conceived as part of the
texture of ongoing ways of life. "Sophisticated rational arguments" about
the superiority or philosophical basis of such principles and values necessarily fail to orient themselves toward politics as a way of life: by their very
form, they fundamentally misconstrue the nature of political life and disable the democratic project. To underscore the deficiencies of rational argument, Mouffe gives pride of place to the mobilization of affect ("passions
and sentiments") in the advancement of political aims. By sharpened contrast, rational argument and context-transcending claims are themselves
definitively barred from contextualist meaningfulness and effectivity.

It is this set of assumptions, with their framing opposition between rationality and ethos, that these essays collectively challenge. A conceptual
dynamic that opposes rationality to ethos, and that in turn conflates ethos
and affect, projects the idea that various discursive practices of rationality
—such as critique, argument, or procedure—are unable to realize themselves as a viable and positive ethos. Moreover, by simply assigning ethos a
kind of unchallenged privilege—something in need of cultivation, but hazy
enough in definition to seem not to carry with it any sense of coercion or
power—the possibility for a more precise and comprehensive study of the
ways that ethos informs all manner of theory and argument goes missing.

· · ·

The book divides into three sections, which are linked not only to conceptual unities, but also, by and large, to the chronology of composition.
The first pair of essays examines the topos of detachment and reflective
distance in contemporary theory, isolating the underdeveloped normative dimensions of those forms of poststructuralist theory that have influenced work in literary studies, cultural studies, and political theory.
The aim in both of these pieces, which concentrate on formations within
feminist and queer theory, is to explore and assess vying conceptions of
critical detachment.

The first chapter, "Debatable Performances," addresses a prominent
debate in feminist and queer theory in the nineties, one which coalesced
in an encounter between Judith Butler and Seyla Benhabib. Like Mouffe,
Butler exemplifies a widely shared poststructuralist tendency to accuse

[18] Chantal Mouffe, "Introduction," in Simon Critchley, Jacques Derrida, Ernesto Laclau,
and Richard Rorty, *Deconstruction and Pragmatism*, ed. Chantal Mouffe (New York:
Routledge, 1996), 5.

Habermasian critical theory (here represented by Benhabib) of the delusion that philosophy can solve the messy, embedded problems of ongoing political life. Interestingly, then, a certain form of philosophical detachment—here associated with rational reflection, proceduralist forms of debate, and universalist principle—is positioned as hopelessly cut off from anything that could authentically count as politics.

In this essay I first analyze the contours of the debate and then suggest a way beyond the impasse presented by it. My argument is that both critical and queer theory are interested in postures of cultivated detachment: critical theory in its promotion of postconventional stances and queer theory in its promotion of persistent denaturalization of imposed identities. Given this common interest in a posture of critique, both sides are unnecessarily defended against each other. On the one hand, Benhabib has an overly narrow conception of what debate or political expression might mean, one that could be usefully expanded through an inclusion of the ironic and theatrical modes of queer politics. On the other hand, Butler produces a fundamental incoherence in her refusal to acknowledge the norms—continuous with those of critical theory—that underwrite her own project. In the end, I suggest that critical theory has the more compelling and comprehensive account of the relation between critical practice, intersubjective ethics, and institutional politics, but I also endorse a pluralist attitude toward the forms through which critical detachment might manifest itself or develop into ongoing, lived practices.

A discernible tension runs throughout this particular essay, and indeed throughout the book as a whole. On the one hand, I am concerned to make a case for Habermasian discourse ethics and democratic proceduralism, which means making the case for a conception of critical rationality underwritten by communicative action. I think not only that this is the most coherent conception of critique on the horizon but also that it is widely misunderstood and often falsely opposed to other theoretical practices. To some extent, theoretical disagreements such as that between Butler and Benhabib stem from divergent views on the basic conditions of linguistic and social life. Poststructuralists insist, in opposition to Habermas, that language is fundamentally unstable, reason fundamentally instrumental, and communicative relations riven by forms of power and violence. I approach these philosophical and political differences by adducing what I claim to be the superior explanatory power of the neo-Kantian position. To that defense I join a critique of poststructuralism, emphasizing its failure to acknowledge or justify its own reliance on critical distance and disputing its portrayal of rationality and procedure. When poststructuralist critics contend that Habermas's ideas of rationality and procedure do not recognize practices as always embedded, embodied, and power-laden, they fail to comprehend that Habermas presents rational, communicative, and procedural norms as guiding or regulative ideals, in both a descriptive and a prescriptive sense. As descriptive concepts, they heuristically allow for the isolation of dimensions of practice that may never exist in any pure form, and as evaluative norms, they do not deny but rather assume the existence of forces and conditions that mitigate against their full realization.

On the other hand, and in some tension with my defense of Habermas, I welcome a plurality of conceptions of detachment and theoretical characterology: in the first essay, I therefore encourage a capacious understanding of forms of critical detachment, one that can comprehend practices that range from reflective endorsement to persistent denaturalization. Thus there is a kind of asymmetry in the project: a strong tendency to favor Habermasian critical theory, and a countervailing claim that critical theory should expand to embrace a wider range of political practices, expressions, modes, and moods. My view is that this is a productive tension, one that informs any attempt to conceptualize a liberal temperament. Inevitably, the postures that liberal pluralism imagines for itself will need to be supplemented by, if not include, an openness to postures and practices different from its own. There thus emerges a felt difference between the principles and orienting postures that one endorses, and those other practices and modes that one takes pains to describe, understand, and sympathetically entertain (as a liberal pluralist). In any event, the tension will be evident throughout the project.

In the second essay, "The Temptations of Aggrandized Agency," I situate the discussion of cultivated postures of critique within an analysis of feminist accounts of gender and modernity. An offshoot of the historical and critical arguments of *The Powers of Distance*, this essay compares theories of gendered modernity across the disciplines of literary criticism and history, with particular focus on differently strained conceptions of ordinary subjectivity and critical detachment in both these theoretical formations. I argue that the intersection of feminist traditions of hagiography with poststructuralist conceptions of subjectivity produces a literary-critical theoretical landscape in which the question of a lived theoretical stance is only fantasmatically present. The essay therefore comprehends both a critique of the failure to represent historical practices of detachment in their complexity and a critique of certain versions of contemporary theory that do not adequately own their own assumptions about the possibilities for critical distance.

The following two chapters shift toward a more specific consideration of ethos and character. The first essay, "Cosmopolitanism, Universalism, and the Divided Legacies of Modernity," seeks to come to terms with the implications of the turn to cosmopolitanism as a key new concept in cultural and political theory. This essay grew out of an interest in exploring the impulses behind new appeals to cosmopolitanism, on the one hand, and universalism, on the other. Those works that deliberately choose to revive and espouse the term "cosmopolitanism" often share a persistent interest in enactment: cosmopolitanism for many scholars becomes a way to imagine a living universalism, one that is guided above all by tact, sensibility, and practical judgment. Cosmopolitanism is, in short, an ethos of universalism. By insisting that an embodied universalism will fundamentally alter, and refine, any universalism conceived in more impersonal or objective terms, it illustrates the very turn to enactment and ethos that this study seeks to anatomize and assess.

The next essay, "Realism, Universalism, and the Science of the Human," examines the relative force exerted by the ethical and epistemological poles of certain influential critiques of postmodernism and poststructuralism. The central aim of the essay is to examine what consequences ensue when normative or ethical dimensions of critique are subordinated to epistemological considerations. Taking the contrasting examples of Satya P. Mohanty's predominantly epistemological critique of postmodernism (in *Literary Theory and the Claims of History*) and Martha C. Nussbaum's predominantly normative or ethical approach (in *Cultivating Humanity*), I suggest that practices of knowledge are always framed by questions of how one should live.[19] Nussbaum's attention to character and self-cultivation is a reflection of this structuring assumption, while Mohanty's avowed "postpositivism," by virtue of its investment in the objectivizing postures of philosophical realism, remains shadowed by that which it aims to overcome.

The final three essays take as their central concern the status of ethos and character in contemporary intellectual debate, particularly in reference to pragmatism, the later Foucault, and proceduralism (with special emphasis on Habermas). "Pragmatism and Character" grew out of the observation that characterological terms were at once persistently present, and yet fundamentally unexamined, in debates over pragmatism. On the one hand, pragmatists are accused of being, among other things, smug, complacent, cynical, blithe, and dismissive. On the other hand, pragmatists themselves claim forms of exemplary character, most prominently through a self-congratulatory relation to their own casual relation to contingency. The contours of the pragmatist case reveal not simply the foreclosure of explicit consideration of character in dominant forms

---

[19] Satya P. Mohanty, *Literary Theory and the Claims of History: Postmodernism, Objectivity, Multicultural Politics* (Ithaca: Cornell University Press, 1997). Martha C. Nussbaum, *Cultivating Humanity: A Classical Defense of Reform in Liberal Education* (Cambridge, Mass.: Harvard University Press, 1997).

of theory within literary and cultural criticism, but also the insistent way in which the characterological dimension continues nonetheless to make itself felt, to seem to *matter*, even when it only appears surreptitiously, or with the appearance of descriptive superfluity (as in the case of the attributions of smugness or complacency).

Ultimately, I read the case of pragmatism critically and symptomatically, arguing that the characterological dimension of recent pragmatist work is curiously narrow, best described as a personification of the fundamental theoretical claim that there is a seamless relation between truth and belief. But an apprehension of contingency need not translate into a governing attitude; indeed, an open-ended approach to character as a project in the making is ultimately more compatible with the historical tradition of pragmatism as promoted by William James and John Dewey. I argue for a pluralist approach to the existential dimensions of contingent vocabularies, such as we find at least partly elaborated by Richard Rorty, whom I assign a productively anomalous place in my account.[20] But more centrally, I also use the pragmatist example to provide an illustration of how an attention to characterology might be incorporated into theoretical analysis, rather than being merely dismissed as a version of ad hominem argument.

The penultimate essay, "Argument and Ethos," continues the diagnosis begun in the essay on pragmatism by turning its attention to the role that the category of ethos plays in the later stages of the scholarly framing, in both literary and political theory, of a fundamental opposition between Foucault and Habermas. The aim here is to show that to the extent that "ethos" emerges as a valued term in this debate, it has been defined principally in opposition to reason. In the case of the reception of Foucault, this mystified understanding of ethos joins with a form of charismatic fallacy that forecloses a more productive elaboration of ethos as a dimension of practice more generally conceived. The second half of this essay attempts to displace the opposition of reason and ethos by exploring the several ways in which a conception of ethos informs Habermas's own critique of Foucault, as well as some of Habermas's central theoretical claims and practices.

---

[20] There is a parallel between the pluralist position I advocate here and Pierre Hadot's pluralist treatment of the existential postures of ancient philosophy. Hadot sees each of the various schools of ancient philosophy—Stoicism, Epicureanism, Platonism, Aristotelianism, Cynicism, and Pyrrhonsim—as manifesting a possibility of the human spirit, one that the complexity of life invites us to treat experimentally and pluralistically. Hadot refuses both the dogma of the individual schools and the attempt to yoke existential modes or moods to specific doctrines in any absolute way. His approach is more generally suggestive for the claims I am trying to advance on the important ways in which notions of character and ethos can enrich our understanding of theoretical practices. See Pierre Hadot, *Philosophy as a Way of Life* (Oxford: Blackwell, 1995).

The final chapter presses this reading of Habermas further, suggesting how we might view the ostensibly abstract and impersonal practice of postconventional critique and proceduralist democracy as an ethos in its own right. This chapter revisits Lionel Trilling's *Sincerity and Authenticity* so as to provide a larger context for understanding the divergent trajectories of poststructuralist and proceduralist political theory. I claim that poststructuralism is in crucial respects the inheritor of the authenticity concept that Trilling saw as coming to dominate over sincerity in the modern period. Proceduralism, by contrast, as a provocative reframing of the sincerity concept, makes it possible to imagine the ways in which cultivated practices of reflection and argument can themselves be articulated as an ethos, at both the individual and collective levels. In its elaboration of an ethicopolitical ideal for posttraditional pluralist societies, Habermasian proceduralism promotes an ethos of ongoing distance-taking from one's most intimate and meaningful cultural identifications. Its presumed impersonality is less a radical denial of the embedded nature of all practices than an expression of the commitment to an ongoing project of reflective distance—or, as Habermas puts it, to the progressive expansion of horizons.

What this final chapter attempts, then, is a displacement of the tendency to oppose reason and ethos, precisely by claiming an ethos of reason and argument. In doing so, I am also pressing for a culture of argument skeptical of the trumping claims made on behalf of the more limiting, antirational conception of ethos—variously conceived as charismatic critique, pregiven identity, or accommodating tact in the face of claims to the primacy of culturally specific systems of belief. This is the most provocative claim of the book: that the dominant paradigms within literary and cultural studies have had an adverse effect on the fostering of public-sphere argument precisely insofar as identity has come to seem the strongest argument of all.

. . .

With the exception of the final essay, all of the essays in this book have appeared previously. Since these essays reflect the time of their composition in important ways, I have chosen not to introduce any substantial revisions, though I have of course corrected errata, regularized style, and changed cross-references so that they refer not to the originally published essays, but rather to the appropriate chapter of this text. The original publication information is contained in the acknowledgments.

PART I

Critical Practices

CHAPTER 1

Debatable Performances

RESTAGING CONTENTIOUS FEMINISMS

THIS ESSAY INVESTIGATES an important feminist rerouting of the Habermas-Foucault debate, as it has been articulated and publicly staged by Seyla Benhabib and Judith Butler. A particularly vivid enactment of this dispute appears in the book *Feminist Contentions: A Philosophical Exchange* (1995). The book has four contributors—Butler, Benhabib, Nancy Fraser, and Drucilla Cornell—but the debate narrows pretty rapidly to a face-off between Butler and Benhabib, with Fraser attempting to mediate, and Cornell pursuing an offbeat, idiosyncratic theoretical project informed by Lacan, Derrida, and Levinas. It's a strange book, and everyone is a little uncomfortable being counted among an elite "gang of four" implicitly authorized to chart the course of feminist debate.[1] The editor, Linda Nicholson, who is also general editor of Routledge's Thinking Gender series (in which this book appears), feels compelled to give a detailed history of the essays collected in the text: beginning as a symposium organized by the Greater Philadelphia Philosophy Consortium in September of 1990 (absent Cornell), the essays were then published in the July 1991 issue of *Praxis International*. After this, "a decision was made" to invite a contribution from Cornell, and then to have a round of responses from all four contributors and publish the eight essays as a book (*FC*, 1). The volume was first published in Germany, where Benhabib is an important Frankfurt School figure, and where the Habermasian position is more regularly and deeply engaged in the debates over postmodernism.[2] Subsequently, it was decided to publish the book in English.

I focus on this book not because it successfully presents a complete picture of the contending positions held by Butler and Benhabib (it in

---

[1] I borrow the use of the term "gang of four" from the editor Linda Nicholson, who uses it in the introduction to *Feminist Contentions: A Philosophical Exchange* (New York: Routledge, 1995), 1. Hereafter cited in the text as *FC*.

[2] For another recent volume in Routledge's Thinking Gender series that helpfully extends the debate on Habermas, see Johanna Meehan, ed., *Feminists Read Habermas: Gendering the Subject of Discourse* (New York: Routledge, 1995). But note that Meehan points out in her introduction that "the authors anthologized here are to some extent rowing against the feminist mainstream" (1).

fact does not), but because it symptomatically displays some of the impasses in the debate. In this essay, I will go beyond *Feminist Contentions* to consider more seriously the arguments put forth in Butler's and Benhabib's relevant published work to date; but I also want to draw out the reasons why *Feminist Contentions* represents such an agonizingly failed speech situation. Any reader of the text cannot fail to register, in particular, Butler's emphatic attempts to distance herself from the whole project. In her second contribution to the volume, she writes,

> I'm struck in many ways by what now appears to me to be the parochialism of these debates, for the four of us certainly are not representative of "feminism" or "feminist theory" as it is currently articulated. Missing from this volume is a sustained discussion of the place of racial difference in contemporary feminist debate; the ethical and political questions raised by reproductive rights and technologies; the ethical and political questions raised by the discourse of victimization which seems to prevail in U.S. public feminist debate and exemplified in the work of Catherine MacKinnon; the contemporary theoretical divergences between sexuality and gender studies initiated by lesbian and gay studies; the transnational problems of translating feminist political goals and their claim to "universality"; the remapping of power by feminist theory in ways that encompass shifting geopolitical terrains; the feminization and racialization of poverty both domestically and abroad. (*FC*, 132)

"Neither does this volume address," Butler goes on, "the 'theory wars,' for as a group, we toil in the domain of philosophy and its critique, and in that way dwell within a presupposed sense that theoretical reflection matters" (*FC*, 132). Butler culminates her indictment of this club, which includes her as a member, by insisting that one cannot really consider this volume as constituting a "debate" on the value or viability of "modernity," "the subject," "progressive history," or "the transcendental norm"; the question is simply whether such terms can serve as "grounds" for political struggle (*FC*, 132). And the answer, for Butler, is simply no. Butler thereby scores one of her sharpest points against critical theory and against Benhabib: politics truly occurs only when such terms are struggled over in more concrete historical and institutional contexts. The kind of debate that tries to resolve such issues "philosophically" is engaged in the insidious practice that imagines one can decide such matters by mere reflection, in advance of actual struggles: "This urge to have philosophy supply the vision that will redeem life, that will make life worth living, this urge is the very sign that the sphere of the political has already been abandoned" (*FC*, 131).

Combining an anxiety about vanguardism and political relevance with a stark claim about the relation between philosophy and politics, Butler indicates that she has moved beyond the debate recorded in the volume, that she is *elsewhere*, which in this case is implied to be the true realm of the political as opposed to the deluded, apolitical realm of philosophical justification. The acknowledgment of complicity (we *all* "toil in the domain of philosophy and its critique") is overshadowed by the cordoning-off of critical theory as *un*self-critical philosophy, as a species of retreat, withdrawal, and mystification against which "real" politics is defined. In making this move, Butler at once frames and dismisses Benhabib, and in a sense refuses to debate her. To be sure, Benhabib herself evinces discomfort about republishing an old essay and lets us know that she needed to be persuaded that the controversy should be made publicly available in a new format. But beyond the anxiety about timeliness, she appears less concerned with the nature of the issues debated than with the wounds reopened by yet another public enactment of a strained disagreement that has taken its toll on "personal loyalties and friendships" (*FC*, 31).

If nothing else, these acts of distancing on both sides indicate that the debate has calcified, and that Linda Nicholson's attempt to vivify it through republication has exacerbated existing tensions. Consequently, one can appreciate Nancy Fraser's attempt to reconcile the opposing positions, however quixotic such an attempt at times appears.[3] The initial impetus for my own commentary on this text came not from any desire to reconcile, I must confess, but from outright frustration with Butler for distortions of Benhabib's position and, by extension, of Habermas's position and the theory of communicative action. In exploring the relation between Butler's position and her vehement rejection of communicative ethics, I suggest that Butler in some sense requires a trumped-up version of normative critical theory in order to secure the pedigree of her politics. Central to her negotiation of critical theory and of performative politics is a complex rhetoric of temporality that emphasizes thresholdism, on the one hand, and belatedness, on the other. By tracing out the implications of temporal nonsynchronicity in Butler I aim to expose her own evasion of normative explicitness, and thereby to vindicate communicative ethics.

At the same time, however, I want to suggest that Benhabib's theory needs a more capacious model of dialogue, one that can accommodate different forms of political practice, particularly the disruptions of spectacle, performance, and what Butler at one point calls "theatrical rage."[4]

---

[3] Fraser's critiques of both thinkers are incisive and illuminating, yet she ultimately takes a pragmatic, consumerist approach to the problem, arguing that we should pick and choose elements from each thinker. The paradigmatic divergences between Butler and Benhabib are far too profound to allow for such a mode of reconciliation.

[4] Judith Butler, *Bodies That Matter: On the Discursive Limits of "Sex"* (New York: Routledge, 1993), 233. Hereafter cited in the text as *BTM*.

Despite her own emphasis on identity as situated, Benhabib's position dubiously diminishes, and even wards off, the importance of political practices and ways of everyday life that dramatically denaturalize commonly held assumptions about identity, imagining that such practices are a threat to feminist political cohesion. I believe that this assumption is misguided and that radical *disidentification* of the type Butler advocates constitutes a practically and theoretically significant form of contemporary politics. But to accept and even promote radical disidentification, or subversive denaturalization, need not entail the abandonment of communicative ethics. There is no necessary reason why disidentification and communicative ethics have to be defined against each other.

If one accepts this conclusion, a significant question still remains. Even if a potential compatibility is asserted between the project of communicative ethics and subversive denaturalization of the Butlerian sort, one might still reasonably ask: to what extent should the dramas of identity, whether affirmative or subversive, dominate or shape a leftist politics? Indeed, Nancy Fraser's subsequent work, whose claims do not significantly animate her (earlier) analyses in *Feminist Contentions*, pursues the question of how we might best combine a politics of recognition oriented around questions of identity and a politics of redistribution oriented around questions of socioeconomic justice.[5] Such a project requires assessing various forms of recognition politics in terms of which forms of state or institutional politics that they seem to enable, advocate, foreclose, play into, or fail to consider. It involves, in other words, asking how we combine a politics of identity, whether conceived affirmatively or subversively, with a politics that reaches beyond that potentially limiting rubric.

The discussion will thus proceed as follows. I will present the salient features of Butler's and Benhabib's positions, assessing them in terms of their key concepts, their implicit politics, and their normative integrity. My goal will be to expose what I take to be misguided and questionable ways of configuring the relations among politics, identity, and norms, and to argue for a refurbished communicative ethics that can accommodate the various politics of disidentification. Throughout, I will revisit the question of how well the two thinkers integrate their theoretical claims into a larger political vision, arguing that Benhabib's communicative ethics, despite some significant shortcomings, is far more developed in ethicopolitical, collective, and institutional terms.

Benhabib's *Critique, Norm, and Utopia* (1986) and *Situating the Self* (1992) both prominently include a feminist appropriation and critique of

---

[5] Nancy Fraser, "From Redistribution to Recognition? Dilemmas of Justice in a 'Post-Socialist' Age," *New Left Review* 212 (July/August 1995): 68–93.

Habermas's critical theory.[6] Unfortunately, the core of Benhabib's position, her own dense elaboration of feminist commmunicative ethics, is nowhere elaborated in the Nicholson volume. Its absence lamentably diminishes the force of her argument that Butler's theory lacks adequate normative resources. Instead, what comes to the fore is Benhabib's critique of the models of agency and subjectivity that emerge in postmodernism, and the problems such models entail for a politics premised on women's oppression. Two unfortunate distortions ensue. First, it can appear as though Benhabib is simply trying to defend an unexamined conception of the deliberative, autonomous self; and second, one misses the complexity and thoughtfulness of Benhabib's own theory of normative justification.

Like Habermas, Benhabib seeks to draw out and justify the norms that underlie critiques of power, inequality, and the negative effects of the forces of modernization. She does so through Habermas's theory of communicative ethics, which is a reformulation of Kantian ethical universalism. As Benhabib writes in *Situating the Self*, "Instead of asking what I as a single rational moral agent can intend or will to be a universal moral maxim for all without contradiction, the communicative ethicist asks: what principles of action can we all recognize or agree to as being valid if we engage in practical discourse or a mutual search for justification?" (*SS*, 28).

Whether such a procedural approach actually helps to yield any substantive normative guidance is an issue of debate. Habermas has sought to justify communicative ethics through appeal to the principles of respect and reciprocity that he claims are inherent in linguistic practices geared toward reaching understanding. Attempting to redress the overwhelmingly negative forms of critique characteristic of both the Frankfurt School and poststructuralist traditions, he argues that the logocentrism of Western thought and the powerful instrumentality of reason are not absolute but rather constitute "a systematic foreshortening and distortion of a potential always already operative in the communicative practice of everyday life." The potential he refers to is the potential for mutual understanding "inscribed into communication in ordinary language."[7] Habermas acknowledges the dominance and reach of instrumental reason—his project is largely devoted to a systematic analysis of the historical conditions and social effects of that dominance—yet at the same time he wishes to retrieve an emancipatory model of *communicative*

[6] Seyla Benhabib, *Critique, Norm, and Utopia: A Study of the Foundations of Critical Theory* (New York: Columbia University Press, 1986), and *Situating the Self: Gender, Community and Postmodernism in Contemporary Ethics* (New York: Routledge, 1992). The latter is hereafter cited in the text as *SS*.

[7] Jürgen Habermas, *The Philosophical Discourse of Modernity*, trans. Frederick Lawrence (Cambridge, Mass.: MIT Press, 1987), 311.

reason derived from a linguistic understanding of intersubjective relations. As Benhabib argues, this form of communicative action, embodied in the highly controversial and pervasively misunderstood concept of the "ideal speech situation," entails strong ethical assumptions, namely the principles of universal moral respect and egalitarian reciprocity (*SS*, 29).

Habermas has famously argued that he does not believe any metaphysical grounding of such norms is possible; he insists instead that we view the normative constraints of the ideal speech community as "universal pragmatic presuppositions" of competent moral actors who have reached the postconventional stage of moral reasoning. Habermas's theory combines a "weak transcendental argument" concerning the four types of validity claims operative in speech acts with an empirical reconstruction of psychosocial development derived from Lawrence Kohlberg. Benhabib, though she, too, appeals to socialization processes, distinguishes her position from Habermas's "weak transcendental argument" by promoting a "historically self-conscious universalism" that locates the ethical principles of respect and reciprocity as "constituents of the moral point of view from within the normative hermeneutic horizon of modernity" (*SS*, 30). Benhabib's work thus constitutes, like Habermas's, a strong defense of specific potentialities of modernity. She differs from him in two key respects, besides the emphasis already outlined. First, she believes that Habermas's emphasis on consensus seriously distorts his account of communicative ethics. Like others who have argued against the conflation of understanding and consensus, Benhabib champions instead a discourse model of ethics that is geared toward keeping the conversation going:

> When we shift the burden of the moral test in communicative ethics from consensus to the idea of an ongoing moral conversation, we begin to ask not what all would or could agree to as a result of practical discourses to be morally permissible or impermissible, but what would be allowed and perhaps even necessary from the standpoint of continuing and sustaining the practice of the moral conversation among us. The emphasis now is less on *rational agreement*, but more on sustaining those normative practices and moral relationships within which reasoned agreement *as a way of life* can flourish and continue. (*SS*, 38)[8]

---

[8] For another helpful revision of Habermas along these lines, see Thomas McCarthy, *Ideals and Illusions: On Reconstruction and Deconstruction in Contemporary Critical Theory* (Cambridge, Mass.: MIT Press, 1991). McCarthy argues that given the diversity of value-orientations in modern culture, we cannot presuppose, and indeed do not presuppose, rational consensus when we engage in practical discourse, and that this fact must fundamentally alter Habermas's procedural model. He calls for "a more flexible and politically serviceable conception of rationally motivated agreement" (182), one that must self-consciously affirm "conciliation, compromise, consent, accommodation, and the like" (197), precisely in the recognition that some value-orientations are recalcitrantly divergent and that what count as reasons for some may not for others.

The second significant difference between Habermas and Benhabib is that Benhabib rejects Habermas's rigid opposition between justice and the good life, an opposition that effectively relegates identity-based politics to a lower plane of moral practice, and that for Benhabib undercuts our ability to apprehend the radical particularity of the other. While she believes in the importance of self-reflexive interrogations of conventional identities and roles, she strongly opposes any ethics or politics that privileges the unencumbered or detached self over the concrete, embodied, situated self. She argues in particular against those liberal models that imagine that conversations of moral justification should take place between individuals who have bracketed their strongest cultural or social identifications and attachments. Instead she promotes what she calls an "interactive universalism":

> Interactive universalism acknowledges the plurality of modes of being human, and differences among humans, without endorsing all these pluralities and differences as morally and politically valid. While agreeing that normative disputes can be settled rationally, and that fairness, reciprocity and some procedure of universalizability are constituents, that is, necessary conditions of the moral standpoint, interactive universalism regards difference as a starting point for reflection and action. In this sense, "universality" is a regulative ideal that does not deny our embodied and embedded identity, but aims at developing moral attitudes and encouraging political transformations that can yield a point of view acceptable to all. Universality is not the ideal consensus of fictitiously defined selves, but the concrete process in politics and morals of the struggle of concrete, embodied selves, striving for autonomy. (SS, 153)

This passage encapsulates the core of Benhabib's position, which attempts to mediate between universalism and particularism as traditionally understood. On the one hand, universalism's informing principles of rational argumentation, fairness, and reciprocity adjudicate between different positions in the ethicopolitical realm, enabling crucial distinctions between those notions of the good life that promote interactive universalism and those that threaten its key principles. It insists, in other words, that there is a specifiable moral standpoint from which—to take a few prominent examples—Serbian aggression, neo-Nazism, and gay bashing can be definitively condemned. On the other hand, universalism "regards difference as a starting point." It understands identity as "embodied and embedded" and promotes encounters with otherness so as to nurture the development of a moral attitude that will "yield a point of view acceptable to all."

Of course it must simultaneously be recognized that the "all" here cannot coherently include those who have, according to universalism's own principles, forfeited their place as equal participants in the ethicopolitical community. Ironically, then, Benhabib's redefinition of universalism insists on inevitable exclusion, but not in the sense that many poststructuralist and postmodernist cultural critics do, as the hardwired effect of universalism's false claims to inclusiveness, and as victimizing those disempowered by race, class, gender, or sexuality. Against naive conceptions of inclusiveness and plurality, which ultimately prove self-undermining in their toleration of communities, individuals, and practices that exclude others *arbitrarily*, interactive universalism claims that certain exclusions are not only justified, but indeed required by the principles of recognition and respect that underpin democratic institutions and practices.

If there is a point of potential strain in this argument, it lies not in the fact that Benhabib's interactive universalism will inevitably exclude or condemn—this seems to me its particular strength and honesty—but rather in its assumptions about embodied identity and whither its development tends. Benhabib takes for granted that the interactive struggles that define her universalist politics are waged on behalf of selves *striving for autonomy*. While it is certainly true that some ideal of freedom must underlie any critique of oppression, Benhabib seems to forward a restrictive notion of autonomous identity as her particular ideal of freedom. Benhabib avoids a monadic understanding of autonomy insofar as she insists that any struggle for autonomy must acknowledge life as shared; she conceives of autonomy as a form of selfhood achieved in and through communicative and social practices that accord with the democratic ideals of recognition and respect. Nonetheless, Benhabib's understanding of autonomy rests on an unexamined privileging of stable, if embodied and situated, identity that is secured through successful socialization processes. It assumes that humans inevitably wish to make positive affiliations with preexistent forms of cultural identity, or to bravely forge newly stabilizing ones. It fails to acknowledge, and hence implicitly devalues, practices and modes of life that *persistently* seek to denaturalize commonly held assumptions about identity, mistakenly conflating such practices with the incoherent accounts of agency and communication that frequently attend the theorizations of those practices.

Benhabib's conception of autonomy in many ways stacks the deck against any productive encounter with Butler, whose own theory operates within an entirely different paradigm of subjectivity, one derived from both Foucault and psychoanalysis. Butler stresses the ways in which identity is both externally constrained and internally unstable from the start. According to Butler, identity is constituted through the repeated enactment of norms via a process that she calls "performativity." She is particularly interested in the production of sexed identity, which she sees as governed by a heterosexual normative regime. Butler has tried to intervene theoretically so as to produce a more fluid, phenomenologically resonant understanding of social constructionism, one that is attentive to the constitution of identity as a temporal process, achieved diachronically through iteration and citation. She subscribes to the Foucauldian understanding of power as productive rather than merely negative, though it should be noted that her Lacanianism involves emphasis on a singular law with restricted resources and imagination, in which sexuality is the main axis of operation and normative heterosexuality the main obsession. In this sense, she privileges a form of law that Foucault himself saw as fundamentally juridical, and for Foucault, of course, juridical forms of law are largely superseded by multiple forms of modern productive power.[9]

In Butler's theory, the process of identity constitution as the forced reiteration of norms is governed by a logic of exclusion. As she states succinctly in "Contingent Foundations," her opening essay in *Feminist Contentions*, "Identity categories are never merely descriptive, but always normative, and as such, exclusionary" (*FC*, 50). Identity's exclusionary logic generates baleful effects for both normative subjects and for what she terms, adapting Kristeva, "figures of abjection": those who, with respect to norms established by the dominant regime, are not accorded full status as subjects, and are thereby relegated to "unlivable" and "uninhabitable" regions of social existence (*FC*, 47; *BTM*, 3). For Butler, the speaking subject is formed through the process of "assuming a sex," which is governed by a "heterosexual imperative [that] enables certain sexed identifications and forecloses and/or disavows other identifications." A repudiation of certain identifications in favor of others thus founds the constitution of the subject, and undergirds the subject's illusory claims to "autonomy and to life" (*BTM*, 3). And since such repudiations are generated by a distinctly heterosexual imperative or regulative norm, they refer primarily to the abjected figures of homosexuality, despite Butler's increasing efforts to assimilate into her model exclusions occurring along other axes of domination, most notably race.[10]

[9] The tension between Foucault and Lacan runs throughout Butler's work. Benhabib herself points to this theoretical rift in a cogently argued footnote in *Feminist Contentions*. See 120–21n5.

[10] Both Nicholson and Fraser criticize Butler for her assumption that the constitution of subjectivity necessarily and always produces negative, and specifically exclusionary, effects. In Fraser's memorable statement: "Is subject-authorization *inherently* a zero-sum game?" (*FC*, 68). In other words, in authorizing myself as a subject do I necessarily deauthorize others? In what can only be called a moment of radical self-contradiction and incoherent recantation, Butler responds that "the exclusionary formation of the 'subject' is neither good nor bad, but, rather a psychoanalytic premise that one might usefully employ in the service of a political critique" (*FC*, 139). I genuinely do not think that Butler can maintain this suddenly neutral meaning of exclusion without unwriting *Gender Trouble* and *Bodies That Matter*.

One might better understand at this point the distance between Benhabib's and Butler's conceptions of "autonomy." Benhabib represents ethicopolitical life as an ongoing struggle for autonomy on the part of embodied, concrete selves, a process that is enabled by the historically specific form of socialization that promotes interactive universalism. It is this socially articulated universal framework, as it were, that makes possible the recognition and preservation of difference. Butler represents ethicopolitical life as the ongoing struggle to overcome the pernicious forms of exclusion and subordination that underwrite the so-called universal and autonomous subject of modernity. For Benhabib, politics involves consolidating autonomy for the greatest collectivity; for Butler, politics involves deconstructing autonomy as the basis of any individual or collective life.

Paralleling these divergent understandings of autonomy are fundamentally different conceptions of "norms." For Benhabib, a norm is a rule or principle that provides criteria for evaluating the rightness or wrongness of an action or practice. One might specify such norms as *evaluative* norms. While Benhabib believes the norms of reciprocity and respect are embedded in communicative practices and reproduced through socialization, she follows Habermas in calling for our self-reflexive justification and extension of such norms. For Butler, by contrast, norms are mechanisms of social reproduction and identity formation internal to hegemonic social structures. One might specify these norms as functional or *normalizing* norms. Whereas Benhabib would certainly distinguish between these two senses of norm and fully admit the existence of the latter, it is not at all clear that Butler admits a distinction in kind between them. Indeed it would seem for her that all normativity ultimately reduces to normalization. Even more: Butler feels that evaluative norms are insidious precisely insofar as they attempt to mask their normalizing power.[11]

Not surprisingly, the paradigmatic divergences between the two thinkers produce radically different understandings of public political life. Like Habermas's, Benhabib's conception of autonomy is rooted in the notions of the "political public sphere" and "deliberative democracy." Benhabib values modernity precisely insofar as it fosters the development and extension of a broad spectrum of participatory forums for public debate, and "democracy" is considered the institutional expression of the ideals

---

[11] In the remainder of the essay, when encountering the term "norm" and its cognates, the reader should assume the sense of the term that applies to the thinker under discussion. Where the context does not make the specific sense of the terms clear, or where I am using one thinker's sense of norm against the other's, I will indicate this by using phrases like "evaluative norms" (for the Benhabibian sense) and "normalizing norms" (for the Butlerian). Wherever possible, I will avoid such cumbersome locutions.

of respect, recognition, and participation that are embodied in discourse ethics. But in this conception, discursive will formation encompasses more than the narrow formal institutions of democracy as traditionally understood: it encompasses the whole range of social and cultural spheres in which the issues most vital to the public are debated. "Participating in a citizen's initiative to clean up a polluted harbor is no less political than debating in cultural journals the pejorative presentation of certain groups in terms of stereotypical images (combating sexism and racism in the media)" (*SS*, 104). It is important to note that Benhabib persistently connects what might look to be a narrowly philosophical project of communicative ethics to a larger political program, as did Habermas in his work on the public sphere. She approvingly cites the following summation by Jean Cohen:

> Both the complexity and the diversity within contemporary civil societies call for the posing of the issue of democratization in terms of a variety of differentiated processes, forms, and *loci* depending on the axis of division considered. Indeed, there is an elective affinity between the discourse ethic and modern civil society as the terrain on which an institutionalized plurality of democracies can emerge. (Quoted in *SS*, 105)[12]

For Butler, reflecting a very different version of the linguistic turn than does Habermas, the discursive constitution of subjects necessarily disables the possibilities for collective democratic life. How, then, according to her, should ethics and politics proceed? Well, there are essentially two routes to political practice in Butler: one based on performative subversion, the other on acknowledging and redressing the logic of exclusion. Both forms of practice derive from Butler's poststructuralist argument that the normative constitution of identity is the ineluctable and foundational form of power that any politics must engage and (re)enact. And both forms of practice are fundamentally cultural and, even at times, restrictively therapeutic: despite appeals to collective action, identity remains the privileged topos of political practice, which, as Fraser argues, is conceived too restrictively from an *intra*subjective perspective.[13] The two forms can be distinguished from each other, in part, by their divergent temporal rhetorics. Thresholdism, or futurity, marks the performative politics, while belatedness

---

[12] For a related discussion on the public sphere, see Nancy Fraser, "Rethinking the Public Sphere: A Contribution to the Critique of Actually Existing Democracy," in Craig Calhoun, ed., *Habermas and the Public Sphere* (Cambridge, Mass.: MIT Press, 1992), 109–42. For further elaborations of Benhabib's theorization of democracy, see Seyla Benhabib, ed., *Democracy and Difference: Contesting the Boundaries of the Political* (Princeton: Princeton University Press, 1996).

[13] Also see Amanda Anderson, "Cryptonormativism and Double Gestures: The Politics of Post-structuralism," *Cultural Critique* 21 (spring 1992): 63–95.

defines the antiexclusionary practices. In both instances, I shall argue, temporal nonsynchronicity negotiates the perceived threat of a resurgent evaluative normativity.[14]

Let me begin with the notion, most prominent in *Gender Trouble* (1990), that politics should proceed through performative subversion.[15] In her original elaboration of the idea of identity as both normative and performative, Butler advocated a cultural politics that would expose the constructedness of all identity. The most famous example was drag: through its potential to reveal the imitative nature of all sexual and gendered identity, drag and other gender-bending practices were celebrated as performing the important work of denaturalizing identity. Since power operates through the naturalizing of identity, which in turn produces constraint, loss, and exclusion, denaturalizing identity is assumed to be politically efficacious. This aspect of Butler's theory has been widely criticized for its voluntarism and its inattention to the shifting and variable meanings and effects of such gender-bending practices, which are not necessarily and obviously in the service of subversion, but can easily reconsolidate gender norms. Butler acknowledges the latter criticism in *Bodies That Matter* (1993), and a more nuanced understanding of the multiple uses of denaturalization informs her reading of *Paris Is Burning* and drag melancholia in that text. But she remains recalcitrant on the voluntarism issue, insisting that her notion of agency is a supple one derived from "the notion of gender as the effect of productive constraint" (*BTM*, x). To that extent she insists on repeating the verbal acrobatics of *Gender Trouble* in relation to the question of agency. Here's one of her (many) reformulations of the issue from *Bodies That Matter*:

> There is a tendency to think that sexuality is either constructed or determined; to think that if it is constructed, it is in some sense free, and if it is determined, it is in some sense fixed. These oppositions do not describe the complexity of what is at stake in any effort to take account of the conditions under which sex and sexuality are assumed. The "performative" dimension of construction is precisely the forced reiteration of norms. In this sense, then, it is not only that there are constraints to performativity; rather, constraint calls to be rethought as the very condition of performativity. Performativity is neither free play nor theatrical self-presentation; nor can it simply be equated with performance. Moreover, constraint is not necessarily that which sets a limit to performativity; constraint is, rather, that which impels and sustains performativity. (*BTM*, 94–95)

---

[14] This mapping is not absolute. Futural rhetoric does occasionally attend antiexclusionary politics, and belatedness can attend performativity. But by and large, the emphases are as I have stated them.

[15] Judith Butler, *Gender Trouble: Feminism and the Subversion of Identity* (New York: Routledge, 1990).

I have no problem with the notion that we must always act within conditions that are not of our own making, but Butler wants to retain a strong version of constraint, or the reiteration of norms, as something that is compelled or forced even as she argues for the possibilities of critical resignification. And it seems to me that for this reason the charge of voluntarism retains its force. Because when she shifts from the systemic perspective—or the descriptions of the law as producing identity and compelling citation—to the standpoint of the performing agent, she necessarily evokes a subject who is actively and deliberately reworking the law, and thus not under compulsion. She produces an insufficiently acknowledged challenge, that is, to her own assumption of norms as normalizing. This challenge is rendered even more visible by the fact that Butler also insists that subversions of the law are simultaneously *guaranteed* at the systemic level: the law is destined to fail, either because full conformity to its dictates is impossible, or because repetition introduces the possibility of failed repetition, or because exclusions come back to haunt and subvert it. From this perspective, it would appear that deliberate subversion is gratuitous and, hence, all the more obtrusively voluntaristic.[16]

When Butler elaborates the model of performative subversion, she continually suggests the possibility that denaturalization and resignification might eventually issue in a thoroughgoing reworking of the symbolic, but this possibility is always cast in elusively futural terms. In *Gender Trouble*, she gestures somewhat cryptically toward actions that might "[proliferate] beyond the binary limits imposed by the apparent binary of sex."[17] In *Bodies That Matter*, she writes, "If there is a 'normative' dimension to this work"—she insists on putting this rare evaluative use of "normative" in quotes—"it consists precisely in assisting a radical resignification of the symbolic, *deviating the citational chain toward a more possible future* to expand the very meaning of what counts as a valued and valuable body in the world" (*BTM*, 21–22; my emphasis).

In some ways, this is understandable as utopian writing, with recognizable antecedents throughout the history of leftist thought. But what is distinctive in Butler's writing is the way temporal rhetoric emerges precisely at the site of uneasy normative commitment. In the case of performative subversion, a futural rhetoric displaces the problems surrounding agency, symbolic constraint, and poststructuralist ethics. Since symbolic constraint is constitutive of who we can become and what we can enact,

---

[16] For a related analysis of the voluntarism and political inefficacy of Butler's notion of performativity, see Molly Anne Rothenberg and Joseph Valente, "Identification Trouble" (unpublished manuscript).

[17] Butler, *Gender Trouble*, 112.

there is clearly no way to truly envision a reworked symbolic. And since embracing an alternative symbolic would necessarily involve the imposition of newly exclusionary and normalizing norms, to do more than gesture would mean lapsing into the very practices that need to be superseded. Indeed, despite Butler's insistence in *Feminist Contentions* that we must always risk new foundations, she evinces a fastidious reluctance to do so herself.

The forward-looking articulation of performative politics increasingly gives way, in *Bodies That Matter*, to a more reflective, and now strangely belated, antiexclusionary politics. Less sanguine about the efficacy of outright subversion, Butler more soberly attends to ways we might respond to the politically and ontologically *necessary* error of identity categories. We cannot choose *not* to put such categories into play, but once they are *in* play, we can begin to interrogate them for the exclusions they harbor and generate. Butler here is closely following Gayatri Chakravorty Spivak's position on essentialism, a position Butler earlier sought to sublate through the more exclusive emphasis on the unremitting subversion of identity.[18] If performative subversion aimed to denaturalize identity and thus derail its pernicious effects, here, by contrast, one realizes the processes of identity formation will perforce proceed, and one simply attempts to register and redress those processes in a necessarily incomplete way. The production of exclusion, or a constitutive outside, is "the necessary and founding violence of any truth-regime," but we should not simply accept that fact passively:

> The task is to refigure this necessary "outside" as a future horizon, one in which the violence of exclusion is perpetually in the process of being overcome. But of equal importance is the preservation of the outside, the site where discourse meets its limits, where the opacity of what is not included in a given regime of truth acts as a disruptive site of linguistic impropriety and unrepresentability, illuminating the violent and contingent boundaries of that normative regime precisely through the inability of that regime to represent that which might pose a fundamental threat to its continuity. . . . If there is a violence necessary to the language of politics, then the risk of that violation might well be followed by another in which we begin, without ending, without mastering, to own—and yet never fully to own—the exclusions by which we proceed. (*BTM*, 53)

Because the exclusionary process is productive of who and what we are, even in our oppositional politics, our attempts to acknowledge and redress it are always post hoc. Here the future horizon is ever-receding

---

[18] For a discussion of Butler's earlier position in relation to Spivak, see Anderson, "Cryptonormativism and Double Gestures."

precisely because our own belated making of amends will never, and should never, tame the contingency that also begets violence. But the question arises: does Butler ever propose that we might use the evaluative criteria governing that belated critical recognition to guard against such processes of exclusion in the first place? Well, in rare moments she does project the possibility of cultivating practices that would actually disarm exclusion (and I will be discussing one such moment presently). But she invariably returns to the bleak insistence on the impossibility of ever achieving this. This retreat is necessitated, fundamentally, by Butler's failure to distinguish evaluative criteria from the power-laden mechanisms of normalization. Yet the distinction does reappear, unacknowledged, in the rhetoric of belatedness, which, like performative thresholdism, serves to underwrite her political purism. As belated, the incomplete acts of "owning" one's exclusions are more seemingly reactive and can appear not to be themselves normatively implicated.

We can see a similar maneuver in Butler's discussion of universalist traditions in *Feminist Contentions*. Here she insists that Benhabib's universalism is perniciously grounded in a transcendental account of language (communicative reason), and is hence not able to examine its own exclusionary effects or situated quality (*FC*, 128–32). This is, to begin with, a mischaracterization. Benhabib's account of communicative reason *is* historically situated (if somewhat loosely within the horizon of modernity) and aims to justify an ongoing and self-critical process of interactive universalism—not merely through the philosophical project of articulating a theory of universal pragmatics but more significantly through the identification and cultivation of practices that enable democratic will formation.[19] Butler then introduces, in contrast to Benhabib, an exemplary practice of what she calls "misappropriating" universals (Paul Gilroy's *The Black Atlantic* is cited here). Now, it is hard not to see this as a species of dogmatism. Bad people reinscribe or reinforce universals, good people "misappropriate" them. Benhabib calls for the *reconstruction* of Enlightenment universals, but presumably even reconstruction is tainted. The key point, however, is that misappropriation is a specifically protected derivative process, one whose own belatedness and honorific disobedience are guaranteed to displace the violence of its predecessor discourse.

Let me pursue here for a moment why I find this approach unsatisfactory. Simply because the activity of acknowledging exclusion or misappropriating universals is belated or derivative does not mean that such

---

[19] Benhabib remarks in her second essay in *Feminist Contentions* that foundations are "of course, as Butler observes, contingent, for the project of modernity itself is a contingent historical project" (*FC*, 118).

an activity is not itself as powerfully normative as the "normative political philosophy" to which Butler refers with such disdain. There is a sleight of hand occurring here: Butler attempts to imply that because such activities exist at a temporal and critical remove from "founding regimes of truth," they more successfully avoid the insidious ruse of critical theory. But who's rusing who here? Because Butler finds it impossible to conceive of normativity outside of normalization, she evades the challenging task of directly confronting her own normative assumptions. Yet Butler in fact advocates ethical practices that are animated by the same evaluative principles as communicative ethics: the rigorous scrutiny of all oppositional discourse for its own newly generated exclusions, and the reconfiguration of debilitating identity terms such as "women" as sites "of permanent openness and resignifiability" (FC, 50). Both these central practices rely fundamentally on democratic principles of inclusion and open contestation. Communicative ethics does no more than to clarify where among our primary social practices we might locate the preconditions for such activities of critique and transformation. By justifying its own evaluative assumptions and resources it aims not to posit a realm free of power but rather to clarify our own ongoing critiques of power. This does not mean that such critiques will not themselves require rigorous scrutiny for harboring blindnesses and further exclusions, but neither does it mean that such critiques will necessarily be driven by exclusionary logic. And communicative ethics is by no means a "merely theoretical" or "philosophical" project inasmuch as it can identify particular social and institutional practices that foster democratic ends. By casting all attempts to characterize such practices as pernicious normalizing, Butler effectively disables her own project and leaves herself no recourse but to issue dogmatic condemnations and approvals.

I want to return now to Butler's attempts to define politics against philosophy (at least the brand of critical theory represented by Benhabib) and her discomfort at seeming to endorse the activity of "philosophical exchange" represented by Feminist Contentions. Butler characterizes Benhabib's position as the desire to let "philosophy" redeem life, claiming that such a desire reveals an abandonment of politics itself. I have argued that it is not such an abandonment. But I also want to underscore the irony of Butler's position here, which attempts to set a realm of "pure" politics against any activity that lapses into the project of normative justification. Butler herself argues that we can never avoid laying down foundations and positing universals. She also argues that we must continually subject our use of contingent foundations to rigorous critique, so as to promote not the deconstruction of universality itself, but its greater inclusiveness. The fact that "the scope of rights considered to be universal" is governed by contingent conditions "simply means that the claim to universality has not yet received a full or final articulation and that it remains to be seen how and whether it will be articulated further" (*FC*, 130). Butler here unmistakably projects an ideal of progress toward such a desired telos (even if it is not guaranteed, and is necessarily asymptotic).[20] And it is precisely at this point in her argument, when she actually begins to sound like a critical theorist, that she feels compelled to distinguish herself fully from critical theory, producing the passages about normative philosophy as the abandonment of politics.

If nothing else, it is clear that a lot is at stake here for Butler. Why does Butler attempt to disqualify *in advance* (to adopt one of her favorite phrases) any politics that employs the normative principles and procedures of communicative ethics, which are simply attempts to justify and promote practices and institutions that might allow the fullest possible scope to universal rights and public contestation? First, as I argued earlier, Benhabib's investment in a specific form of socialized autonomy goes entirely against Butler's ongoing attempts to elaborate a theory of performative agency. Second, the theory of communicative action, as a species of "philosophy," ironically operates for Butler as a useful foil against which to define a protected conception of political purity. Third, Butler conceives of critical theory as tainted by a form of imperialism, valorizing Western notions of universality at the expense of other cultures' rights to sovereignty. Not accidentally, her passage on increasing the scope of universal rights is separated from her condemnation of normative philosophy by a short paragraph on the problems of "translation" in an international arena. Likewise, "Contingent Foundations" argues strenuously for the furtherance of "democratic contestation within a postcolonial horizon" (*FC*, 41).

But once again, Butler seems to mischaracterize Benhabib's critical theory in order to secure the pedigree of her own politics. To begin with, Benhabib's "interactive universalism" is not incompatible with Butler's calls for intercultural dialogue here. In addition, Benhabib writes in *Situating the Self* that it is precisely the horizon of *modernity* generally that has seen not simply a unidirectional and efficient imperialism, but also complex exchange and self-reflective dialogue between cultures: the West has not monolithically maintained hegemony but has itself been continually transformed by conflictual and cooperative exchanges with other cultures. Benhabib wants to extend processes of intercultural exchange and understanding, precisely by means of the regulative ideals of dialogue and democracy (*SS*, 61–63n48). That may leave her open to the charge of valorizing Western democracy, but surely Butler is left open to the

[20] On the insufficiently acknowledged ideals of progress animating much work on the cultural left, see Bruce Robbins, "The Weird Heights: On Cosmopolitanism, Feeling, and Power," *differences* 7, no. 1 (spring 1995): 165–87.

same charge when she champions universal rights and refuses a concept of radical incommensurability between cultures (*FC*, 131).

There remains yet another reason why the theory of communicative ethics cannot answer Butler's theoretical investments. Despite Butler's obvious political commitment, and her intermittent attention to race, internationalism, and institutions, her theories dwell overwhelmingly at the level of individual, intrapsychic drama. Nancy Fraser, who herself criticizes Butler's intrasubjective focus, suggests that perhaps Butler's recent appeals to radical democracy, though at this point only gestural, are the beginnings of a more sustained working out of normative commitments and collective practices. Perhaps. But I read these more as compensatory moments in a theory whose real focus often lies elsewhere. In *Gender Trouble*, because the field of politics remains fully focused on questions of identity, performative subversions necessarily emphasize the self's relation to the law, or the self's relation to the self (or to the normative identity the self inhabits). Given the exclusionary effects of any assumption of identity, one might assume that denaturalizing that process of assumption will have positive intersubjective consequences, but we are not told how this works.

The problem reemerges in *Bodies That Matter*, most pronouncedly in the essay "Phantasmatic Identification and the Assumption of Sex." Here Butler makes an impassioned plea for the ethicopolitical efficacy of incoherent identity: since the assumption of coherent identity always comes at a cost, and harbors exclusions, we need to cultivate incoherent identity, or forms of identity that remain open to multiple, and what now appear as contradictory, identifications. Only then can we begin the ongoing process of overcoming a situation in which "the specificity of identity is purchased through the loss and degradation of connection" (*BTM*, 114). Not only does this account fail to elaborate any basis for its normative commitments, but there is an unexamined assumption that intrapsychic maneuvers translate directly into political realities, which seems to me to be a highly questionable claim. This comes out more sharply in the following gesture toward more positive psychic practices: "If [the] subject produces its coherence at the cost of its own complexity, the crossings of identifications of which it is itself composed, then that subject forecloses the kinds of contestatory connections that might *democratize the field of its own operation*" (*BTM*, 115; my emphasis). As was the case with performative subversion, the primary drama here is one of self-constitution. Democracy can be achieved internally, via the self's own internal operations. Intersubjective effects simply follow naturally from the form of identification undergone. At best, this constitutes an argument by analogy.

This is one of those rare passages where Butler admits the possibility, indirectly and negatively to be sure, that we might actually foster antiexclusionary practices that would not require belatedness as a constitutive feature. Characteristically, Butler draws back somewhat from this utopian moment, stressing in subsequent paragraphs that processes of exclusion can never be eradicated. In the light of that sobering truth, she then offers a variant version of future possibility: by avowing our exclusionary identifications, we will glimpse an expanded community. In her words, we should "[trace] the ways in which identification is implicated in what it excludes, and [follow] the lines of that implication for the map of future community it might yield" (*BTM*, 119). In other words, to recognize that one is what one repudiates will help to effect a possible avowal of connection with those now constituted as irredeemably other. This passage more readily acknowledges the gap between intrapsychic and collective transformation, yet it still installs the former as the template for the latter.

Butler's work is not devoid of all references to public and collective political practices. Indeed, she clearly aligns herself with specific activist communities—the feminist and gay and lesbian, most prominently—and seeks to articulate collective moments, most notably in "Gender Is Burning" and "Critically Queer," two of the essays in *Bodies That Matter*. But there is a distinctly unmapped connection between her intrapsychic model and her collective model, an attempt to imagine that intrapsychic transformation will automatically yield social transformation, just as the assumption of identity has automatically produced all the exclusions that structure our social and political world. I think there is a real problem with this emphasis on intrapsychic identity, which will continue to disable Butler's attempts to project positive political norms or to explain why she regards certain activist communities or moments as more "democratic" than others. Butler's theory needs an account of how intersubjective and collective associations might be forged and nurtured beyond the moment of "contestatory connections." This would necessarily require the risk of a greater normative clarity about democratic *procedure* (might not she at least risk a contingent proceduralism?).

Having stressed the deficiencies in Butler's theory, not only its normative incoherence but its failure to articulate its primary theoretical claims into a coherent collective or institutional politics, I now want to explore the implications of Benhabib's tendency to dismiss the kinds of cultural politics that Butler advocates. My larger question is whether the theory of communicative ethics can encompass political practices that involve the subversive staging of identifications and disidentifications such as Butler elaborates and, if not, whether this is a serious drawback to that theory.

As I stated earlier, Benhabib strongly challenges the emphasis on ethical neutrality and generalized otherness in liberal as well as Habermasian theory. To that extent she wants to bring questions of identity into the ethicopolitical arena and not subordinate them to questions of justice, as do Rawls and Habermas. But it is revealing to examine precisely how Benhabib formulates her plea for the importance of recognizing and foregrounding concrete otherness in ethicopolitical practices: "In conversations of moral justification, it is not necessary for individuals to define themselves independently either of the ends they cherish or of the constitutive attachments which make them what they are" (*SS*, 73). Benhabib emphasizes an *affirmative* relation to cultural identity: she envisions a plurality in which many different conceptions of selfhood and the good life are given positive expression. What Butler emphasizes, by contrast, is a form of politics that directly challenges stable conceptions of cultural identity, which for her always underwrite hierarchies of power. One need not believe in Butler's zero-sum game or in the political efficacy of mere destabilization to acknowledge the importance of challenging those forms of identity and identification that depend on hierarchy for their articulation: heterosexism, patriarchy, and racism. I believe Benhabib would acknowledge this—recall, for example, her recognition of the importance of cultural critiques of stereotyping—but I do not think that her theories give enough play to the multiple forms of politics that enact and stage a *radically* critical relation to stable identity, particularly the subversively theatrical and spectacular forms that Butler so cherishes and that have defined so much of queer politics in the nineties. And such theatrical displays in queer politics, as Butler's work carefully reminds us, are not simple attempts to *épater le bourgeois*, but frequently a form of rage against "the killing inattention of public policymakers on the issue of AIDS" (*BTM*, 233). Queer theatricalization in groups such as ACT UP and Queer Nation is *not* mere aestheticist politics or a flamboyant indulgence in the politics of identity. Performance is doing important political work here.

There is, in fact, something of a tension within Benhabib's work on the question of identity as "situated." On the one hand, over and against those postmodernists, pragmatists, and communitarians who suggest that our activities as critics are always determined by the norms of our communities, Benhabib argues that social criticism *needs* philosophy, and "precisely because the narratives of our cultures are so conflictual and irreconcilable that, even when one appeals to them, a certain ordering of one's normative priorities and a clarification of those principles in the name of which one speaks is unavoidable" (*FC*, 27). In extreme instances, Benhabib warns, cultural conditions might even require the social critic to become an exile, to radically separate him- or herself from the reified customs and practices of a corrupt society. In this conception, then, some form of disidentification (as a radicalization of postconventionality) structures social criticism itself, and may lead in rare instances to separation from cultures.

On the other hand, at other moments in her work, Benhabib seems to assume that by challenging "constitutive attachments," by promoting oneself as willfully detached, one risks either assuming a false neutrality or toppling the whole edifice of communicative ethics through a postmodernist celebration of negative freedom. The fact that exile is conceived as an extraordinary recourse that must be undertaken in the name of revitalization indicates, I think, that Benhabib's emphasis remains on the need for stable identifications and the socialization processes that make them possible. Butler's work helps to remind us that communicative ethics may have a tendency to reinforce stable conceptions of identity, thereby closing off important political practices and resources. We need an enlarged conception of public dialogue, one that is open to the radical disruptions of spectacle, disidentification, and transgressive experimentation, which of course themselves derive from the vertiginous insights of the postconventional moral position. In other words, we need to explore the most radical possibilities of permanent internal exile, not to hold it up as a heroicized or ideal position, but to test the assumptions of communicative ethics.

Take, for example, sadomasochism, an issue that has spanned debate within both feminist and gay politics, from the "sex wars" of the 1980s to the more recent political battles over NEA funding. In *Situating the Self*, Benhabib herself brings up the practice of sadomasochism as a kind of limit case in her outline of the principles governing communicative ethics. Some practitioners and defenders of S/M have justified the practice in libertarian terms, arguing that what consensual adults do in privacy cannot and should not be open to any formal condemnation by others who are not harmed by the practice. Others have taken more radical stands, suggesting that transgressive sexual practices—and their representation in publicly available artistic media—can work to destabilize regimes of power, therapeutically enact power relations, or fundamentally challenge oppressive conceptions of normalcy or indeed the very idea of consent itself, which derives from a liberal model of the deliberative, autonomous self.[21] Given Benhabib's emphasis on the importance

[21] For discussions of the S/M debates, and of the various perspectives I go on to discuss throughout this example, see Lisa Duggan and Nan D. Hunter, *Sex Wars: Sexual Dissent and Political Culture* (New York: Routledge, 1995); Carole S. Vance, ed., *Pleasure and Danger: Exploring Female Sexuality* (London: Pandora, 1989); Pat Califia, *Public Sex: The Culture of Radical Sex* (San Francisco: Cleis, 1994); SAMOIS, *Coming to Power* (Boston: Alyson Publications, 1982).

of the ethical principles of recognition and respect, there is no doubt that S/M presents a potential challenge to her, and she is fairly candid about that fact in a footnote. She meets the challenge with a strong set of claims:

> The psychosexual complexity of this practice [sadomasochism] is not sufficient argument against the immorality of sado-masochism, insofar as it violates the principles of moral respect and egalitarian reciprocity among humans. Nevertheless, I would agree with the libertarian position and also maintain that as long as these practices are engaged in with the explicit consent of two adults and do not result in "cruel and unusual injury" to the parties, they must be tolerated in the liberal-democratic polity. It is not the business of the modern state to promote virtue in private life; however, the standpoint of the discourse ethicist has to go beyond the perspective of the "legislator" to a utopian promotion of modes of social interaction and solidarity that realize the norm of egalitarian reciprocity. In arguing that the sado-masochists may be wrong in the perception of their own interests as lying in inflicting and receiving bodily punishment, I am not arguing as a Kantian legislator but as a moral theorist who realizes that morality is part of a larger universe of culture and values. Communicative ethics projects a utopian way of life in which mutuality, respect, and reciprocity become the norm among humans as concrete selves and not just as juridical agents. (*SS*, 59–60n34)

The first thing to notice about Benhabib's remarks here—and it obviously does not require much effort to notice it—is her baseline belief that S/M is immoral. There is no conceivable way, in her view, that a communicative ethicist can endorse a set of practices that involve "inflicting and receiving bodily punishment." As a private act undertaken between consenting adults, S/M must be tolerated by the state, but on some fundamental level Benhabib herself cannot respect the integrity of that consent: the practitioners are ultimately self-deceived about their interests, so much so that in certain instances state intervention may be required to halt or redress "cruel and unusual injury."

Benhabib's approach entirely forecloses the radical understandings of S/M outlined above, and a number of other possible conceptions of it besides. A list of such conceptions might include: S/M as an insistence on or recognition of the inescapability of power in any relations of pleasure; S/M as the expression or highlighting of the potentially liberatory fluidity of sexual and gendered roles (here it would be akin to Butler's performative subversion); S/M as a form of respect for the complex psychic needs and desires of another; S/M as a form of solidarity—a mutual understanding of how power is practiced, and of how it informs our personal history and our most intimate relations. Moreover, Benhabib implies that these practices should remain private and dyadic, thereby skirting the issue of whether representations of S/M can themselves participate in any valuable cultural or political work. But public representations of S/M that play on performative conceptions of selfhood or radically denaturalize stable conceptions of gendered roles can themselves accomplish vital political work. Admittedly, such political effects depend upon concretely situated interpretive moments and are not achieved automatically. Moreover, there is certainly no guarantee, as Butler herself admits in *Bodies That Matter*, that denaturalizing representations will serve the cause of subversion or radical transformation. Denaturalizing representations, whether framed within S/M scenarios or not, are not immune to ethicopolitical critique; S/M is not inherently immoral, pathological, or oppressive, just as vanilla sex is not inherently egalitarian and expressive of the principles of recognition and respect. Rather than seek to condemn or defend S/M in absolute terms, we should seek to foster rigorous public debate on the meanings and effects of various public representations of gender and sexuality. Here is where critical theory's conception of the deliberative processes of the public sphere must augment and modify any claim for the practical political importance of performativity.

The value of communicative ethics, in contrast to the deficiencies of Butler's position, is that it clarifies the conditions of possibility for the cultivation of specific ethicopolitical practices and stances: self-reflexive questioning of cultural norms, openness toward difference, reciprocal recognition, and respect. It demands constant interrogation of any attempts to restrict access to the rights of full citizenship in the human community and persistently argues for the most capacious and flexible forms of respect. Benhabib's failure to accord the practitioners of S/M a genuine respect does not, as one might assume, reveal the incommensurable relativity of the very idea of respect, and thereby disable communicative ethics at the core. Rather, by its own terms, communicative ethics must judge Benhabib's understanding of S/M as narrow, and highly suspicious in its attempt to relegate S/M to the realm of the private.[22]

In its elaboration of a moral ideal and its reliance on the attainment of enabling intersubjective practices, communicative ethics is not fatally compromised by identity logic and hegemonic normalization. I would suggest

[22] I particularly want to thank Joseph Valente, who served as a respondent to a colloquium version of this essay, for pressing me on this very issue of conflicting ideals of respect (within the context of another example of his own).

that the best use we can make of the Butler-Benhabib dispute is to begin the difficult work of thinking beyond this impasse, especially since Butler herself is implicitly endorsing some version of individual and social ethics. Normative political philosophy justifies itself through appeal to communicative practices: it defines the subject in relational, intersubjective, and communicative terms. Promoting communicative action and rational argumentation in its broadest sense need not, and indeed does not, translate into procedures that restrict the political imagination or the subject's relations to the multiple cultural communities in which he or she might be embedded. The subject's relation to a specific cultural identity may extend from strongly expressed attachment, to radical redefinition, to outright rejection and negation. Communicative ethics should promote practices that can remain flexible and open-ended in the face of multiple and shifting attachments and detachments.

What is most significant in this conception of communicative ethics is holding self-reflexive questioning of norms, or postconventionality, as the moral ideal that undergirds the subject's acts of affiliation and disaffiliation. A reflective return to the various cultural identities that define one can thus be as critically aware as a persistent detachment. There is no single stance, no particular politics of recognition, that can be held up as the exemplary form. Fraser's recent work has been highly illuminating in its careful mapping of the ways recognition and redistribution politics intersect with one another. As I stated at the outset, her work cogently makes the case that we must assess recognition politics in terms of political aims that extend beyond the rubric of identity. But her ultimate privileging of "deconstructive" recognition politics over "affirmative" recognition politics, and her yoking of deconstructive practices to a radically transformative politics of redistribution, seems problematic and potentially as constricting as Benhabib's tendency to privilege affirmative politics. If "deconstructive" only means "postconventional," then I agree that deconstructive recognition politics holds more promise than the potentially reifying and essentializing effects of "affirmative" approaches. But this does not appear to be her meaning, and she thereby effectively subordinates affirmative expressions of cultural affiliation, which can be just as self-reflexive and antiessentialist as deconstructive practices and certainly need not disable struggles for redistribution.

Fraser's ambitious and provocative mapping of recognition and redistribution politics is expressive of a deeply held desire for radical transformation in the socioeconomic sphere; communicative ethics, despite all the claims about its utopianism, and despite its links to the profound systematic and Marxist elements in critical theory, suggests a more pluralized conception of political practices and spheres.[23] It is in the hopes of forwarding such a conception, while retaining the normative edge of critical theory, that I have argued for a more productive dialogue between the theorists of performativity and the proponents of communicative ethics.

[23] Actually, Fraser's position in "Rethinking the Public Sphere" is closer to what I am asserting here, with the important difference that she retains the fundamental conviction that a transformative politics of redistribution must take absolute political precedence insofar as a truly pluralized public sphere can only be enacted in conditions of social and economic parity. Her understanding of the politics of identity, interestingly, is more affirmatively inflected in that earlier essay. In criticizing the Habermasian emphasis on rational procedures of justification, she writes: "This means that participation is not simply a matter of being able to state propositional contents that are neutral with respect to form of expression. Rather, as I argued in the previous section, participation means being able to speak in one's own voice, and thereby simultaneously to construct and express one's cultural identity through idiom and style" (125–26). Only in a footnote does she go on to mention deconstructive relations to identity as forms of expression she means to include. In "From Redistribution to Recognition?", by contrast, she advances deconstruction's "utopian image of a culture in which ever new constructions of identity and difference are freely elaborated and then swiftly deconstructed," arguing that this can only be achieved, of course, "on the basis of rough social equality" (90). Again, I am arguing that what is important is that relations to identity and difference be undertaken from a critically reflective vantage point; "swift deconstruction" may be effective for certain purposes, or cherished by certain individuals and groups, but it is certainly not *required*.

CHAPTER 2

The Temptations of Aggrandized Agency

FEMINIST HISTORIES AND THE HORIZON OF MODERNITY

IN THE 1980s feminist cultural history of the Victorian period manifested a decisive shift toward asserting the centrality of gender to the ideological advent of modernity. In her influential essay, "Gender: A Useful Category of Historical Analysis," Joan Wallach Scott gave prominence to the notion that feminist history ideally aspires not only to uncover women in history, but to argue for the primacy of gender to the symbolic formations of culture and the political arrangements shaping social life.[1] Such an agenda has been dramatically evident in theoretically minded feminist scholarship on the modern period, which has positioned women and cultural forms of femininity as vital structuring agents within history. A prime example of this approach would be Nancy Armstrong's *Desire and Domestic Fiction: A Political History of the Novel*, which provocatively asserts, "the modern individual is first and foremost a female."[2] A Foucauldian understanding of the advent of modern power and its development throughout the eighteenth and nineteenth centuries underwrites Armstrong's bold claim, even as her work also aligns itself with the tradition of cultural materialism.[3] Armstrong's book, as well as Mary Poovey's roughly contemporaneous *Uneven Developments: The Ideological Construction of Gender in Mid-Victorian England*, locates gender, and more specifically the construction of ideal middle-class femininity, at the heart of the ideological formation of the modern bourgeois subject and its articulation in literary and social narratives.[4] Similarly, Elizabeth

---

[1] Joan Wallach Scott, "Gender: A Useful Category of Historical Analysis," in *Gender and the Politics of History* (New York: Columbia University Press, 1988), 28–50.

[2] Nancy Armstrong, *Desire and Domestic Fiction: A Political History of the Novel* (New York: Oxford University Press, 1987), 66. Subsequent page number references will be cited parenthetically in the text.

[3] For a helpful analysis of the way these different paradigms inform Armstrong's study, see Judith Newton, "History as Usual?: Feminism and the 'New Historicism,'" *Cultural Critique* 9 (1988): 87–121.

[4] Mary Poovey, *Uneven Developments: The Ideological Work of Gender in Mid-Victorian England* (Chicago: University of Chicago Press, 1988). Subsequent page number references will be cited parenthetically in the text.

Langland's *Nobody's Angels: Middle-Class Women and Domestic Ideology in Victorian Culture* assigns to women the primary task of consolidating and regulating cultural capital, a key form of bourgeois hegemonic power.[5]

In laying claim to forms of feminine power, and to the primacy of gender within modern ideologies, these critics nonetheless display a certain discomfort with the question of just how critically reflective modern women subjects might be presumed to be. On the one hand, as I will show, feminine agency is imagined as continuous with unreflective forms of power that are simply transmitted by culturally embedded subjects. Yet on the other hand, strange exceptions occur, wherein certain historical subjects are exempted from networks of power, and consequently accorded what I will characterize as "aggrandized agency," which is marked by both critical lucidity and political potency. I consider such exceptions to be worth our scrutiny for two important reasons that extend beyond the simple satisfaction of exposing inconsistency. First, the impulse to imagine a form of agency fueled by the insights of critical detachment reveals an unexamined limit in the general theories of power to which these critics otherwise ascribe, theories that typically do not allow for the possibility that subjects might achieve any such sharpened distance from their own cultural context. Indeed, an incoherence about critical detachment itself shadows much of contemporary theoretical debate. From one perspective, detachment is cast in a negative light and opposed to a valorized conception of situatedness or avowed positionality, as in critiques of liberal neutrality or in the multiple incarnations of standpoint epistemology and identity politics. Yet, from another perspective, through a logic of exceptionalism similar to the one that characterizes work on gender and modernity, detachment is implicitly celebrated as the negative freedom that permits parodic performativity or the exposure of constructed identities. This conflict is often especially acute within feminist theory, where aesthetic or constructionist tendencies exist in some tension with longstanding critiques of those conceptions of disembodied or detached subjectivity that seem to deny or exclude the body, the feminine, the particular.

If the symptomatic moments of aggrandized agency illuminate current theoretical problems, however, they also warrant scrutiny for their effect on our understanding of Victorian culture. This, then, is the second reason for the present critique: the moments of exceptionalism, as

[5] Elizabeth Langland, *Nobody's Angels: Middle-Class Women and Domestic Ideology in Victorian Culture* (Ithaca: Cornell University Press, 1995). Subsequent page number references will be cited parenthetically in the text.

well as the more general theories of power from which they depart, ultimately forestall analysis of the ways in which Victorian subjects themselves conceived questions about critical detachment, which were fundamental to their own vexed encounter with the promises and challenges of modernity. This is a larger historical question, with ramifications for our understanding of the ways in which we have inherited this problem from the Victorians. An ideal of critical distance, itself deriving from the project of the Enlightenment, lies behind many Victorian aesthetic and intellectual projects, including the emergent human sciences and allied projects of social reform; various ideals of cosmopolitanism that sought to disrupt or complicate nationalist identifications; literary forms such as omniscient realism and dramatic monologue; and the ideal of *Bildung*, or the self-reflexive cultivation of character, which animated much of Victorian ethics and aesthetics, from John Stuart Mill to Matthew Arnold and beyond. Yet, at the same time, many Victorians were wary of the negative effects of modern life, the forms of alienation, estrangement, and rootlessness that accompanied modern disenchantment. With varying degrees of self-consciousness and explicitness, Victorian writers grappled with this problem, and its pressures affected their ideologies of gender in profound ways. Studies that bracket the question of detachment at the theoretical and methodological levels therefore cannot examine this dimension of the culture. And it is a dimension of modern life that continues to affect our own debates. Contemporary theorists have often inverted the values that Victorians assigned to different forms of detachment, valorizing irony over disinterestedness, for example, but the fundamental questions sustain their force: Are we capable of detachment from cultural forms? How do we best cultivate such detachment? Do we need to distinguish between good and bad forms of detachment? What are the ethical and political implications of the forms of detachment that we cultivate?

This essay will touch on these broader issues only briefly, and largely by way of conclusion, though they remain central to the perspective of critique adopted here, and especially to my conviction that feminist analyses of the modern period have insufficiently examined or confronted the question of critical detachment. My discussion first examines the assumptions, strategies, and symptoms that appear in the studies by Armstrong, Poovey, and Langland. I then compare these works, written by scholars trained in literary criticism and theory, with two contemporaneous feminist studies issuing from the discipline of history: Leonore Davidoff and Catherine Hall's *Family Fortunes: Men and Women of the English Middle Class, 1780–1850* and Judith R. Walkowitz's *City of Dreadful Delight: Narratives of Sexual Danger in*

Late-Victorian London.[6] My aim is to map the divergent ways in which the question of agency has emerged across the two disciplines that have together provided our most ambitious feminist cultural histories of the Victorian period. I attribute the rhetorical patterns I locate to conditions very specific to the history of feminism and the tradition of work on the separate-spheres ideology, as well as to the peculiar interactions between the separate-spheres ideology and the specific theoretical frameworks used by Armstrong, Poovey, and Langland. As I will show, Davidoff and Hall as well as Walkowitz might justifiably be said to avoid certain theoretical problems evident in the other critics, quite probably because of the influence of cultural materialism and the more theoretically modest tendencies of history as a discipline. Yet it is also the case that their studies taken alone will not enable an extensive analysis of the relation between gender and detachment in the account of modernity. For this reason, I will conclude by considering Rita Felski's *The Gender of Modernity*, which usefully thematizes and presses beyond some of the theoretical problems that first emerge in Poovey and Armstrong, allowing a fuller consideration of the larger theoretical and historical issues that I have introduced here.[7]

· · ·

The critical formations that appear in Armstrong's and Poovey's texts are governed, from one perspective, by the trope of metalepsis, the transformation of an effect into a cause. For within historicist-theoretical feminism of the late 1980s, the lure of a constructionist victimology was repudiated and to a large extent replaced by a conception of women as instrumental agents of those forms of power that were potentially seen to determine them. Poovey's and Armstrong's studies would be two versions of this formation. Vigorously debunking the understanding of women as mere objects of power, and insisting on the unacknowledged centrality of gender to the rise of modern bourgeois and disciplinary institutions, both scholars grant to middle-class women a form of influence coextensive with the practices of power that their studies always at least implicitly critique. Middle-class women become

[6] Leonore Davidoff and Catherine Hall, *Family Fortunes: Men and Women of the English Middle Class, 1780–1850* (Chicago: University of Chicago Press, 1987); Judith R. Walkowitz, *City of Dreadful Delight: Narratives of Sexual Danger in Late-Victorian London* (Chicago: University of Chicago Press, 1992). Subsequent page number references to these works will be cited parenthetically in the text.

[7] Rita Felski, *The Gender of Modernity* (Cambridge, Mass.: Harvard University Press, 1995). Subsequent page number references will be cited parenthetically in the text.

the paradoxically potent agents of a power that effectively speaks through them.[8]

The description of women as instruments of modern power may at first glance seem better to describe Armstrong than Poovey, since Poovey's principal claim is that the feminine domestic ideal serves simply as symbolic anchor to Victorian ideological reproduction across many registers. Her textual analyses in *Uneven Developments* repeatedly establish what she at one point calls the "epistemological centrality of woman's self-consistency to the oppositional structure of Victorian ideas" (9). An emphasis on the symbolic function of gender, that is, need not involve the claim that women serve as primary instruments of power. Nonetheless, on the level of social practices, Poovey's idealized middle-class wife unmistakably serves as the crucial conduit for the forms of power that secure modern identity. In Poovey's reading of Charles Dickens's *David Copperfield*, for example, the feminine domestic ideal consolidates masculine identity and guides the narrative of individual fulfillment that underwrites bourgeois ideology:

> Because her domestic authority—indeed, her self-realization—depended on her ability to regulate her own desire, the faithful woman as wife anchored her husband's desire along with her own, giving it an object as she gave him a home. In this model, self-regulation was a particularly valuable and valued form of labor, for it domesticated man's (sexual) desire in the private sphere without curtailing his ambition in the economy. (115)

Poovey's analysis here is consonant with Armstrong's insistence on the centrality of the female subject, and of feminine forms of power and surveillance, to the development and consolidation of bourgeois identity.

This manner of establishing the vital significance of gender within the history of power is shared by Langland's *Nobody's Angels*, as well. Drawing on the sociology of Pierre Bourdieu, Langland argues that Victorian middle-class women were defined by the broadly social and public task of regulating cultural capital. Rather than simply playing a key role in the making of modern privatized selfhood, the domestic woman enforced

---

[8] I don't mean to suggest that alternatives to victimology in feminist history only began to occur with the publication of these studies in the late 1980s. In the 1970s, the reconsiderations of women's place within history by cultural feminists was accompanied by assertions of women's influence on history, and by conceptualizations of women's forms of community and solidarity. Indeed, some feminists have insisted that work in women's history in the seventies was cognizant of the issues of power and agency that are often attributed to poststructuralism, new historicism, and Foucault. See Catherine Hall, *White, Male, and Middle-Class: Explorations in Feminism and History* (Cambridge: Polity Press, 1992), 14–15. My discussion of the trope of metalepsis here has to do with feminist historiographical developments within established poststructuralist and new historicist horizons.

elaborate distinctions of class that subtly demarcated and defined an emergent middle class. Langland insists that there was a more complex model of feminine management than either Armstrong or Poovey identifies: women performed the crucial work of establishing and maintaining social hierarchy; they did not merely represent privatized virtue or self-regulating interiority. Yet despite this difference, there is an underlying continuity of approach here: Langland may support a different vision of how social practices articulate relations of power, but her inscription of femininity into the narrative of modernity is similar. As in the case of Poovey and Armstrong, the middle-class woman is the principal instrument of a power that is instantiated in her fundamental practices, yet falls below the level of conscious strategy. An adept manager and social tactician, the middle-class woman nonetheless cannot be said to reflect critically upon the power that she represents. Neither victim nor plotter, she yet remains entirely continuous with the modern form of power that she promulgates. She is powerful but not critical, profoundly effective but not self-reflective. As Langland puts it, in a passage elaborating Bourdieu's conception of *habitus*, "Whereas genteel women oriented themselves toward specific goals of class hegemony, their actions were rarely the product of conscious deliberation and calculation, rather the result of an unconscious disposition (inscribed even in the body through speech and bearing) to act in certain ways" (10).

In focusing on the middle-class woman, these theorists clearly wish to bring to the fore a submerged chapter in the rise of the middle class and of modern disciplinary power. They considerably complicate the traditional materialist feminist insight that middle-class women are empowered by their class and disempowered by their gender, arguing that the convergence of class and gender ideology produced a distinctive subject-position that served to secure bourgeois hegemony. In this respect gender becomes the site of power's enactment, not the occasion for oppression. Indeed, given the particular set of ambitions and anxieties guiding these projects, one can see why the middle-class woman would become the privileged site of interrogation. First, such an approach gives to women, and to the ideology of gender, a central role in modernization and class consolidation: this may seem more empowering, ultimately, than recovering submerged voices within radical or working-class culture, which appear doomed to a certain marginality to this main story.[9] Second, it

---

[9] An important body of feminist scholarship treats the place of women in working-class culture and working-class radical politics. See Hall, *White, Male, and Middle Class*, 124–50. See also Dorothy Thompson, "Women and Nineteenth-Century Radical Politics: A Lost Dimension," in *The Rights and Wrongs of Women*, ed. Juliet Mitchell and Ann Oakley (Harmondsworth: Penguin, 1976), 112–38; Barbara Taylor, *Eve and the New Jerusalem: Socialism and Feminism in the Nineteenth Century* (London: Virago, 1983).

also serves to acknowledge middle-class complicity in practices of power, thereby answering to prominent charges in the late seventies and early eighties that middle-class women were blindly projecting their particular experience as a universal one for all women. The analyses of the distinctive power of middle-class women within the larger society overcomes this blindness, as have more recent studies of the ways in which the Victorian ideology of femininity supported the larger project of Empire.

Influential work on women and British imperialism—by Deirdre David, Jenny Sharpe, and Raina Lewis—can in some measure be seen to draw on, or reproduce, the paradigm under discussion, insofar as middle-class women become conduits for modern imperial power, which is linked to the disciplinary project of subject formation within the domestic sphere (in both the familial and national sense).[10] David's *Rule Britannia*, in particular, stresses how the conception of women's moral influence played into imperial ideas, especially in light of the symbolic importance of the queen. But the work on gender and imperialism in the Victorian period has a distinctive theoretical legacy, and in some significant ways these studies do not fit the paradigm I identify in works focusing more narrowly on national class culture. Influenced by the postcolonial theories of Gayatri Chakravorty Spivak and Homi Bhahba, these analyses of gender and imperialism tend to focus on the ways in which white middle-class women consolidated their sense of self against an excluded, racialized, native other. Such accounts position themselves primarily against liberal feminist approaches that try to celebrate women's autonomy or finding of voice, arguing that liberal projects involve the exclusion of others. They are not so much interested in repudiating victimology, then, as in repudiating problematic claims to agency. Similarly, these studies often highlight the conflicted nature of women's relation to

---

There is a tendency to emphasize particularism, resistance, and the materiality of labor in analyses of working-class women, insofar as working women cannot be assimilated to hegemonic modernizing processes in the way that middle-class woman are. For a book that manifests, and ruminates powerfully on, these tendencies, see Carolyn Kay Steedman, *Landscape for a Good Woman: A Story of Two Lives* (New Brunswick: Rutgers University Press, 1987). For an instance of this tendency within one of the studies I am discussing, see the analysis of Hannah Cullwick in Langland, *Nobody's Angels*, 209–21. For an interesting study of solidarity and community within a subculture of working-class prostitutes, see Judith R. Walkowitz, *Prostitution and Victorian Society: Women, Class, and the State* (Cambridge: Cambridge University Press, 1980).

[10] Deirdre David, *Rule Britannia: Women, Empire, and Victorian Writing* (Ithaca: Cornell University Press, 1995); Jenny Sharpe, *Allegories of Empire: The Figure of the Woman in the Colonial Text* (Minneapolis: University of Minnesota Press, 1993); Raina Lewis, *Gendering Orientalism: Race, Femininity, and Representation* (New York: Routledge, 1996).

imperial ideology, tracing a complex psychic interplay between complicity and critique, as well as the ways in which women are positioned allegorically in relation to the imperial project. In their intrasubjective focus, in their relentlessly negative critique of the liberal feminist model, and in their focus on internal textual oscillations, they do not prosecute the claim of women as central agents of modern power in the way that the metaleptical models do.[11]

It is the specific sources and effects of the metaleptical models that I want to explore for a moment. In general terms, the highlighting of middle-class women's histories and interests, and the insistence that these interests are linked to the interests of bourgeois and imperial hegemony, has enabled feminist scholars to reframe their acknowledgment of women's power within a legitimating hermeneutics of suspicion. One might be tempted, in a further turning of the screw of suspicion, to read the scholarly disavowal of deliberate calculation by the domestic woman as an attempt to diminish her responsibility, to hold to the inspiration of her profound efficacy without having to construct her as a malign oppressor. Without dismissing such a reading, I would also like to suggest that we may here be encountering a moment in which historical ideologies exert a certain force upon the interpretive present. For as in the traditional nineteenth-century representation of feminine virtue, which ideally had many desirable social and moral ramifications and diffused itself through many capillaries, certain contemporary images of feminine power project a form of agency that, while far-reaching in its effects, has no real capacity for the detached examination and critique of its aims and motives. The Victorian domestic angel was often described as making her presence and influence felt without any element of deliberation, calculation, or even self-awareness. This ideological formation conforms uncannily to the current reconstruction of domestic power as, to adapt a formulation of Foucault's, "both intentional and nonsubjective."[12]

Interestingly, however, this feminist theorization of gender and power, which combines a nuanced social constructionism with a distinctive enlargement of feminine efficacy, typically exhibits points of symptomatic strain. Indeed, in tension with the understanding of feminine power that undergirds their central arguments, there frequently appears within these accounts a privileged and anomalous figure or two who are granted

[11] For an interesting analysis that centers, within this postcolonial framework, on the relation between ideologies of femininity and conceptions of hybridity, or racial impurity, see Jennifer Brody, *Impossible Purities: Blackness, Femininity, and Victorian Culture* (Durham: Duke University Press, 1998).

[12] Michel Foucault, *The History of Sexuality: An Introduction*, vol. 1, trans. Robert Hurley (New York: Random House, 1978), 94.

deeper insight into the workings of power, and who seem not simply to instantiate modern power but to manipulate if not inaugurate it. These are the exceptional and aggrandized figures I invoked at the outset of the essay. I have in mind here, for example, Armstrong's treatment of the Brontës, who hold the dubious honor of "[establishing] a tradition of reading that would universalize modern desire in order to implant it within every individual as the very thing that makes him or her human" (202). Another instance would be Poovey's treatment of Florence Nightingale, portrayed as deftly deploying different elements of Victorian ideology so as to secure the professionalization of nursing. Generally, a certain higher-order reflexivity is at least implicitly granted to *authors* of realist texts whose *characters* represent unselfconscious modes of power: this is true not only of Armstrong's treatment of the Brontës, but also of Langland's approach to Elizabeth Gaskell and Margaret Oliphant. That is, whereas Gaskell's and Oliphant's characters might be said to be the embedded but also blinkered tacticians that Langland wants to retrieve from history, the authors are granted a larger understanding of the philosophical and social beliefs undergirding the identification of such practices. As Langland baldly puts it at one moment, Gaskell "represents reality as a construction" (120). Indeed, Langland explicitly assimilates Gaskell to the position of the privileged theorist with insight into the ruses of power: "[Gaskell's] narrative procedures suggest we should heed Michel Foucault, who recognizes behind 'minute material detail' the presence of 'alien strategies' of power and knowledge" (114). Margaret Oliphant is presented as an even more impressive poststructuralist *avant la lettre*, with full awareness of the free play of signification and the performative identities that her heroines less reflectively inhabit (165–66).

Similarly striking, and perhaps most dramatic among the examples, is the manner in which Mary Poovey's Florence Nightingale becomes endowed with an uncanny ability to understand and manipulate the whole of Victorian ideology. Not simply a woman who serves as a conduit for power, or whose influence draws on the larger forces that work through her, Florence Nightingale appears at a crucial point in Poovey's analysis actually to take a read on the current ideological formation and then selectively deploy its variables to open up a space for professional nursing in the Crimean War. I quote at some length to give the full flavor of Poovey's analysis, which begins by showing how Nightingale stressed the potency inherent in the domestic ideal:

> If Nightingale's exploitation of the militancy inherent in the domestic ideal helped authorize the supremacy of nursing, it also aligned her vision of the nurse with another enterprise gaining momentum at midcentury. To appreciate

the connection between these two campaigns, it is helpful to cast Nightingale's project in terms only slightly more militaristic than the ones she provided. If we view her campaign for nursing as an imperialistic program, we can see that it had two related fronts. The first was the "domestic" front within medicine; in this battle, Nightingale's opponents were medical men; her object was to carve out an autonomous—and ultimately superior—realm for female nursing. The second front was the "foreign" front of class; in this skirmish, her enemies were the "dirt, drink, diet, damp, draughts, drains" that made lower-class homes unsanitary; her object here was to bring the poor and their environment under the salutary sway of their middle-class betters. *Nightingale's strategy was to foreground the second campaign, which was a project shared by middle-class men, to mask the subversive character of the first, domestic campaign, which decidedly was not.* But the rhetoric in which this strategy was accomplished made Nightingale's vision of nursing particularly amenable to appropriation by English politicians and imperialists, who had their own foreign front to conquer. (188–89; my emphasis)

One might welcome this kind of analysis as giving back what the *David Copperfield* analysis seems to preclude: the capacity for reflexive critique of the ideologies encountered by the situated historical subject. This positive explanation could of course equally be applied to Langland's descriptions of Gaskell and Oliphant. But one might also question why the representation is taken so far: indeed, what is interesting here is that Nightingale becomes almost indistinguishable from Poovey herself, in the same manner that Gaskell and Oliphant become ersatz Langlands. While Nightingale clearly is an actor in a complex cultural field, she also manifests a capacity to survey from above, like a battle commander planning out tactics on a scale model. One might immediately wonder, upon reading this description, whether Nightingale may be not strategically foregrounding the "second campaign" but rather simply inhabiting it as ideology. That is, her "strategy" may have been effective but nonintentional. Why, one is led to ask, does Poovey want to ascribe such superagency to Nightingale?

It answers a need, I suggest, to get beyond the models of agency and power that affect the metaleptic formations analyzed earlier, in which "empowered" subjects simply exercise or transmit modern disciplinary power. Here, at least, however fantastically, the woman uses power formations to advance women's entry into professional practices, practices that are not reducible to disciplinary power but that share some of its aims and effects. Through figures such as Nightingale, I would argue, the critics awkwardly displace an anxiety in their own self-conceptions, awarding the valorized individual a detached understanding of the very ideological formations that they otherwise imply operate unreflectively through historical subjects. On one level these critics are skeptical that any such detachment is possible, yet on another level they rely on such detachment for the promulgation of their critical social theories. This problematic gets symptomatically displayed in strangely aggrandized portraits of historically situated subjects, which sit uneasily next to the other figurations of women as unreflexively coextensive with forms of power.

The forms of detachment, critique, and transformative intervention that I have been examining have all been associated with individuals presented as extraordinary by the critic or historian of culture: this certainly might be adduced as a reason for the overstatements that I (perhaps uncharitably) call "aggrandized agency." It is inevitable that feminists would want to bring heroic or otherwise prominent women within the annals of history, and some celebration of their historical influence is surely in order. But I want to hold to the significance of the distinction I have been drawing. It is precisely because agency and critical reflection are insufficiently or confusedly theorized that such exaggerated representations occur. They can escape notice because they approximate conventions in hagiographic recovery work or, alternately, the marriage of auteur theory and constructionism in much recent poststructuralist theory, where manipulative detachment by otherwise constrained subjects rather capriciously appears. The particularly strong claims about the subject-constituting effects of modern power or cultural capital virtually invite symptomatic excesses in the work of critics simultaneously committed to the critical and transformative potential of feminist and materialist traditions. Less wild swings occur in feminist histories with more modest, and more tempered, approaches to the question of power and agency. Walkowitz's *City of Dreadful Delight*, for example, positions itself quite explicitly as a mediated response to the influence of Foucault and poststructuralism on contemporary scholarship. Acknowledging that all subjects are situated within systems of power, Walkowitz also insists, with a very explicit appeal to the principles animating the discipline of history, on a cultural materialist conception of situated agency: "That individuals do not fully author their texts does not falsify Marx's insight that men (and women) make their own history, albeit under circumstances they do not produce or fully control. The historian's task still remains to explain cultural expressions in terms of "historically situated authorial consciousness" and to track how historic figures mobilized existing cultural tools" (9). While similar claims can be found in the introductions of Armstrong, Poovey, and Langland, the dialectical conception of agency voiced here is more consistently deployed in Walkowitz's study than in the others'. Invoking a feminist conception of the "heterogeneous public sphere" (80), Walkowitz provides a richly textured cultural analysis of the dramatic sexual narratives that circulated through London in the 1880s, treating exposés of child prostitution, scientific theories of sexuality, conceptions of lunacy, and media representations of Jack the Ripper. The absence of rhetorically extreme conceptions of agency may reflect in part the fact that Walkowitz is not interested in making any fundamental claims about the relation of gender to the advent of modernity; she charts crucial changes in the makeup and figuration of public spaces, identifies a wide range of differently gendered social actors, and describes the conventions animating dominant cultural narratives, but she does not aspire to the form of theorizing that is evident in Armstrong, Poovey, and Langland.

Because of her clearly stated aim of writing history through the reconstruction of situated social actors, Walkowitz's analyses typically center on individuals who were prominently placed within cultural dramas of gender and sexuality. Such a methodology does not, however, issue in the forms of aggrandized agency we saw elsewhere, though Walkowitz certainly is eager to grant her early feminists a strong and transformative role in the production and contestation of cultural meanings. For example, after analyzing a number of Josephine Butler's writings on her work with fallen women and as an activist in favor of the repeal of the Contagious Diseases Acts, Walkowitz draws the following conclusions about Butler's use of melodrama:

> Butler gave a radical meaning to the melodramatic narrative of sexual danger by vindicating female activism, by dignifying the figure of the suffering fallen woman, and by inserting herself as heroine/victim. She also celebrated a deferential politics of motherhood that aimed at subverting patriarchal authority: it gave mothers, not fathers, the right to control sexual access to the daughters. Butler tried to deploy the melodramatic convention of suffering womanhood to invert the prevailing view of "fallen women" as pollutants of men; instead she defended them as victims of male pollution, as women who had been invaded by men's bodies, men's laws, and by that steel penis, the speculum.
>
> In other respects, her propaganda against the Acts adhered to the gender and class expectations of traditional stage melodrama. (92)

Walkowitz portrays her subject as a privileged historical actor engaged in a complex self-representation. Butler is not credited with an institutional transformation achieved by the ruse of ideological manipulation but rather with an attempt, only partly successful, to use and transform certain cultural narratives that were ready-to-hand. This articulation, by a feminist historian using the methodologies of cultural studies, seems to be most successful among the examples I have presented in avoiding the tendency to transfer the extremes of Victorian gender construction onto contemporary analysis; and it does so by refusing the understandings of

power and agency that align so easily with those gender constructions. I
have already discussed how the theorization of diffusive, potent agency
(along the lines of Foucault or Bourdieu) is virtually invited by the Victorian conception of the domestic angel; representations of the fallen woman,
alternately, can all too easily encourage victimological or starkly constructionist accounts.[13] Walkowitz, who is keenly aware of the seductions of these hermeneutics, evades them skillfully. Here Butler is an
aware participant, one who challenges conventions from within a situated rather than omniscient perspective, one who is perspicacious and
effective, neither unconsciously instrumental nor fully detached.

Davidoff and Hall's magisterial *Family Fortunes* is interesting to place
next to Walkowitz's *City of Dreadful Delight*, insofar as it also aims to
reconstruct a mediated understanding of agency; it also makes major
claims about the role of gender, and a specifically gendered middle-class
ideology, in the formation of modern industrial society. It therefore at
least partly undertakes the same form of ambitious account that we see
in Poovey's and Armstrong's work. Indeed, there are several close parallels between the claims that underpin Poovey's study and those that are
advanced in the discussion of methodology in Davidoff and Hall's pro-
logue. Most prominently, both scholarly ventures manifest strong allegiances to materialist criticism and feminist recovery work. Like Scott
and Poovey, Davidoff and Hall see the articulation of sexual difference
as "central to the social world" and "structured by the institutions not
only of family and kinship but at every level of the legal, political, economic and social formation" (29). Drawing on the Gramscian concept
of "common sense" that has been crucial to work in cultural studies,
Davidoff and Hall stress that conceptions of femininity and masculinity
are "continually being forged, contested, reworked and reaffirmed in social institutions and practices as well as a range of ideologies" (29).

A number of elements in Davidoff and Hall's study, however, config-
ure its effects in ways that contrast with Poovey's study. Concentrating
on the emergence of the English middle class during the period
1780–1850, Davidoff and Hall typically present gender ideologies in the
process of formation, rather than positing gender difference as an established binary animating the logic of an encompassing network of ideologies. Poovey, treating the end period covered by *Family Fortunes*, assumes the binary of gendered relations to undergird a range of
ideologies, even if it is open to exposure, challenge, and transformation.
Poovey tends to locate the productive destabilization of this underlying

---

[13] This tendency is critiqued in Amanda Anderson, *Tainted Souls and Painted Faces:
The Rhetoric of Fallenness in Victorian Culture* (Ithaca: Cornell University Press, 1993),
198–203.

binary in the recurring faltering of the domestic ideal, which can never successfully disavow or suppress the forms of feminine sexual aggression that belie it.

Second, Davidoff and Hall take as their object of study the local and everyday activities structuring the town of Birmingham and the counties of Essex and Suffolk. Through the archival exploration of an exhaustive number of local records, they reconstruct the quotidian life of communities coming increasingly under the sway of industrial capitalism, which had a profound effect on family relations, local economies, the understanding of private and public relations, and practices of production and consumption. Although *Family Fortunes* does showcase nationally known writers and events that found their way into, and inflected, local culture, it tends not to isolate the power or effects of single agents. Its more common tendency is to stress the way that emergent practices positioned women as important collective agents in the overall processes of historical transformation.

Let me focus for a moment on Davidoff and Hall's discussion of Ann Taylor, one of the early proponents of "professional motherhood," a crucial element in the claims to moral authority underpinning emergent middle-class ideology. A local writer on gender roles who became nationally prominent, Taylor spent most of her married life in Essex, and was the author of, among other works, *Maternal Solicitude For a Daughter's Best Interests* (1814), *Practical Hints to Young Females on the Duties of a Wife, a Mother and the Mistress of a Family* (1815), and *Reciprocal Duties of Parents and Children* (1818). Her main stress throughout her works lay on the responsibilities parents, and particularly mothers, held for the proper moral and spiritual instruction of their children, and on the great need for system and order in the parental education of children. Taylor's mentors were Hannah More and Maria Edgeworth, and her advice grew in large part out of her own experience as a mother and domestic manager.

Davidoff and Hall characterize Taylor as one of the early supporters of an ideology that would not achieve full articulation until the 1830s and 1840s. Here is their summary description of Taylor's views and practices, one which follows directly after a detailing of the arguments contained in her advice manuals:

> These were the views of people who know that their values were not shared by the majority. Until such cultural patterns became more widely accepted, the ideologues of domesticity thought of themselves as Christian warriors, using what swords and bows they had at their disposal, in a society which was careless of spiritual life. Mrs. Taylor's pen and ink and her connections with evangelical publishing houses were her weapons. She was at one and the same time

making sense of her own experience and making it available to others. Her
writing, initially for her own purposes, forced her to be self-conscious and explicit about her maternal practices, and she no doubt presented them as more
consistent and coherent than they were in practice. In part she was giving the
work she had done as a mother a weight and public recognition which had to be
fought for. It was women like Ann Taylor who were insisting on the vital tasks
associated with motherhood, not men who were imposing it on them. (176)

A number of things about this passage are noteworthy. First, Taylor is
immediately situated within a larger group of vanguard ideologues, rather
than singled out. And while Davidoff and Hall clearly are writing
against the idea that women were in any sense simple victims of domestic ideology, they also do not aggrandize them as empowered instruments
of that ideology. Taylor's influence and experience originates locally, is in
the process of formation and diffusion, and does not singlehandedly effect any definitive transformation of motherhood. The tactic it most
prominently uses—Christian exhortation—it uses in good faith, not
manipulatively, and the misrepresentations it generates—a dubious consistency and coherence—are cast as a genuine effect of self-exploration
and self-authorization.

We are at some distance indeed from Nightingale's omniscient and ex
nihilo creation of professionalized nursing. Obviously Davidoff and Hall
have presented us with a conception of feminine critical consciousness
that raises less suspicion because its claims are not quite so dramatic.
Taylor is situated as one groping mortal within an emergent ideology,
Nightingale as an avenging angel cannily rearranging a series of ideological blocks and thereby opening a space for a new form of professionalized womanhood. But it would be wrong to simply praise Davidoff and
Hall's more modest and mediated understanding of female agency, expose Poovey's as deludedly fantastic, and stop there. In different ways,
both versions of feminist analysis have failed adequately to account for
the forms of critical reflection that enable systemic critique, either their
own or those of the historical actors they treat. The accounts that position women as continuous with modern discipline or regulation create
not exactly an empowered but rather simply a powered subject, whose
limited consciousness is symptomatically recompensed in the anomalous
portraits of aggrandized agency, born precisely of an otherwise disavowed critical detachment. The accounts that generate a more mediated conception of participatory agency, largely under the influence of
cultural materialism and more traditional historical method, certainly
provide a better description of many forms of human cultural practice,
but fail adequately to theorize the forms of critical detachment that underwrite aspirations to systemic understandings of the social totality,

and the forms of political action that might fuel, accompany, or issue from such understandings. It is crucial to reconstruct the forms and uses of detachment in their theoretical and historical complexity if we are properly to understand and distinguish among the contributions of distinctive historical individuals, the complexities of literary characterization and authorial stance, and the forms of systemic critique that animate modern and postmodern disciplinary formations.

Felski's *The Gender of Modernity* enables us to further pursue the effects of a troubling disjunction between participatory agency and critical reflection. Exploring how forms of consciousness were mapped onto gender in the rise of modernism and the theorization of modernity, Felski grapples with the topic of detachment in very interesting ways. Her account is enriched by her simultaneous investment in two accounts of modernity that frequently do not cohabit: those that, following Habermas, locate specific potentialities of modernity in the practices of critical reflection that constitute the public sphere, and those that focus more somberly on the modern extension of disciplinary power, logics of commodification, or the consolidation of cultural capital.[14] This dual focus prompts a more explicit and potentially balanced consideration of critical detachment, since reflective distance is valorized by Habermas yet viewed skeptically by the critics of modernity. Ultimately, it might be more accurate to say that Felski's competing theoretical investments, as well as her attentiveness to gender, result in a treatment of detachment that manifests more ambivalence than balance. When tracing the forms of detachment that emerge in the late nineteenth century and are associated with aestheticism and modernism, Felski highlights the many ways in which women are constructed as lacking the self-reflexivity that defines the modern male subject. Such a critique seems implicitly to acknowledge self-reflexivity as a desirable model for self-authorization and cultural interrogation. At the same time, however, Felski explicitly and implicitly criticizes the extreme forms of disengagement and detachment that she sees as underwriting masculinist aesthetics. This double gesture is clearly visible, for example, in her chapter on commodification and consumerism.

Felski opens her discussion in this chapter with a brief history of the treatment of women's consumerism in critiques of modernity, showing that until recently a victimological approach has dominated, one that portrays women as manipulated by the ideology of consumerism, "trapped in a web of objectified images which alienate them from their

---

[14] There is certainly attention to both traditions in Davidoff and Hall as well as Walkowitz: both studies pay attention to women's distinctive participation in public spheres variously construed. But Felski's study pursues further the theoretical implications of the approaches to power and rationality underlying the two traditions.

true identity" (63). But Felski does not make this point in order to join forces with recent work in cultural studies that emphasizes women's consumerist practices as the site of resistance or the pursuit of pleasures that cannot be reduced to the manipulation thesis. Although she concedes the importance of this critique, she redirects attention to a particular rhetorical configuration in modernity's representation of consumption: the voracious female consumer. Felski locates in the modernist rhetoric the same pattern of victimization-transmuted-into-threatening-superagent that we saw in Victorian ideology, and in the critical recapitulations of that rhetoric. In its most extreme manifestation, the female consumer becomes the instrument of modern capitalism precisely through the operation of metalepsis: "Depicted as the victim of modernity, she is also its privileged agent; epitomizing the subjection of women by the tyranny of capital, she simultaneously promotes the feminization of society through a burgeoning materialism and hedonistic excess" (66).

In the modern imagination, the consuming woman—and Felski's analyses single out the figures of the prostitute and the shopper—comes to figure a threatening and negative form of modern power, in this case the encroachment of consumerism, uncontainable desire, and irrationality into the traditional masculine public sphere. Crucially, however, Felski is careful to distinguish the fantasmatic figurations of such forms of power from the actual practices of women consuming in public, which were linked to democratizing gains and greater freedom of access. Felski's account also usefully serves to supplement the Habermasian understanding of the rise of the public sphere by showing how the public realm of consumption not only operated by a democratizing logic of open access (everyone was free to enter the department store), but also was distinctly gendered and played to the impulses of desire rather than the deliberative debate associated with the bourgeois public sphere as traditionally conceived. Here, as in the study as a whole, Felski mediates between an approach that stresses the encroachment of power and one that reconstructs the democratizing practices of modernity.

Yet even given her important reconceptualization of gendered practices within modernity, Felski's understanding of detachment in the study is still not fully worked out. The chapter on consumerism tries to provide an alternative not only to the rational-debate model of public participation, but also to the pejorative form of masculine detachment attributed to the flâneur. Extending her argument in relation to a quotation from Griselda Pollock, Felski writes,

If "the flâneur embodies the gaze of modernity which is both covetous and erotic," then such a gaze was by no means limited to men, but emerged as a determining feature of women's voyeuristic relationship to the commodity. Yet the flâneur's aloof detachment was, perhaps, replaced by a more intimate relationship between surveyor and surveyed, a complex intermingling of active desire and surrender to the lures of images, objects, and lifestyles. (70)

Another version of this intimate, eroticized alternative to masculine detachment appears in Felski's reconstruction of female sadism in her chapter on Marguerite Rachilde, where an abstract, depersonalized male sadism is counterposed to a feminine sadism based on the more dialogical model of seduction: cruelty is mediated through tactics of performance and masquerade that actively engage the other, rather than enacted in a "brutal, corporeal, imposition of the will" from above (190). These models of what we might call "immersed" disengagement and reengagement, while laudably dialectical, may cede too much in their flight from the reflective detachment that, by sharpened contrast, now gets associated with the indifferent violence and deluded freedom of the masculine subject. Felski's reconstruction of feminine modes of modern consciousness certainly helps to imagine and theorize different versions of being-in-public. In that sense it answers the call of cultural critic Janet Wolff, who insists that rather than invent a female flâneuse, we should attempt to characterize both the private forms in which nineteenth-century women experienced modernity and the actual ways in which they negotiated public space.[15] Nonetheless, Felski's positing of an ideal or at least approximate dialogism in feminine practices inadvertently precludes a more rigorous theoretical consideration of the gains and relative freedom enabled by detachment cultivated in the service of more systemic critique. Indeed, Felski's tantalizing analysis of Rachilde's angry heroines makes this absence all the more acutely felt, for it brings to mind a series of excessive or "perverse" representations of feminine critical consciousness in nineteenth-century British literary culture: Rosa Dartle in *David Copperfield*, Miss Wade in *Little Dorrit*, Edith Dombey in *Dombey and Son*; the Alcharasi in *Daniel Deronda*; Marian Halcombe in *The Woman in White*; Lucy Snowe in *Villette*.[16] These are just a few characters who, like certain historical actors, profoundly exceed the feminine typologies of Victorian ideology, as well as its theoretical recapitulations. Many of them do so by instantiating available practices of self-reflection, from cosmopolitan and travel-writing traditions, vanguard

---

[15] See Janet Wolff, "The Invisible Flâneuse: Women and the Literature of Modernity," in *Feminine Sentences: Essays on Women, Class, and the State* (Berkeley: University of California Press, 1990), 34–50.

[16] For discussion of several of these characters along these lines, see the chapters on Brontë, Dickens, and Eliot in Amanda Anderson, *The Powers of Distance: Cosmopolitanism and the Cultivation of Detachment* (Princeton: Princeton University Press, 2001).

aesthetics, omniscient realism, the social sciences, and even from models of professional authority ranging from medicine to motherhood. Let me make my position as clear as I can here: I consider the capacity for self-reflection both a function of human self-consciousness more generally but also as something that never can be exercised or understood apart from specific historical forms. Hence my argument here is as much against particular historical or literary claims as it is against certain theoretical tendencies, as I indicated at the outset of this essay. Much of the work on nineteenth-century gender ideology—despite the important ways in which it has established women's roles as public actors, professionals, or observers—has precluded fuller recognition of how Victorians themselves understood and grappled with the question of detachment.[17] In ways that should not seem entirely foreign to us, Victorian cultural self-understanding manifested a recurring structure of ambivalence about detachment: there was a tendency, on the one hand, to lament modern forms of rootlessness, compromised belonging, or cultural exile, and an impulse, on the other hand, to celebrate and defend the powers of distance associated with modern society, particularly the forms of cultivated detachment that shaped the emergent methodologies of the human sciences, the ambitions of omniscient realist narration, and a cosmopolitanism of art, travel, and knowledge.

The category of gender, of course, often became a key site at which this ambivalence played itself out, in ways similar to those Felski describes when treating the culture of modernism. The domestic ideal was regularly defined as lacking the capacity for admirable forms of cultivated detachment, or constructed not as a self-authorizing subject but rather as the symbolic guarantor of family, community, and nation—the nonreflective ground of those projects of reflective endorsement or affiliation undertaken by more privileged subjects. Impure women frequently rep-

---

[17] Women's use of available cultural forms are of course noted and analyzed in many of the texts I have been discussing, as my examples should make clear. In addition, important groundwork for the analysis of women's roles as observers, public actors, and professionals is provided in Deborah Epstein Nord, *Walking the Victorian Streets: Women, Representation, and the City* (Ithaca: Cornell University Press, 1995); Barbara Leah Harman, *The Feminine Political Novel in Victorian England* (Charlottesville: University Press of Virginia, 1998), and Monica F. Cohen, *Professional Domesticity in the Victorian Novel: Women, Work, and Home* (Cambridge: Cambridge University Press, 1998). The tendency in these more recent literary studies, however, is toward the mode of descriptive analysis that was evidenced in the work of the historians. This is part of a larger trend toward less theoretically bold, more historically attuned work in many areas of literary and cultural studies. My focus here is on the need for a theory and methodology that can account not only for historical forms of detachment, but also for 1) the specific ways the Victorians grappled with the issue of detachment, and 2) our own disciplinary practices of critical detachment and reflexive critique.

resented negative versions of modernity: the fallen woman symbolized acute forms of modern alienation, as someone both buffeted by impersonal forces and condemned to nonliberatory modes of self-consciousness, doomed to a perpetual self-objectification.[18] Recent work on Victorian masculinity has shown, moreover, how precarious were practices of masculine *ascesis*, itself a cultivated relation to self-development haunted by fears of compromised autonomy.[19] Any adequate understanding of gender and detachment in the Victorian period must acknowledge these cultural formations in their complexity, as well as the many challenges, implicit and explicit, to these formations. To isolate simply one internal complexity that is lost to view in the analyses I have been critiquing: at the same time that women novelists themselves often could not fully escape less enlightened economies of gender, they were themselves participating in the larger project of the novel as a practice of critical detachment through the mode of realism, which aspired to a systemic representation of social life.[20]

To the extent that the question of detachment is a focus in contemporary work on the nineteenth century, it has been primarily within the sphere of late Victorian culture, and above all within queer analyses of the aesthetic movement, and, in particular, of Oscar Wilde, who is singled out for his artful denaturalization of social norms and accepted truths.[21] In large measure this focus on Wilde and aestheticism is driven by the privileging of ironic over other forms of detachment in contemporary queer and postmodern theory. Indeed, there is a tendency among postmodern critics to valorize detachment only when it is fully ironized or otherwise defined against reflective reason. As I indicated earlier, this tendency paradoxically exists alongside an opposing tendency to disparage critical reason as a disavowal of situatedness, embodiedness, and particularity. My own position is that the valorized form of ironic detachment in queer and postmodern theory is ultimately a species of—and hence should not be opposed to—the postconventional critical reflection appealed to

[18] Anderson, *Tainted Souls and Painted Faces*.

[19] See James Eli Adams, *Dandies and Desert Saints: Styles of Victorian Manhood* (Ithaca: Cornell University Press, 1995).

[20] For an analysis keenly attuned to the tension between observer and observed within women's writing (fictional and nonliterary works of social investigation), see Nord, *Walking the Victorian Streets*. Feminist narratologists are also more alert to this kind of informing tension: see, for example, Susan Sniader Lanser, *Fictions of Authority: Women Writers and Narrative Voice* (Ithaca: Cornell University Press, 1992).

[21] See, for example, Jonathan Dollimore, *Sexual Dissidence: Augustine to Wilde, Freud to Foucault* (Oxford: Oxford University Press, 1991); Lee Edelman, *Homographesis: Essays in Gay Literary and Cultural Theory* (New York: Routledge, 1994); Christopher Craft, *Another Kind of Love: Male Homosexual Desire in English Discourse, 1850–1920* (Berkeley: University of California Press, 1994).

as the basis for critical social theory.[22] It involves the same cultivated distance from conventions, norms, and habits that characterizes critical reason. And it typically involves similar utopian or universalist aspirations, however encrypted or explicitly disavowed.

My interest in the historical enactment of modes of detachment stems from a desire to explore these utopian and universalist aspirations in their concrete manifestations. In that sense my argument here is in the service of a larger defense of the critical, dialogical, and even emancipatory potential of cultivated detachment—a potential that can be expressed in aesthetic modes like irony and parody as well as through the more serious mode of critical social theory. I should make clear, however, that I am not arguing that all modes of cultivated detachment express this potential. Scientific, systemic, and postconventional knowledge can and have been allied to motives of domination—they have even been pursued, at times, with indifference.[23] At the very least, the various forms of detachment I have alluded to render some normative dimensions of social life more explicit. More frequently, they problematize these norms, thereby opening up new possibilities of reconceptualization and new spaces of action. It is the relation between these practices of detachment and the forms of agency that they express and engender that is occluded in the feminist analyses I have been examining here. In cases where critical detachment is denied to historically situated subjects, the relation is simply absent; in what I have identified as the compensatory case of the aggrandized agents, by contrast, we see a fantastic conflation of omniscience and ominipotence: reflective distance immediately translates into large-scale transformative action. But the cultivation of detachment—which in some sense is only another name for the examined life— is always an ongoing, partial project, whose interrelated ethical and epistemological dimensions promote the reflexive interrogation of norms and the possibility for individual and collective self-determination.

[22] See the previous essay in this volume, "Debatable Performances."

[23] I should also make clear that in defending detachment I do not mean to suggest that I believe that absolute objectivity is ever achieved. I am interested in detachment as a set of historically situated, modern practices that aim to objectify facets of human existence so as to better understand, criticize, and potentially transform them. When I refer to the cultivation of detachment, I am referring to the aspiration to a distanced view, the forms it takes, the potentialities it has.

PART II

Living Universalism

CHAPTER 3

Cosmopolitanism, Universalism, and the Divided Legacies of Modernity

ONE OF THE MORE REMARKABLE developments in contemporary cultural criticism has been the surge of interest in the idea and history of universalism, a concept that has frequently been viewed as unrecuperable by practitioners of poststructuralism, postmodernism, and cultural studies more broadly. Partly in reaction to the excesses of identity politics, and partly in response to the political and ethical impasses of a strictly negative critique of Enlightenment, a number of theorists have begun to reexamine universalism, asking how we might best combine the critique of partial or false universals with the pursuit of those emancipatory ideals associated with traditional universalism. I have in mind here not the neo-Kantian versions of universalism promoted by Jürgen Habermas and his followers, which in any event already have a lengthier history, but rather the more guarded, poststructuralist-inflected analyses forwarded by critics such as Etienne Balibar, Judith Butler, Ernesto Laclau, Naomi Schor, and Joan Scott.[1]

In some respects, the reconsiderations of universalism reenact the strategies and approaches that characterized reconsiderations of essentialism in the late 1980s and early 1990s. That is to say, like the advocates of "strategic essentialism," the current theorists frequently adduce universalism's practical necessity, political efficacy, or sheer unavoidability. Similarly, many of these theorists deploy the deconstructive double gesture characteristic of the essentialism debates, arguing, on the one hand, that universalism is necessary or practically desirable, and, on the other, that

---

[1] See Etienne Balibar, "Ambiguous Universality," *differences* 7, no. 1 (1995): 48–74; Judith Butler, "Kantians in Every Culture?" *Boston Review* 19, no. 5 (1994): 18, and "For a Careful Reading," in Linda Nicholson, ed., *Feminist Contentions: A Philosophical Exchange* (New York: Routledge, 1995), 127–43; Ernesto Laclau, "Universalism, Particularism, and the Question of Identity," in John Rajchman, ed., *The Identity in Question* (New York: Routledge, 1995), 93–108, and "Subject of Politics, Politics of the Subject," *differences* 7, no. 1 (1995): 146–64; Naomi Schor, "French Feminism is a Universalism," *differences* 7, no. 1 (1995): 15–47; and Joan W. Scott, "Universalism and the History of Feminism," *differences* 7, no. 1 (1995): 1–14. *Differences* 7, no. 1 (spring 1995), is a special issue devoted to the topic of universalism. Page number references to Balibar and Butler ("For a Careful Reading") will be cited parenthetically in the text.

exclusion and violence will nonetheless attend any projection of unity or commonality.[2]

Still, one cannot simply assimilate the recent discussions of universalism and particularism to the earlier debates over essentialism and constructionism. First, essentialism and constructionism are sharply opposed to each other, whereas universalism and particularism are more easily articulated in a nuanced, mutually constitutive relationship. It is for this reason, I think, that the exchanges over universalism hold more promise than the highly polarized essentialism debates, which ultimately became so stale. Second, there is a long and significant history of universalism within Marxism, a body of thought to which many progressive poststructuralists feel some allegiance, however tempered or conditional. Consequently, there is less need to formulate one's relation to universalism in overwhelmingly strategic or suspicious terms. Indeed, it is no accident that some of the most developed contemporary poststructuralist thought on universalism emanates from critics deeply versed in Marxism, such as Ernesto Laclau and Etienne Balibar. Third, and I think most important, the reconsiderations of universalism are being made in the face of grave concerns over resurgent nationalisms and the often atomizing politics of identity. Whereas the reconsiderations of essentialism sought to address the felt needs and insistent self-understandings of marginalized groups, the reconsiderations of universalism are frequently responses to the limitations and dangers involved in a too-protectionist approach to assertions of identity or primary affiliation. In this sense, the recuperation of universalism is diametrically opposed to the recuperation of essentialism, insofar as the new universalism focuses on those ideals and practices that propel individuals and groups beyond the confines of restricted or circumscribed identities.

There is, of course, a term that throughout its long philosophical, aesthetic, and political history has been used to denote cultivated detachment from restrictive forms of identity, and that term is "cosmopolitanism." Interestingly, despite a prevalent prejudice in favor of neologisms, this rearguard term with close ties to universalism is itself making provocative appearances across a range of writings in anthropology, cultural studies, literary criticism, intellectual history, and contemporary theory broadly construed. Many of these appearances are simply gestural or nonce-descriptive, and involve no sustained analysis or endorsement of the term. Such appearances are often passing moments within a larger attempt to describe or promote self-consciously global perspectives and

---

[2] For an overview and analysis of the essentialism debates, see Amanda Anderson, "Cryptonormativism and Double Gestures: The Politics of Poststructuralism," *Cultural Critique* 21 (1992): 63–95.

methodologies. But there have been more sustained recuperative analyses of the term, which together considerably complicate and enrich the reconsiderations of universalism.

In this essay, I want to try to characterize the new appeals to cosmopolitanism, and to situate them in relation to both the new poststructuralist versions of universalism and the neo-Kantian universalisms of Habermas and the proponents of communicative ethics. My premise is that the idea of cosmopolitanism is worthy of a focused genealogy in its own right, and that current endorsements of the term have valuable contributions to make to contemporary academic and cultural debates about the politics of identity. A rigorous genealogy of cosmopolitanism would, I believe, contribute to more calibrated analyses of the history of universalism, rendering reductive oppositions between modernity and countermodernity obsolete by bringing into sharp relief modernity's own divided histories, and by disallowing any easy identification of modernity with abstract universalism. For the present purposes, however, I intend to concentrate on the current manifestations of cosmopolitanism, with only passing discussion of the history of Enlightenment and classical cosmopolitanism, to name just two Western forms of cosmopolitanism.

Unlike the reconsiderations of universalism, which have been undertaken by some of the most theoretically ambitious and philosophically inclined of contemporary thinkers, the new cosmopolitanism has tended to emerge within the more exoteric, historically minded disciplines and modes: anthropology, cultural criticism, history of the intelligentsia. To take three prominent examples, sustained recuperative analyses of the term occur in James Clifford's "Traveling Cultures" (anthropology), Bruce Robbins's *Secular Vocations* (cultural criticism; history of the intelligentsia) and David A. Hollinger's *Postethnic America* (American cultural and intellectual history).[3] Within this disciplinary matrix there is a tendency toward more popular venues and more casual genres. Moreover, many proponents of cosmopolitanism who may otherwise produce highly esoteric writings honor the topic by seeking a wider audience both through choice of publisher and style of address. Thus Julia Kristeva deliberately recast the self-avowedly cosmopolitan ideas in *Strangers to Ourselves* in the more journalistic and accessible essays of *Nations Without Nationalism*, and Martha C. Nussbaum and the editors

---

[3] James Clifford, "Traveling Cultures," in Larry Grossberg, Cary Nelson, and Paula Treichler, eds., *Cultural Studies: Now and In the Future* (New York: Routledge, 1992) 96–112; Bruce Robbins, *Secular Vocations: Intellectuals, Professionalism, Culture* (London: Verso, 1993); and David A. Hollinger, *Postethnic America: Beyond Multiculturalism* (New York: Basic Books, 1995). Page number references to these three studies will be cited parenthetically in the text.

of the *Boston Review* saw "Patriotism and Cosmopolitanism" as the occasion for a wide-ranging forum.[4]

Before going on to consider individual arguments in favor of a rehabilitated or reconfigured cosmopolitanism, I want to sketch briefly some of the main features of the concept. It is important to realize that cosmopolitanism is a flexible term, whose forms of detachment and multiple affiliation can be variously articulated and variously motivated. In general, cosmopolitanism endorses reflective distance from one's cultural affiliations, a broad understanding of other cultures and customs, and a belief in universal humanity. The relative weight assigned to these three constitutive elements can vary, as can the cultural identities against which "reflective distance" is defined. In antiquity, with the initial elaborations of cosmopolitanism by the Cynics and Stoics, cosmopolitan detachment was defined against the restricted perspective and interests of the polis. In the Enlightenment, it was defined against the constricting allegiances of religion, class, and the state. In the twentieth century, I think we can fairly say that it is defined against those parochialisms emanating from extreme allegiances to nation, race, and ethnos. In very recent defenses of cosmopolitanism, the ethnos rhetorically reaches to include any identity politics conceived along the model of the ethnic enclave.[5]

Yet the forms of distance from cultural identification that are advocated within specific cosmopolitanisms can range from the rigorously negative or exclusionary, as in the Stoic position of eschewing petty allegiances in favor of a universal standard, to the expansively inclusionary, as in those cosmopolitanisms that promote understanding of many different cultures and experiences.[6] In exclusionary cosmopolitanism, little

---

[4] "[In] the present context, a reflection involving an audience wider than that of academic circles seems necessary where the concept of the nation is concerned—a concept that has welded the coherence of individuals in Western history since the eighteenth century." Julia Kristeva, *Nations Without Nationalism*, trans. Leon S. Roudiez (New York: Columbia University Press, 1993), 6. Page number references will be cited parenthetically in the text. See also Julia Kristeva, *Strangers to Ourselves*, trans. Leon S. Roudiez (New York: Columbia University Press, 1991). Nussbaum's essay, along with twenty-nine responses, appeared in the *Boston Review* 19, no. 5 (1994): 3–34. It was subsequently published in book form, along with eleven of the original replies and five additional ones. See Martha C. Nussbaum with Respondents, *For Love of Country: Debating the Limits of Patriotism*, ed. Joshua Cohen (Boston: Beacon, 1996).

[5] This brief sketch of the historical shifts in cosmopolitan detachment is partly indebted to Max H. Boehm, "Cosmopolitanism," *Encyclopedia of the Social Sciences* (New York: Macmillan, 1931) 4:457–61.

[6] For a useful discussion of the difference between exclusive and inclusive cosmopolitanism in the eighteenth century, see Alan D. McKillop, "Local Attachment and Cosmopolitanism: The Eighteenth-Century Pattern," in Frederick W. Hilles and Harold Bloom, eds., *From Sensibility to Romanticism* (New York: Oxford University Press, 1965), 191–218. I am indebted to McKillop's terminology here.

to no weight is given to exploration of disparate cultures: all value lies in an abstract or "cosmic" universalism. In inclusionary cosmopolitanism, by contrast, universalism finds expression through sympathetic imagination and intercultural exchange. This tension, between bracketing affiliations, on the one hand, and appreciating and sometimes integrating them, on the other, appears throughout the history of cosmopolitan thought, including its contemporary articulations, which tend to argue for a redefined dialectic between the two.

Cosmopolitanism also typically manifests a complex tension between elitism and egalitarianism. It frequently advances itself as a specifically intellectual ideal or depends on a mobility that is the luxury of social, economic, or cultural privilege. In the eighteenth century, the cultivation of international communication and travel among scholars was often embraced as the symbolic or even actual enactment of cosmopolitan ideals. Here, privileged mobility among elites synecdochally masquerades as global community, or the coming together of humanity, bespeaking a profound investment in the exceptional individualism of the intellectual class, their enabling but anomalous detachment from ordinary, provincial loyalties. At the same time, the cosmopolitan identification with the larger sphere of the world, or with humanity, or with standards assumed to transcend any locale, is ostensibly inspired by the deep-seated belief in the humanity of all, wherever positioned.[7]

Still, despite its awkward elitism, which can manifest different degrees of self-consciousness, one virtue that cosmopolitanism has over a more abstract universalism is that it situates the question of universalism in relation to the position and role of the intellectual and the intellectual enterprise. It is also commonly articulated in relation to new geopolitical configurations and within the context of destabilizing experiences of intercultural contact and exchange. In the context of Stoical cosmopolitanism, the sense of an expanded world traces to Alexander the Great's program of cultural fusion and his far-reaching world conquests. Likewise in the eighteenth century the opening up of trade routes and the advancement of imperial ventures caused powerful self-interrogation among thinkers in Europe. The results of such interrogations often appear naively unaware of their own imbrication in relations of power, or their relation to the logic of capitalist expansion, as instanced in the common Enlightenment view that international commerce would foster world peace. But if we truly wish to historicize universalism, and locate

---

[7] For discussion of the tension between elitism and egalitarianism in Enlightenment cosmopolitanism, see Thomas J. Schlereth, *The Cosmopolitan Ideal in Enlightenment Thought: Its Form and Function in the Ideas of Franklin, Hume, and Voltaire, 1694–1790* (South Bend, Ind.: University of Notre Dame Press, 1977), 14.

it within an international framework of cultural contact, exchange, and conflict, then the specificity of cosmopolitanism must be traced, and analyzed in relation to the history of universalism.

Cosmopolitanism also tends to be exercised by the specifically ethical challenges of perceived cultural relativisms; it aims to articulate not simply intellectual programs but also ethical ideals for cultivating character and negotiating the experience of otherness. It is no accident, in this regard, that one primary site for the elaboration of a new cosmopolitanism is within contemporary anthropology, whose intellectual project perforce involves complex ethical questions. Although cosmopolitanism has strongly individualist elements (in its advocacy of detachment from shared identities and its emphasis on affiliation as voluntary), it nonetheless often aims to foster reciprocal and transformative encounters between strangers variously construed. In this respect, it partakes of the same intersubjective turn with regard to liberal autonomy as communicative ethics does with regard to Kantian moral theory. Its liberal tenets and ethical values frequently result in a mood of optimism that contrasts rather sharply with the hermeneutics of suspicion dominating much work on the cultural left. Although this optimism can appear at times to shade into cultivated naivete, it is often an acutely self-conscious departure from prevailing practices of negative critique, and moreover is often offset by a sophisticated attentiveness to geopolitical and multicultural complexities.

In *Secular Vocations*, Bruce Robbins provides one of the more thoughtful and developed defenses of cosmopolitanism that has appeared in recent years, one that attempts self-consciously to reconfigure the tension between elitism and egalitarianism. Invoking Edward W. Said's concept of "secular criticism," as well as James Clifford's idea of "discrepant cosmopolitanisms," Robbins sketches an intellectual and professional ideal that is very far indeed from the universal humanism of the Enlightenment philosophes.[8] Robbins finds the disparate connotations of the word "cosmopolitanism" exactly suited to his goal of articulating a self-conscious professionalism among academics that acknowledges its own privileges and interests, but without imagining that such an acknowledgment irrevocably taints its practices, or fundamentally disarms its attempts to forward progressive principles and strive against prejudice and partiality. He wants cosmopolitanism to cover a less anxious, though by no means complacent, acknowledgment of the intellectual's inability to transcend relations of power. Cosmopolitanism enables an embrace of worldliness in two senses: "1) planetary expansiveness of subject-matter,

---

[8] See Edward W. Said, *The World, the Text, and the Critic* (Cambridge, Mass.: Harvard University Press, 1983), 1–30; James Clifford, "Traveling Cultures."

on the one hand, and 2) unembarrassed acceptance of professional self-interest, on the other" (181).

Robbins, that is, acknowledges and accepts the privilege associated with the term. He does so in the knowledge that a significant Marxist tradition, still very much alive, uses the term against intellectuals pejoratively, precisely to describe forms of illusory or politically disastrous detachment from important affiliations. For example, drawing on Antonio Gramsci, Tim Brennan has recently used the term "cosmopolitan" to describe third world metropolitan intellectuals such as Salman Rushdie, Isabel Allende, and Bharati Mukherjee. In "Cosmopolitanism and Celebrities," he argues that these writers have been selected by Western reviewers as interpreters and public spokespeople for the third world.[9] "Cosmopolitans" are writers who make Western audiences less uncomfortable, and whose work importantly shares the following characteristics:

> a harsh questioning of radical decolonisation theory; a dismissive or parodic attitude towards the project of national culture; a manipulation of imperial imagery and local legend as a means of politicising "current events"; and a declaration of cultural "hybridity"—a hybridity claimed to offer certain advantages in negotiating the collisions of language, race and art in a world of disparate peoples comprising a single, if not exactly unified, world. (7)

While not dismissive of the important pedagogical and mediating roles of celebrity cosmopolitans, Brennan believes that their attitudes toward the collective popular struggles of national peoples, and their Western reception, must be analyzed in political and cultural terms. To begin this analytic of cosmopolitanism, he invokes Gramsci's critical conception of the cosmopolitan intellectual, whose historically determined emergence thwarts the crucial task of developing "national culture" (10).[10]

According to Gramsci, the Italian intellectual's disconnected relation to national culture traces back to the culturally homogenizing effects of the Roman Empire: "[It is] necessary to go back to the times of the Roman Empire when Italy, through the territory of Rome, became the melting pot of the cultured classes from throughout the Empire. Its ruling classes became ever more imperial and ever less Latin: they became cosmopolitan" (quoted in Brennan 12). Cosmopolitanism here translates into a culturally conditioned, disastrous detachment that is specifically linked to imperialism, the false universal ecumenicism of the Catholic Church,

---

[9] Tim Brennan, "Cosmopolitans and Celebrities," *Race & Class* 31, no. 1 (1989): 1–19. Page number references will be cited parenthetically in the text. A somewhat expanded version of this essay appears in Tim Brennan, *Salman Rushdie and the Third World* (New York: St. Martin's Press, 1989).

[10] This obviously has resonances with Fanon as well, as Brennan notes. See "Cosmopolitans and Celebrities," 16–18.

and the development of a rootless, intellectualized, managerial class. Over and against this, Gramsci sets the activist intellectual, one who helps to forward the development of national culture through the vigorous and direct expression not of some nostalgically unified national mythos but of the complex intercultural engagements that define the national history. Here, against Rome, Gramsci invokes ancient Greece and Renaissance England, both cultures whose distinctiveness was achieved through rich intercultural exchange. A contrast is developed, then, between a lifeless imperial disengagement—what Gramsci pejoratively calls "cosmopolitanism"—and a more local and agonistic intellectual practice. Along a Gramscian model, the development of national culture is conceived not in romantic terms, as the recognition of inward essence, a *Volksgeist*, but rather as the dynamic product of social transfer across borders of ethnicity, language, class, taste, and scientific outlook.

Brennan's fascinating, though selective, genealogy of cosmopolitanism enables a careful situating of the intellectual in relation to geopolitical history and, in particular, the *disparate* histories of various empires. The fact that he uses the term critically does not diminish the analytic richness of his arguments. It is striking to note, however, that the Gramscian alternative to a negative "cosmopolitanism" actually comes close to positive versions of the idea. Although cosmopolitanism manifests, or can be constructed as manifesting, varying degrees of detachment and engagement, the salient point here is that as an analytic category it tends to invite a layered geopolitical understanding. This does not mean that all conceptions of cosmopolitanism—whether positive or negative, naive or sophisticated—achieve a high level of analytical insight, but simply that they tend to be self-consciously articulated in the context of intercultural contact and exchange. Precisely for this reason, a fresh look at the history of cosmopolitanism, including its current manifestations, promises to enrich certain revisionary projects aimed at the analysis of terms such as "modernity" and "universalism."

Take, for example, Paul Gilroy's *The Black Atlantic*.[11] This book resituates the cultural history of slavery, as well as the history of the West, by insisting on an antinational transcultural rubric, the black Atlantic. Gilroy's study is an exemplary instance of the new attempts to do cultural analysis within a genuinely transnational frame: accordingly, Gilroy is critical of cultural studies' investment in the topos and integrity of *national* histories. He also announces as one of the book's main goals the attempt to seriously rethink the project of modernity. He thus ana-

---

[11] Paul Gilroy, *The Black Atlantic: Modernity and Double Consciousness* (Cambridge, Mass.: Harvard University Press, 1993). Page number references will be cited parenthetically in the text.

lyzes the racist logics and rhetorics at work in the theorists of modernity beginning with the Enlightenment, while at the same time affirming the promise of the universalist project. In an eloquent introductory passage describing why he focuses so persistently on the dislocating image of the ship—with its illumination of transmigration, intercultural contact, and the middle passage—Gilroy remarks, "Getting on board promises a means to reconceptualise the orthodox relationship between modernity and what passes for its prehistory. It provides a different sense of where modernity might itself be thought to begin in the constitutive relationships with outsiders that both found and temper a self-conscious sense of western civilisation" (17).

This idea central to the rethinking of modernity—that its claims to a culturally superior form of self-consciousness are inseparable from its constitutive relations to otherness—can be further refined, and rendered immediately more vivid, through an examination of the history of cosmopolitanism. Gilroy's profound reframing of cultural history reinforces the limitations of a too-restrictive conception of modernity. I want to suggest as well that the cosmopolitan tradition usefully complicates the idea of an insular Western modernity, and moreover, may provide resources for the critique of modernity within modernity itself. To reiterate, cosmopolitanism is characteristically elaborated within an experience of cultural multiplicity and at least limited self-reflexivity, and against a specific form of parochialism. Cosmopolitanism has repeatedly emerged at times when the world has suddenly seemed to expand in unassimilable ways; it is at these moments that universalism needs the rhetoric of worldliness that cosmopolitanism provides. Contemporary revitalizations of universalism, and the frequency with which the imperative of *translation* is invoked in current theoretical debates, can be seen as an instance of the same moment of radical destabilization.[12] This is not to say that articulations of cosmopolitanism will magically be less likely to impose their own particulars as a false universal. The Enlightenment conception of horizon-expanding travel and communication among scholars was often narrowly limited to Europe, even as many of their researches extended to other regions of the world. Likewise the philosophes's constructions of universal human nature often bore all too markedly the imprint of European culture and history. These points are by now ones that we expect to be made. What is more interesting is to follow out the complex forms of cultural positioning, and the more radical potentialities, that are implicit and explicit in the articulation of different cosmopolitan ideals.

[12] For invocations of the need for translation, see Jacques Derrida, *The Other Heading: Reflections on Today's Europe*, trans. Pascale-Anne Brault and Michael B. Naas (Bloomington: Indiana University Press, 1992), and Judith Butler, "Kantians in Every Culture?"

Many of the new cosmopolitanisms aim to realize such radical poten-tialities through the studied integration of their intellectual and ethical ideals. And whereas the balancing of intellectual and ethicopolitical prin-ciples may be said to characterize a vast range of contemporary work in the human sciences, I want to argue that cosmopolitanism has carved out a distinctive place for itself in regard to this animating tension. Let me be-gin to address this issue by elaborating more fully the contributions of Robbins and Clifford, paying attention now to the ways in which their egalitarianism reconfigures the traditional elitism of cosmopolitanism. One might view Robbins's text as symptomatic of the new cosmopoli-tanism insofar as what looked like an intellectual or pedagogical project, "planetary expansiveness of subject-matter," slowly develops into a sug-gestive ethical meditation. Robbins's ethical orientation begins to an-nounce itself when he makes clear that he is not advocating cosmopoli-tanism as a negative detachment from any and all affiliations, stressing instead "a density of overlapping allegiances" (184). He then goes on to favorably present Clifford's notion of "discrepant cosmopolitanisms."

Clifford himself argues for an expanded conception of cosmopoli-tanism, one that extends beyond its usual associations with the West, the metropolis, and the intellectual. His central claim is that "the normative practices of twentieth-century anthropology" have "privileged relations of dwelling over relations of travel" (99). He rejects stabilizing concep-tions of "native" culture by drawing out the many ways in which "na-tives" are travelers within complex webs of intercultural communication and exchange. Clifford employs descriptive terms such as "hybridity" and "diaspora cultures," and commends the work of Paul Gilroy, Mar-cus Rediker, Kobena Mercer, and Stuart Hall. Although he does not shy away from the more current theoretical terms, it is clear that a redefined cosmopolitanism is his term of choice. After citing Mercer's and Hall's provocative work on how diasporic cultures unsettle conventional con-ceptions of ethnicity and identity, Clifford writes:

> Such cultures of displacement and transplantation are inseparable from spe-cific, often violent, histories of economic, political, and cultural interaction, histories that generate what might be called *discrepant cosmopolitanisms*. In this emphasis we avoid, at least, the excessive localism of particularist cultural relativism, as well as the overly global vision of a capitalist or technocratic monoculture. (108)

The virtue of Clifford's work, for Robbins, lies in its skillful disman-tling of the opposition between cosmopolitan and local, its insistence on multiple cosmopolitanisms partly rooted in local cultures, partly posi-tioned in global networks. No longer conceivable as the prerogative of the West, cosmopolitanisms manifest themselves in any instance of sustained intercultural contact and exchange. Robbins draws this conclusion from Clifford: "Instead of renouncing cosmopolitanism as a false universal, one can embrace it as an impulse to knowledge that is shared with others, a striving to transcend partiality that is itself partial, but no more so than the similar cognitive strivings of many diverse peoples" (194). As an integral part of an intellectual program, then, Robbins attempts to formulate an ethos, a receptive attitude toward otherness that will stimulate what he at one point calls "mobile, reciprocal interconnectedness" (197). The term functions as an umbrella for all attempts to get beyond ethnocentrism, and for the multiple secularisms and syncretisms of a complex world. Robbins also advocates the retrieval and circulation of non-Western formulations of cosmopolitanism, citing among a few other tantalizing examples Levi-Strauss's essay "Cosmopolitanism and Schizophrenia," which presents "the syncretic mythology of Native Americans along the Pacific Northwest Coast" (194). Ultimately, Robbins's cosmopolitanism aims to foster communication and to promote a "long-term process of trans-local connecting that is both political and educational at once" (196).

Robbins's cosmopolitanism attempts to mediate between the particular and the universal in both intellectual and ethical terms. First, there is an insistence on a plurality of situated cosmopolitanisms: the will to transcend local or restrictive identities does not issue in a gray universalism, but rather a vivid spectrum of diverse dialectics of detachment, displacement, and affiliation. Second, cosmopolitanism is seen to involve a vigilant attentiveness to otherness, an ethical stance that cannot be separated from the will to knowledge: "transcending partiality" is fundamentally both an ethical and an intellectual ideal. Thus, despite the appeal to multiplicity, this cosmopolitanism deliberately contrasts itself with moral relativism: "transcending partiality" is the regulative ideal against which both intellectual projects and intersubjective practices can be judged.

Robbins himself does not make the principles underlying his claims quite as explicit as I have rendered them, however. Indeed, he claims that cosmopolitanism "better describes the sensibility of our moment" in part because "the word is not as philosophically ambitious as the term 'universalism'" (196). He thereby would appear to dissociate himself from a program of explicit normative justification. Yet, at the same time, Robbins asserts provocatively the claim that cosmopolitanism "produces normative pressure against such alternatives as, say, the fashionable hybridization" (196). It is important to recognize that this is not a simple case of inconsistency or underdevelopment of ideas. There exists a genuine tension between the universalist ethical assumptions of the new cosmopolitanisms and their simultaneous desire to cultivate ethical practices that do not impose false universals. It is precisely this tension that has led to the distinctly casual normativity of the cosmopolitan.

In contrast to neo-Kantian universalism, then, proponents of cosmopolitanism simply do not appear anxious about justification. They want to assert a strong normative claim against other positions seen to be normatively weak or undeveloped, but do so through a process of incremental, casual description rather than philosophical justification (or, to anticipate, deconstructive double gestures).[13] This casual normativity may be seen as both stemming from and potentially dictating issues of genre and address. Cosmopolitanism generally invites a description from the perspective of the participant as he or she negotiates a dense array of affiliations and commitments. Although there are developed and ongoing philosophical debates on cosmopolitanism and nationalism, the articulations of cosmopolitanism often occur not within a philosophic or high theoretical mode, but rather within genres more classically literary or eclectic: the essay, the autobiography, travel writing, and works of literature generally. The prevailing mode is descriptive and occasional.

Ultimately, a too-rigorous or bald universalism seems at odds, for the cosmopolitan, with the requisite moral task of developing a delicate intersubjective competence within a culturally diverse horizon. I deliberately use this somewhat jarring phrase, "delicate intersubjective competence," which joins the language of universalist ethics with an emphasis entirely foreign to that tradition—an emphasis on tact, sensibility, and judgment (*phronesis*), which seem fundamental to the cosmopolitan's reconfigured relation to universality. Obviously, one can read this element of cosmopolitanism as itself insufficiently conscious of its investment in an elitist *habitus*, yet the refinement advocated here is precisely an attentiveness to the "uninhibited universalizing," as Robbins puts it, that is itself an elitist prerogative (196). Normative explicitness is felt, somehow, to violate the cosmopolitan spirit, even though the cosmopolitan project is animated by the conviction that delicate intersubjective competence derives from our shared commonalities. As Paul Rabinow writes, when describing "critical, cosmopolitan intellectuals" as one among four loosely federated groups with which he as an anthropologist identifies:

> The ethical is the guiding value. This is an oppositional position, one suspicious of sovereign powers, universal truths, overly relativized preciousness, local authenticity, moralisms high and low. Understanding is its second value,

---

[13] Cosmopolitanism's casual normativity might also be described as a kind of pragmatism, a position with which it appears to share some affinities. For a discussion of the connections between cosmopolitan ethics and liberal pragmatism, see Tobin Siebers, "The Ethics of Anti-Ethnocentrism," *Michigan Quarterly Review* 32, no. 1 (1993): 41–70. Siebers especially emphasizes the fundamental optimism and hopefulness characterizing both.

but an understanding suspicious of its own imperial tendencies. It attempts to be highly attentive to (and respectful of) difference, but is also wary of the tendency to essentialize difference. What we share as a condition of existence, heightened today by our ability, and at times our eagerness, to obliterate one another, is a specificity of historical experience and place, however complex and contestable they might be, and a worldwide macro-interdependency encompassing any local particularity. . . . Although we are all cosmopolitans, *Homo sapiens* has done rather poorly in interpreting this condition. We seem to have trouble with the balancing act, preferring to reify local identities or construct universal ones. We live in-between.[14]

The cosmopolitan manifests an acute awareness of living in between, displaying a temperamental (one might even say principled) discomfort with a too-explicit affirmation of the universalism that nonetheless prompts suspicion of "overly relativized preciousness" or "local authenticity." Most of the current articulations of cosmopolitanism exhibit some version of this balancing act.[15]

As the preceding discussion makes clear, the ethical stance characterizing new articulations of cosmopolitanism has been especially influenced by the disciplinary crises of (post)modern anthropology. Partly because of this influence, cosmopolitan ethics can appear at times to be narrow and contrived, modeled as they are on a relatively bracketed encounter between strangers or travelers. Even given the demand for historical and geopolitical analysis in the "discrepant cosmopolitanisms" of Robbins and Clifford, the cosmopolitan encounter can appear restrictively dyadic, transient, thin, and protected, unlikely to have any effect on larger

[14] Paul Rabinow, "Representations Are Social Facts: Modernity and Post-modernity in Anthropology," in James Clifford and George E. Marcus, eds., *Writing Culture: The Poetics and Politics of Ethnography* (Berkeley: University of California Press, 1986), 258.

[15] The concern with how to conduct oneself amid a destabilizing diversity of cultures and norms also exercised the eighteenth-century cosmopolites. In key ways this was linked to their aspirations to develop a science of human nature, a humanist project that is not really in the same spirit as some of these new articulations of cosmopolitanism. But there was also the sense that being a "citizen of the world" required a specific form of character and a rigorous cultivation of virtue. The altruistic, expansive forms of cosmopolitanism so linked to our notion of eighteenth-century sentimentalism is partly an attempt to express an ideal of sympathetic encounter with broad varieties of experience. The eighteenth-century elaboration of codes of conduct, manners, and mores is far too momentous and complex a cultural development to go into here, and was linked to the breakdown in aristocratic privilege and the rearticulations of the concept of virtue in the midst of a developing bourgeois ideology. There are of course deeply suspicious readings to be done—and that have been done—of all of this. But such rigorous attention to conduct and manners also was tied to attempts to facilitate the challenges of intercultural contact and exchange. See Schlereth, *The Cosmopolitan Ideal*; Peter Gay, *The Enlightenment: An Interpretation*, 2 vols. (New York: Alfred A. Knopf, 1966, 1969).

political structures and forces, to which it can seem culpably inattentive in its valorization and cultivation of "mobile, reciprocal interconnectedness."

But one must guard against giving disproportionate emphasis to the anthropological ethics influencing current articulations of cosmopolitanism. As I also stated at the outset, the new interest in cosmopolitanism stems largely from a concern with the question of nationalism and, by extension, with attendant issues of domestic governance and international politics. David A. Hollinger's *Postethnic America* engages this matrix of cosmopolitan concerns, while simultaneously giving voice to those intersubjective ideals I have just articulated. The debate in the *Boston Review* over Martha C. Nussbaum's "Patriotism and Cosmopolitanism" also brings larger political issues to the fore. Indeed, the conflicts generated by Nussbaum's piece, which dramatically opposes cosmopolitan ideals to the dangers of provincial patriotism, symptomatically register tensions over nationalism internal to the new cosmopolitanisms. Lastly, Julia Kristeva has written with insight and eloquence on the relation between cosmopolitanism and nationalism. Because her approach in many ways reconciles the oppositions driving the divergences between cosmopolitanism and the new universalisms, I will reserve discussion of her work until the end of the essay.

Although Hollinger describes and endorses a form of cosmopolitanism that he sees operative in the current debates over multiculturalism, the phrase "postethnic perspective" ultimately stands in as his ethicopolitical ideal, partly, I believe, because it more readily adopts the lexical features of our time: the obligatory "post-" and the recognition of the centrality of the category of ethnicity to many people's self-understandings. But Hollinger underscores the continuities between his postethnic perspective and the cosmopolitanism articulated by American intellectuals earlier in the century. Indeed, Randolph Bourne's 1916 essay, "Trans-National America," a remarkably resonant endorsement of hyphenated identities, serves as a kind of touchstone for Hollinger's entire study.[16]

Hollinger advocates cosmopolitanism because it places a check on the proliferation of ethnic enclaves and the divisive idea of race-based descent. At the same time, he affirms the value of civic nationalism for an historically multicultural United States. One virtue of Hollinger's argument is that he does not engage in the facile and quixotic rejection of nationalism tout court, but rather follows out Liah Greenfeld's distinction between ethnic and civic nationalism in an attempt to preserve the values of the latter: its emphasis on voluntary association, democratic

[16] Interestingly, Bourne also is held up as exemplary in Mitchell Cohen, "Rooted Cosmopolitanism: Thoughts on the Left, Nationalism, and Multiculturalism," *Dissent* (Fall 1992): 478–83.

will formation, and tolerance of cultural difference.[17] He specifically argues that the importance of civic nation-states in protecting rights and providing basic welfare programs (such as health care and social security) is undervalued by proponents of postnationality, such as Arjun Appadurai.[18]

As evidenced particularly in the *Boston Review*'s forum, many thinkers have affirmed a mutually reinforcing relationship between cosmopolitanism and patriotism. This argument can take different forms. One can simply enfold patriotism into an inclusive cosmopolitanism, arguing that our affiliations can be multilayered and nonantagonistic. A corollary of this argument is often that we need to make identifications on a scale smaller than the "world" or "humanity": by this account, an exclusionary cosmopolitanism is "thin," "bloodless," "airless," "superficial." One can also assert an affinity between civic nationalism and cosmopolitanism; both share liberal-humanist values and privilege democratic practices, voluntary associations, and a self-reflective relation to cultural heritage and cultural difference.[19] This is the route Hollinger predominantly takes, though within the context of an elaborate endorsement of inclusive cosmopolitanism.

Of course, as Jacques Derrida has argued in the case of France and Europe, it is quite possible for the alliance between nationalism and cosmopolitanism to support a cultural imperialism that is difficult to distinguish from a refurbished ethnic nationalism. Ventriloquizing this position, Derrida writes: "I am (we are) all the more national for being European, all the more European for being trans-European and international; no one is more cosmopolitan and authentically universal than the one, than this 'we,' who is speaking to you."[20] Yet, a potentially problematic rhetoric of exemplarity can attend not only cosmopolitanism, but also endorsements of postnational or transnational identity. Indeed, Appadurai himself looks hopefully to the United States as a place where postnationality might particularly thrive. The problem is not, however, with the aspiration to exemplarity per se, but rather with the forms of unexamined elitism or complacent universalism that such aspiration may, but certainly need not,

---

[17] See Liah Greenfeld, *Nationalism: Five Roads to Modernity* (Cambridge, Mass.: Harvard University Press, 1992).

[18] Hollinger specifically discusses Arjun Appadurai, "Patriotism and Its Futures," *Public Culture* 5 (1993): 411–29.

[19] For examples of these arguments in the *Boston Review*'s forum, see the responses by Anthony Appiah, Robert Pinsky, Benjamin R. Barber, Leo Marx, Paul Berman, Charles Beitz, Charles Taylor, Anthony Kronman, and Lawrence Blum. For an argument that contests the charge that cosmopolitanism will somehow fail to promote the emotionally rich forms of affiliation associated with nationalism or communities of smaller scale, see Bruce Robbins, "The Weird Heights: On Cosmopolitanism, Feeling, and Power," *differences* 7, no. 1 (1995): 165–87.

[20] Derrida, *The Other Heading*, 48.

generate. The more promising and vigilant versions of cosmopolitanism avoid this danger (as do, for that matter, provocative articulations of post-nationality like Appadurai's). If the coimbrication of nationalism and cosmopolitanism issues in claims to be the universal subject, then the excesses of a narrow universalism have overwhelmed the promising openness of cosmopolitanism. But this is not necessarily what is happening when one makes appeal to particular national histories; there are reasons why the democratic traditions of America and France might have something to teach us about cosmopolitan ideals.

Hollinger aims to highlight cosmopolitanism as a significant intellectual and political tradition in the United States, whose current manifestations are sometimes lost within an insufficiently analyzed multiculturalist debate. He argues that there are two distinct strains within contemporary discourse on ethnicity: the cosmopolitan and the pluralist. While he believes that both strains have been united in their struggle for greater tolerance and diversity, they have different inflections:

> Pluralism differs from cosmopolitanism in the degree to which it endows with privilege particular groups, especially the communities that are well established at whatever time the ideal of pluralism is invoked. While cosmopolitanism is willing to put the future of every culture at risk through the sympathetic but critical scrutiny of other cultures, pluralism is more concerned to protect and perpetuate particular, existing cultures. . . . If cosmopolitanism can be casual about community building and community maintenance and tends to seek voluntary affiliations of wide compass, pluralism promotes affiliations on the narrower grounds of shared history and is more quick to see reasons for drawing boundaries between communities.
>
> Cosmopolitanism is more oriented to the individual, whom it is likely to understand as a member of a number of different communities simultaneously. Pluralism is more oriented to the group, and is likely to identify each individual with reference to a single, primary community. (85–86)

In keeping with his inclusive cosmopolitanism, Hollinger takes pains to say that his notion of postethnicity is not meant to constitute an absolute break with ethnic identifications; rather, it develops cosmopolitan ideals of voluntary affiliation in light of "the past quarter-century's greater appreciation for a variety of kinds of ethnic connectedness" (4). From a postethnic perspective, one does not dissociate oneself from particular attachments in a purely negative way, but rather reflectively relates to overlapping communities, and sees the individual's relation to its multiple attachments as voluntary, shifting, and part of an ongoing process. Hollinger thus does not want to rule out practices of reflective return to ethnic and other communities, but he wishes such practices to be undertaken in light of broader commitments to civic-democratic culture at the national level.

Clearly, Hollinger sees cosmopolitanism exerting normative pressure when it questions attachments that are unquestioned from the pluralist perspective, though like Robbins he does not really flesh this out. Individuals or groups that threaten civic-democratic ideals, such as neo-Nazis and advocates of ethnic cleansing, can presumably be condemned from the cosmopolitan perspective, but not so straightforwardly from the pluralist one. Hollinger thus articulates a cosmopolitanism that serves as the basis for a specific form of national government, civic democracy; moreover, he argues that his nationalist perspective is compatible with increased global awareness and the fostering of international relations modeled on democratic institutions.

In its advocacy of specific political institutions that promote cultural self-reflexivity, voluntary affiliation, and openness to diversity, Hollinger's program shares affinities with the ambitious ethicopolitical agendas of Habermas and Seyla Benhabib, both of whom he approvingly cites. Habermas differs from the cosmopolitans insofar as he attempts a justification of democratic institutions through appeal to a universal conception of communicative reason and its attendant ideals of equality and reciprocity. His formalistic approach, as I have already suggested, is temperamentally at odds with the new cosmopolitan sensibility, which feels that formal universalism violates the very diversity it aims to accommodate. Hollinger voices this concern about universalism quite directly: "We can distinguish a universalist will to find common ground from a cosmopolitan will to engage human diversity" (84). Interestingly, Benhabib, who has been critical of the extreme formalism of traditional communicative ethics, particularly its privileging of a generalized and rationalistic conception of otherness over a more attentive and at least in part *felt* relation to the specificity of the other, has articulated a new "interactive universalism" that moves communicative ethics closer to the spirit of the new cosmopolitanisms with their "recognition, acceptance, and eager exploration of diversity" (84).[21] Indeed, the possible convergence of a more culturally sensitive universalism and a more politically ambitious

---

[21] "Interactive universalism acknowledges the plurality of modes of being human, and differences among humans, without endorsing all these pluralities and differences as morally and politically valid. While agreeing that normative disputes can be settled rationally, and that fairness, reciprocity and some procedure of universalizability are constituents, that is, necessary conditions of the moral standpoint, interactive universalism regards difference as a starting point for reflection and action. In this sense, 'universality' is a regulative ideal that does not deny our embodied and embedded identity, but aims at developing moral attitudes and encouraging political transformations that can yield a point of view acceptable to all. Universality is not the ideal consensus of fictitiously defined selves, but the concrete process in politics and morals of the struggle of concrete, embodied selves, striving for autonomy." Seyla Benhabib, *Situating the Self: Gender, Community and Postmodernism in Contemporary Ethics* (New York: Routledge, 1992), 153.

cosmopolitanism reveals the potential complementarity of these two self-conscious inheritors of the divided legacies of modernity.

Thus far I have been discussing cosmopolitanism's relationship to universalism conceived in traditionally humanist, Enlightenment, or neo-Kantian terms. I now want to pursue the relationship between the new cosmopolitanisms and those poststructuralist reconsiderations of universalism that I invoked at the beginning of this essay. I will do so by briefly comparing the new cosmopolitanisms to two recent approaches to universality, Judith Butler's "For a Careful Reading" in *Feminist Contentions*, which in fact largely replicates her response to Nussbaum in the *Boston Review*, and Etienne Balibar's arguments in "Ambiguous Universality," an essay that appeared in a special issue of *differences* devoted to reconsiderations of universalism. By way of conclusion, I will then turn to Kristeva's provocative and potentially bridge building arguments in *Nations Without Nationalism*.

In *Feminist Contentions*, Butler's assertions about universality take place in the context of her general belief that modern identity formation is fundamentally exclusionary insofar as it takes place within a normative heterosexual regime. In keeping with arguments that structured influential poststructuralist responses to the essentialism debates, and actually in contrast to her own earlier arguments in *Gender Trouble*, Butler enacts a double gesture.[22] On the one hand, she insists, we must rigorously critique and expose the exclusions that attend any attempt to assert individual and collective identity. On the other hand, we must recognize that we cannot and ultimately should not avoid such acts of identity assertion: "To set norms, to affirm aspirations, to articulate the possibilities of a more fully democratic and participatory political life is, nevertheless, a necessity. And I would claim the same for the contested status of 'universality'" (129).

As in the case of Ernesto Laclau, Butler's recuperated universalism is articulated almost exclusively in relation to rights, the claim for which is assumed as the primary political act. According to Butler, any actual claim for rights will always be situated and hence can never be truly universal: we can never know that we have achieved a full articulation of universality because we might always encounter a divergent or contestatory articulation of what it means to be universal. There are always cultural conventions that delimit, in her phrase, "the scope of rights considered to be

---

[22] Judith Butler, *Gender Trouble: Feminism and the Subversion of Identity* (New York: Routledge, 1990). In enacting this double gesture, Butler here is closely following Gayatri Chakravorty Spivak's position on essentialism, a position Butler earlier sought to sublate through the more exclusive emphasis on the unremitting subversion of identity, and on the need to derive politics directly and consistently from a constructionist position. For a discussion of Butler's earlier position in relation to Spivak, see Anderson, "Cryptonormativism and Double Gestures."

universal" (130). Still, despite this fact, and as the earlier quote indicates, this does not mean that we should not deploy the term "universal"; we should in fact continuously attempt to give it a fuller articulation, so as to include groups that have hitherto been excluded from its purview. One key way to forward this goal is to set different conceptions of universality and of rights in dialogue with one another, in order to aggravate our awareness of cultural divergence and to hone our capacity for transformative intercultural encounters. Thus emerges the call for *translation*: we must engage in the task of "[articulating] universality through a difficult labor of translation, one in which the terms made to stand for one another are transformed in the process, and where the movement of that unanticipated transformation establishes the universal as that which is yet to be achieved, and which, in order to resist domestication, may never be fully or finally achievable" (130–31).

A double awareness of what we might call an ideal universality, on the one hand, and actual (and thereby inevitably false) universalities, on the other, conditions the political attitude Butler advocates. The elusiveness of the universal, its function as a receding goal, keeps the political process vital for Butler, and she specifically opposes her position to the normative philosophy of communicative ethics, which for her is too certain of its claims for the universality of communicative reason. Butler views appeals to shared rationality as attempts to secure in advance those political principles that need to take shape through the very enactment of political struggle and conflict; this is why the universal must be construed as a horizon rather than a foundation. For Butler, a universality that is true to the primacy of political struggle must be articulated in terms of the immediate political claims of oppressed or excluded groups.

The democratic forms of cosmopolitanism differ from Butler's reconstructed universality in that they favor those political institutions that ensure the autonomy and freedom required for critically reflective practices of affiliation, disaffiliation, and reaffiliation, for the fullest expression of what we might call "hybrid individuality" in a multicultural context. Although democratic cosmopolitanism certainly can encompass those forms of political struggle and conflict that seek to secure the democratic conditions for the full flowering of cosmopolitanism, it nonetheless imagines democratic institutions as a desired precondition (if never fully secure) rather than a necessarily receding horizon. This emphasis on securing the conditions for the free enactment of individuality places cosmopolitanism closer to liberalism than to the radical traditions of critique upon which Butler relies.

Butler's emphasis on rights claims might be seen as falling within the logic of pluralism described by Hollinger, because it would appear to aim simply for greater inclusion of already constituted groups. But Butler clearly wishes this to be not merely an additive but a radically transformative process. The sense of the human will alter radically and remain unstable as competing versions come into contact and seek to translate one another. One might be tempted to claim that the emphasis on translation constitutes an ethos analogous to the one characterizing the new cosmopolitanisms, but there are significant differences between this conception of translation and the cultivated intersubjective sensibilities promoted by Robbins and Clifford. It is important to notice that Butler locates the enabling disruption of any given universality at the linguistic level: it is the conflicting *terms* of universality that are transformed in the process of translation, and it is that "unanticipated transformation" that effectively thwarts any static universalism. A linguistic destabilization guarantees the vitality of the political process. The discussion of universality thus focuses on a semiological level, where the disruptive vicissitudes of the given norms of universality are more primary than an elaboration of intersubjective conduct in a diverse world. It is precisely this abstractive ascent to a level that exceeds the interpretive and interactive practices of individuals and groups that cosmopolitan ethics so assiduously refuses.

Balibar's discussion of universality enables us to press these distinctions further. He provisionally specifies three different types of universality: real universality, fictive universality, and ideal universality. *Real universality* refers to the fact that given the global reach of economic, political, cultural, and communicative structures, we exist within a world that has effectively become unified. For this reason, the historic ideal of "establishing universality by connecting humankind with itself, creating a cosmopolis" is now obsolete because it is redundant. Balibar stresses, however, that real universality has exacerbated rather than alleviated social and cultural differences, antagonisms, and conflicts. *Fictive universality* is closer to what we think of when we discuss the ideals of the Enlightenment: it is for Balibar entirely constructed, but felicitous insofar as it leads dominated groups to struggle for inclusion under the rubric of the Rights of Man. The price to be paid for such inclusion is, however, normalization. In acceding to the status of a subject guaranteed rights under the banner of universality, the subject also is constrained to be "normal" by various regimes of power. *Ideal universality* can be set against the constraints of fictive universality. It refers to the fundamental insurrection of individuals and collectivities against normalcy and in the name of noncoercion and nondiscrimination (what for Balibar is collected under the term "equaliberty" an ideal of freedom and equality together).

Both Butler and Balibar rearticulate the universal ideals that inform political struggle and drive political critique, while at the same time acknowledging the historicity, the fictiveness, of any particular universalism. Like the new cosmopolitanisms, the reconsiderations of universalism are marked by heightened sensitivity to the potential violence and coerciveness of imperial thinking. But, importantly, the ideals of intersubjective recognition and engagement so prominent within cosmopolitanism do not emerge forcefully in these discussions of universalism. I attribute this in part to the fact that the non-normalizing universal, or ideal universality, is so fundamentally linked to a conception of radical freedom rather than the complex negotiations of multiple affiliations that characterize cosmopolitanism. Butler and Balibar foreground what one might call the "drama of subjection" entailed by fictive universality: its normalizing and hence exclusionary effects. What serves as the condition of possibility for a vital political struggle is a subversive force of negative freedom: the instability precipitated by the act of translation in Butler's case, and the insurrectionary force that resists all coercion and normalization in Balibar's. A less radical conception of freedom animates the cosmopolitan desire for reflective relations to cultural heritages and for noncoercive, reciprocal exchanges between variously situated people.[23] The new universalisms, by contrast, tend to oscillate between a profound conviction that all intersubjective encounters are marked by exclusion and violence, saturated with power-laden effects, and an assertion of radical potentialities for transformation or subversion.

Julia Kristeva presents a special case in this regard, because her writings on cosmopolitanism actually integrate elements of both the new universalisms and the new cosmopolitanisms, and in a way that vivifies the tensions that I have been drawing out. To put it simply, she shares the suspiciousness of the new universalisms and the utopianism of the new cosmopolitanisms. Here, first, is Kristeva's defense of cosmopolitan universalism:

> It would seem to me that to uphold a universal, transnational principle of Humanity that is distinct from the historical realities of nation and citizenship constitutes, on the one hand, a continuation of the Stoic and Augustinian legacy, of that ancient and Christian cosmopolitanism that finds its place among the most valuable assets of our civilization and that we henceforth must go back to and bring up to date. But above all and on the other hand, such upholding of universality appears to me as a rampart against a nationalist, regionalist, and religious fragmentation whose integrative contractions are only too visible today. (26–27)

---

[23] Cosmopolitanism as a deliberate alternative to "hybridity" bears on this discussion insofar as many poststructuralist appeals to hybridity rely on a similar conception of destabilizing subversion.

Kristeva eloquently articulates the need for a renewed cosmopolitanism and aims to vindicate its earlier traditions. In general, *Nations Without Nationalism* defends the Enlightenment against reductive and overwhelmingly negative critique, arguing that we should resuscitate some of its most promising ideas and writers. She herself focuses especially on Montesquieu's *esprit général*, suggesting that the concept might aid us in articulating new transitional nationalisms that will hasten the development of international or polynational confederations. Like Hollinger, Kristeva finds invocations of postnationalism quixotic, and believes we must support national forms that protect democratic practices and the voluntary affiliations that promote cosmopolitanism generally. That is, she, too, defends civic forms of nationalism over and against the dangerous destructiveness of ethnic nationalisms.

Yet, unlike some proponents of cosmopolitanism, Kristeva remains wary of the potentially exclusionary effects of universalist programs. Indeed, her own highly developed psychoanalytic theory of abjection, which claims that coherent identity is achieved through the process of excluding and denigrating forms of otherness, has been fundamental to Butler's arguments about the violence of heteronormativity. Thus Kristeva goes on to sound an important caveat directly after asserting the importance of universalism:

> Yes, let us have universality for the rights of man, provided we integrate in that universality not only the smug principle according to which "all men are brothers" but also that portion of conflict, hatred, violence, and destructiveness that for two centuries since the *Declaration* has ceaselessly been unloaded upon the realities of wars and fratricidal closeness and that the Freudian discovery of the unconscious tells us is a surely modifiable but yet constituent part of the human psyche. (27)

Kristeva's sense of the modifiability of a nonetheless universal destructiveness acts as a wedge of hope enabling belief in the ethical efficacy of cosmopolitanism. Derived from psychoanalysis, Kristeva's cosmopolitanism is defined both by detachment from provincial identities and by the therapeutic exploration of strangeness within and outside of the self. It serves as the foundation for an individual ethical practice and as the primary principle animating the democratic and fundamentally liberal practices of civic and transitional "nations without nationalism." For Kristeva, only through the exploration of otherness, and the crucial acknowledgment of strangeness within the self, can people begin to "give up hunting for the scapegoat outside their group" (51). Psychoanalysis can contribute to a renewed universalist project insofar as it teaches the ethically enabling truth that "only strangeness is universal" (21). By acknowledging this truth, we will cease to consolidate the self over and against a foreign other.

Kristeva thus sublates the opposition, articulated by Hollinger, whereby universalism asserts sameness and cosmopolitanism explores and embraces diversity and otherness. She herself may at times sound too optimistic about the seemingly magical capacity of therapeutic transformations to transfigure national politics, yet she also tempers the idealism of cosmopolitanism with a stern warning about the power of psychically driven forms of destructiveness, violence, exclusion, and hatred. This cautionary element in Kristeva's writings, I think, distinguishes her sharply from many current articulations of cosmopolitanism, and in fact renders more obtrusive their generally low levels of anxiety and suspicion. Cosmopolitanism embraces rather than scrutinizes its fascination with otherness, resisting the idea that it is tainted by aestheticist or erotic elements. It values interest in otherness for its own sake, and does not think that such interest either can or should be reduced to self-interest or some monolithic conception of pervasive power. In part, such optimism and casualness must be viewed as a studied reaction to the forms of negative critique dominating much cultural criticism. But absence of anxiety can also indicate absence of duress and, by extension, certain forms of privilege or unacknowledged elitism.

Let me stress here that all current manifestations of cosmopolitanism tend to be highly self-reflexive about the problem of elitism. One impulse behind using the term "cosmopolitanism" seems to be, as I have indicated, an attempt to clearly situate the putatively universal Western observer or metropolitan intellectual, at the same time that one sees the mobility and self-reflexivity associated with the ideal as characterizing any number of positions hitherto cast as local or native.[24] Still, one might reasonably ask whether the avowal of cosmopolitanism is destined to have a retrograde effect in the current debates. Why dredge up this tainted and problematic word? Robbins probably has the most defensible answer when he says, in effect, dredge it up so we know our hands are always dirty anyway. Clifford would undoubtedly say that if we extend the term to cover multiple cultural positions, it will cease to be the elitist epithet it once was. Hollinger and Kristeva would be more adamant about the honorable tradition of cosmopolitanism, and its applicability to the ethicopolitical

[24] Of course this immediately raises the question of the relation between the terms "cosmopolitan" and "postcolonial," especially as descriptors for individuals. While there are sharp debates about the perceived diluting effect of the term "postcolonial" and its lack of clear positioning in relation to third world struggles, it nonetheless may seem more attentive to situatedness than the word "cosmopolitanism," which celebrates mobility, detachment, and voluntary identification. But it is important to recognize that "cosmopolitanism" is an ethicopolitical ideal as well as a description of global positioning, and thus is open to appropriation by those situated more specifically as postcolonial. For debates on the term "postcolonial," see Ella Shohat, "Notes on the 'Post-Colonial,'" *Social Text* 31/32 (1992): 99–113; Arif Dirlik, "The Postcolonial Aura: Third World Capitalism in the Age of Global Capitalism," *Critical Inquiry* 20 (1994): 328–56.

challenges of our time; indeed, neither Hollinger nor Kristeva is particularly troubled by the way in which the word might be said to be irrevocably invested in its own cultural capital.[25]

There are obvious dangers that attend the new elaborations of cosmopolitanism. The narrowly ethical versions can sometimes appear to overemphasize a heroicized individual cultivating its relation to otherness and to global diversity: here cosmopolitanism risks becoming an art of virtue that stands in for broader-based political programs. The skittishness over more rigorously justified philosophical arguments is also, I believe, ultimately misplaced, if understandable. The continuing refinement of communicative ethics avoids many of the problems plaguing strict Habermasian formalism, and a closer scrutiny of that philosophical dialogue could have much to offer the new cosmopolitanisms, which so far seem content with an ad hoc pragmatic stance. But despite these limitations, there are many aspects of the reconfigured cosmopolitanism that are appealing and certainly analytically useful: its promotion of descriptive analyses from a participatory perspective that is nonetheless self-reflexive and critical; its exoteric genres and modes; its suggestive way of articulating relations between disciplinary formation, global position, and lived ethos; its flexibility as a term that can describe various aesthetics, ethics, and intellectual programs; its desire to exert normative pressure and to refuse the fastidious pieties of negative critique; and its linking of self-conscious positioning to the tasks of translation, receptivity to otherness, and the ongoing project of universalism.

But apart from the question of how fully the new cosmopolitanisms should be endorsed, it remains clear that we do need to recognize and analyze its manifestations, and to distinguish them from universalism, on the one hand, and localism, on the other. As I stated at the beginning of this essay, focusing on the term will also help pluralize the effects and sites of Enlightenment discourse, and complicate our ongoing histories of modernity's effects. Most significantly, I think that attending to a hybrid concept such as this will allow for a more complex conception of detachment, which is often reductively opposed to a valorized conception of situatedness or, alternately, too easily celebrated as negative freedom.

[25] Hollinger's own investment in the cultural capital of the term, as opposed to the crassly economic resonances that Robbins likes so much, becomes apparent when he feels compelled to rant for a moment against Helen Gurley Brown, insisting that a Grand Canyon separates his ideal from the Cosmo girl, which must be blamed for giving the idea much of its current "lightness" (103). Kristeva's own lack of self-reflexivity might be said to indicate itself when she avows, "I am a cosmopolitan" (15), a form of expression that, though certainly conventional within cosmopolitan traditions, is strikingly absent from the current instances, where writers evince a reluctance to claim the term directly in this way. Cosmopolitanism is an advocated ideal, not a fully assumable identity.

CHAPTER 4

Realism, Universalism, and the Science of the Human

IT IS ARGUABLY a peculiar fact that a book announcing itself as a defense of objectivity and realism would begin by assuring readers of the political efficacy of its theories. After all, the critique of objectivity and realism within progressive cultural criticism of the past several decades has taken for granted that claims to objectivity and realism are suspicious in part because of their pretense to value-neutrality. But Satya P. Mohanty's ambitious and wide-ranging *Literary Theory and the Claims of History* joins with other attempts to lay claim to a refurbished realism that not only overcomes variously construed limitations of postmodernism but fully answers to the charges leveled against "traditional" objectivity or "naive" realism.[1] Such a project can in part be analyzed against a broader critique of postmodernism and poststructuralism advanced through reconsideration of Enlightenment ideals, including, most prominently, the ideals of universalism and its less abstract cousin, cosmopolitanism.[2] The reconstructions of both universalism and realism have claimed a greater intellectual integrity and coherence than the forms of postmodernism that they challenge *and* a more promising ethicopolitical vision, one that more convincingly acknowledges the place and claims of marginalized others. These reconstructive projects thus fundamentally challenge the familiar postmodernist idea that claims to universalism or objectivity themselves enact forms of privilege or exclusion that inherently disable any properly egalitarian or nonviolent relation to others.

Mohanty would appear to combine the universalist and realist ambitions, insofar as he asserts a moral position based on Kantian notions of

---

[1] See Satya P. Mohanty, *Literary Theory and the Claims of History: Postmodernism, Objectivity, Multicultural Politics* (Ithaca: Cornell University Press, 1997). Subsequent page number references will be cited parenthetically in the text. For related studies, see Linda Alcoff, *Real Knowing: New Versions of Coherence Theory* (Ithaca: Cornell University Press, 1996); Paisley Livingston, *Literary Knowledge: Humanistic Inquiry and the Philosophy of Science* (Ithaca: Cornell University Press, 1988).

The present essay was originally a review article of Mohanty's book and Martha C. Nussbaum's *Cultivating Humanity: A Classical Defense of Reform in Liberal Education* (cited in full below, n. 3). It appeared in *Diacritics* 29, no. 2 (1999): 3–17.

[2] See chapter 3, "Cosmopolitanism, Universalism, and the Divided Legacies of Modernity."

autonomy and dignity at the same time that, in epistemological terms, he elaborates a "postpositivist realist alternative." Maintaining that the critique of objectivity within postmodernism is propped up by an outdated understanding of scientific method and theory, he argues that the more sophisticated theories within current philosophy of science elaborate epistemological models that are fully compatible with a generalized hermeneutical method, precisely because they acknowledge both the theory-laden nature of all inquiry and the larger social and historical contexts of knowledge and experience. Before elaborating this realist alternative, however, Mohanty situates his project by forwarding a number of critiques of "constructivist postmodernism," critiques that enable us to better gauge the motivations behind his work. Foregrounded at the start are what Mohanty sees as the harmful political and ethical consequences of relativism, skepticism, and constructivism. According to Mohanty, while the claims for diversity and difference in the 1960s "had a political edge," at this historical moment they are used primarily for conservative ends, via a state-sponsored bland multiculturalism that diverts attention from the blunt material issues of race politics (17). In broader ethicopolitical terms, moreover, relativist arguments that display skepticism toward the possibilities for rational exchange between variously construed collectivities and cultures lead not to a proper respect for the other but rather to *indifference.* As Mohanty puts it, to deny the possibility of "general criteria" for "interpretive validity" is "to assert that *all spaces are equivalent,* that they have equal value, that since the lowest common principle of evaluation is all that I can invoke, I cannot—and consequently need not—think about how your space impinges on mine or how my history is defined together with yours. If that is the case, I may have started by declaring a pious political wish, but I end by denying that I need to take you seriously" (131; Mohanty's emphasis).

Beyond these harmful consequences, however, lies a more fundamental problem. In its monolithic assault on Western reason and the unified subject of humanism, constructivist postmodernism has deprived itself of any coherent account of human agency and rationality. Without a philosophical anthropology establishing the "capacities, tasks, and limits that might make up a specifically human existence," Mohanty argues, it becomes impossible to account properly for cultural practices and historical agency, for the self-understanding of cultures and the historical transformations they enact (138). Agreement about a common, if minimal, structure of rational human agency is the precondition, moreover, for any genuine intersubjective and intercultural dialogue. From this perspective, it appears that Mohanty's appeal to an anthropological account of agency potentially undergirds a universalist ethics. But while he intermittently makes appeal to universalist principles, Mohanty's overriding focus in the book is on promoting a specifically *realist* response to contemporary theoretical impasses. What assumes centrality from this perspective is not the universalist project of normatively justifying shared human practices, but rather the transcultural project of giving proper causal accounts of experience and of the world. In other words, the project of developing a coherent account of human agency and rationality is supplanted by a postpositivist account of scientific inquiry and the forms of fallibilistic objectivity it purports to achieve. Whether this latter account can make good on what the former has sought to provide is very much an open question.

For the most part, Mohanty does not specifically address the question of universalism's relation to realism, or the place philosophical anthropology might hold in such a relation, though at a key point late in the text he asserts, "There is no reason to assume that philosophical analysis of agency is necessarily discontinuous with the analyses of the empirical sciences; indeed a naturalistic epistemology of the kind I described in Chapter 6 suggests that there is a necessary continuity of substance and method between the 'empirical-scientific' and the 'philosophical.'" He goes on to say that human rationality is "the province of psychology and the social sciences rather than of speculation and polemic" (200). This is a revealing moment, inasmuch as it positions the claims he has made about rational agency as a potential *finding* of the realist project, rather than a philosophical claim that either precedes or lies outside the province of epistemology. The questions that Mohanty suggests ought to be the occasion for further research are as follows:

> What resources of self-understanding do human agents typically possess, and in what ways do physiological constraints define them? How do humans come to believe what they do, in fact, believe? What relation is there between the way they come to hold certain beliefs and the question of how they ought ideally to justify them? How is rationality not just a matter of ideal justification but also related to our biological and social adaptive functions? (200)

Even as Mohanty appears to grant recognition to the more properly universalist question of justification, he also folds it back into a more narrowly scientific approach (indicated most tellingly by the phrase "not just" in the final question). What this train of questions suggests is that, for Mohanty, the reasons why people act the way they do are ultimately to be explained (or explained away) as socially, psychologically, or biologically adaptive behaviors, that is, as causally produced responses.

Taking Mohanty's book as a whole, there is no doubt that the overriding intellectual cathexis is on realism and the specifically epistemological considerations that drive it. Mohanty's focus on epistemology and realism, and the manner in which he articulates their relation to "progressive politics," in fact helps to locate an interesting fault line in contemporary critiques of postmodernism, that between, to speak in fairly broad terms, epistemological and ethical considerations or, alternately, the emphases of a realist project, and the emphases of a universalist one. I say "emphases" rather than "aims" since the projects of universalism and realism do share some common goals and do not need to be seen as necessarily opposed to one another. But examining Mohanty's project, and placing it next to current reconstructions of universalism, reveals several interesting symptoms and characteristics. Most broadly, the realist project insists upon a mind-independent world, no matter with what sophistication the relation to it is construed, and champions the advance of objective knowledge, again, even if such knowledge is construed as situated or fallibilistic. Likewise, realist projects aim to identify the causal forces at work in the world (both natural and social) and promote the possibility of a distinct science of the human (whether or not they espouse an ultimately unified science). While such concerns can go hand-in-hand with a desire to make universal claims about human action or capacities that will in turn undergird ethical and political practices, the urge to draw on the resources of the natural sciences to help elaborate a more potent social science is paramount. To that extent, it is a disciplinary endeavor, an attempt to articulate a science of the human or of society.

The project of a refurbished universalism, by contrast, places ethicopolitical considerations ahead of epistemological ones, if it attends to the latter at all. For example, in *Cultivating Humanity*, Martha C. Nussbaum's sustained defense of an educational and moral ideal based on rational debate only fleetingly appeals to the ongoing debates about the categories of objectivity and truth. Instead, it dwells almost exclusively on the role a cultivated reason should play in current debates about moral and political issues, particularly within an international or multicultural framework. Nussbaum's project articulates a broadly educative (rather than narrowly disciplinary) model that stresses transformative ethical and intellectual practices at the level of self-understanding and intersubjective interaction, the cultivation of character through practices of reflective affiliation and critical detachment. This educative and ethical model is then articulated to a liberal concept of deliberative debate, as in the manner of the comprehensive liberalism of John Stuart Mill.[3] Even in cases where the orientation is less pedagogical or liberal, arguments on behalf of universalism or cosmopolitanism stress common humanity not

[3] See Martha C. Nussbaum, *Cultivating Humanity: A Classical Defense of Reform in Liberal Education* (Cambridge, Mass.: Harvard University Press, 1997). Subsequent page number references will be cited parenthetically in the text. I borrow the term "comprehensive liberalism" from John Rawls. See John Rawls, *Political Liberalism* (New York: Columbia University Press, 1993, 1996), 199.

primarily for the purposes of increasing knowledge or knowledge-gathering activities, but rather for the purpose of fostering rational reflection and promoting individual or collective self-transformation. To that extent the primary interest is not epistemological, but ethical. Both approaches aim to get beyond relativism, the one the better to articulate an account of the world, both natural and social, the other to cultivate a more integrated, more "human" form of individual or social identity.[4]

A larger question concerns whether or to what extent the two approaches—the epistemological and the normative—are compatible with one another, even if they tend in practice not to be articulated together in a balanced or fully integrated way. I will defer discussion of this question until the conclusion of the essay, where I will make some tentative suggestions about how it might best be conceived. My main goal, however, is to examine what consequences ensue when the normative dimension is subordinated to the epistemological one, as I believe it is in Mohanty's project. Because of this particular focus, and also for reasons of practical necessity, I will not pretend to give an exhaustive account of Mohanty's book, which includes discussion of a vast number of thinkers, including de Man, Bakhtin, Peirce, Putnam, Althusser, Jameson, Winch, Rorty, Quine, and Derrida. More broadly, I hope to contribute to a fuller understanding of how the new universalisms and the new realisms constitute distinctly different approaches to the question of relativism and the perceived failures of postmodernism.

Before reconstructing some of the main lines of argument in Mohanty's densely argued and richly allusive text, I want to suggest what I take to be some of the primary motivations for his project. First of all, Mohanty finds frustrating the fact that much contemporary cultural criticism remains ignorant of developments in the philosophy of science. Insofar as postmodernist projects continue to conceive of objectivity, or Enlightenment thought, or the claims of reason, as their main targets of attack, they are not only attacking obsolete and problematic ideas, but also failing to lay claim to key resources for social and political theory.

---

[4] Again, I must stress that these are differences in emphasis. Typically, the epistemologically driven critiques feel entitled to make universalist claims without entirely pursuing the relation those claims bear to the primary realist aims of the project (as in Mohanty). Likewise, ethically driven models like universalism and cosmopolitanism often make an appeal to potential intellectual gains (for theory formation and knowledge gathering) of the transcendence of partiality or narrow identity interests. See, for example, Bruce Robbins, "Comparative Cosmopolitanisms," in Pheng Cheah and Bruce Robbins, eds., *Cosmopolitics: Thinking and Feeling Beyond the Nation* (Minneapolis: University of Minnesota Press, 1998), 246–64. In Robbins's account, "transcending partiality" serves as both an ethical and an intellectual ideal.

Mohanty believes that work in the philosophy of the natural sciences suggests a model for how we might *reconceive* the project of a science of society. Since the theories being used to make sense of the natural sciences are appropriately hermeneutic, holistic, and context-sensitive, they allow for an account of the world that honors the interpretive nature of all inquiry while not forgoing the explanatory force of scientific inquiry, most prominently, the capacity to reliably identify the causal structures that make the world the way it is. As Mohanty puts it in a key passage: "If the notion of causation is sketched in a naturalist and context-sensitive way, no methodological gulf necessarily separates the 'natural' from the 'human' sciences" (191).

Mohanty appears postpositivist insofar as the natural sciences have begun to take on some of the features of the human sciences that they were, under the logic of traditional positivism, supposed to underwrite. Yet it remains the case, curiously, that he still wants a refurbished science of society that is modeled on developments in (the theory of) the natural sciences. Postpositivism in this sense is still shadowed by the intellectual approach that it claims to transcend. And there is a very clear reason for this. It is not simply that Mohanty wants the science of society to carry an authority that, in this case, is borrowed from the magisterial claims of analytic philosophy of science, but also because he is deeply invested in the realist notion that there is a world out there that we can describe and explain, even if only fallibilistically.

What is underdeveloped in Mohanty's own argument, of course, is one of the key differentiating features of the social as opposed to the natural sciences: the fact that in the case of the social sciences, humans are both subjects and objects of the knowledge-gathering process, capable of reacting upon one another in the very context of inquiry. Thus, even though the epistemic relation between humans and the world has itself become an object of scientific study within sophisticated realist accounts in the philosophy of science, that does not mean that the peculiar hermeneutic attending the social sciences—what Habermas called the "intuitive link" between the subjects studying and subjects studied—does not itself require careful attention and produce distinctive effects.[5] Even if we agree with Mohanty that the hitherto posited "gulf" between the methodologies of the natural and the human sciences is obsolete given holistic developments in the understanding of the natural sciences, it is still necessary to clarify the different interpretive situations that obtain. The key difference is summed up clearly by Anthony Giddens: "The practical consequences of the natural sciences are 'technological'; they

    [5] Jürgen Habermas, *On the Logic of the Social Sciences*, trans. Shierry Weber Nicholsen and Jerry A. Stark (Cambridge, Mass.: MIT Press, 1988), 14.

have to do with the application of humanly attained knowledge to a world of objects which exists independently of that knowledge. Human beings, however, are not merely inert objects of knowledge, but agents able to—and prone to—incorporate social theory and research within their own action."[6] This necessarily has implications for the understanding of causation within the human sciences, as well, for any structures or laws of causation that might obtain within the social sciences have to be understood within the framework of human action, which is, again, structured by intention and not merely observable behavior. To acknowledge the intentional structure of inquiry in the natural sciences—that is, the intentionality of the community of scientists within a specifiable horizon—is not the same as seeking to understand how the intentionality of actors within social practices must necessarily be taken into account in any understanding of "causation" within the social world. This is an insight that has framed much of the debate on the "logic" of the social sciences: it was a point dwelt upon by Mill when he took up the question of human agency in the sixth and final book of his 1843 *System of Logic*, where he pursued the possibility of a science of human action. There Mill argued that we can understand human action as conforming to discoverable laws of causation if and only if we consider the internal motives of individuals as one among several forces conducing to make them act in the way that they choose.[7]

Many of Mohanty's descriptions of social theory and ethicopolitical practice do assume the importance of specifically situated human intentionalities and interpretations. His more programmatic statements, however, reveal a desire to subsume the logic of the social sciences to that of the natural sciences. In so doing, Mohanty's project reinstates a masked version of the explanation/interpretation (*erklären/verstehen*) distinction, with interpretation now fully acknowledged but ultimately enlisted in the service of explanation. This movement becomes most clear in the articulation of a refurbished standpoint epistemology in the final sections of his book.

The most important chapter for securing my claims about the ultimate priorities of Mohanty's project is chapter 6, "On Situating Objective Knowledge." In this chapter Mohanty fleshes out his argument that the social situatedness of knowledge does not necessarily lead to skepticism or relativism. Although his stance here is compatible with versions of pragmatism that have circulated within contemporary postmodernist

---

[6] Anthony Giddens, "Hermeneutics and Social Theory," in *Profiles and Critiques in Social Theory* (Berkeley and Los Angeles: University of California Press, 1982), 16.

[7] John Stuart Mill, *A System of Logic Ratiocinative and Inductive*, vols. 7 and 8 of *Collected Works of John Stuart Mill*, ed. J. M. Robson (Toronto and London: University of Toronto Press and Routledge and Kegan Paul, 1963–91), 8:833.

criticism, Mohanty parts company with the pragmatist view (here represented by Rorty) because it cannot adequately account for historical change and because it blurs the distinction between the natural and the human sciences by subsuming the former to the latter. This is a key move in Mohanty's argument, and in making it he endorses Quine's epistemological holism. The crucial point here is that while Mohanty fully espouses a sophisticated realist holism he requires that the human sciences recognize the existence of causal structures that exceed the boundedness of any one culture. Just as the natural sciences aim to produce increasingly accurate accounts of the natural world, the social sciences, on this view, should create increasingly accurate accounts of how society works. Again the shadow of positivism falls on Mohanty's postpositivism. Mohanty may stress the ways that hermeneutic or holistic theories alter conceptions of knowledge-production in the natural sciences, yet such a point, on the face of it, is potentially irrelevant to a project seeking to lay the foundations for a realist social theory. If the object of study or forms of knowledge within the human sciences differ fundamentally from those within the natural sciences, then it does not particularly advance the project of the human sciences to claim that the natural sciences are now understood to be a specifically social achievement. Mohanty, of course, denies such a difference and seeks to unify the human and natural sciences by appealing to the concept of causality. Indeed, in the passage directly preceding the claim that no methodological gulf need separate the natural from the human sciences, Mohanty claims that notions of cause can be likened to Putnam's "natural kinds," terms such as "gold" and "dog" that "are not determined purely by convention, for their referents are part of the real world" (190, 70). Once causal structures stand out as the objects of study for the human sciences, and once causal structures are likened to the "real" objects under study in the natural sciences, then Mohanty has bridged the gulf that troubled him. But at what cost?

What ultimately makes the human sciences different from the natural sciences, normative inquiries different from explanatory ones, is that the former are directed toward decision as well as insight, action as well as knowledge. Although decision without knowledge and insight is blind— and this fact points to the centrality of science to discussions of normativity, as well as to the need for a distinctly human science—giving priority to the natural sciences by using them as a template for the human sciences will only conduce to empty the human sciences of their fundamental normative dimension. Causes may inform but they are not the same as reasons for action, and reasons must be properly acknowledged by the method and theory of any proper science of the human. As a theorist with deep allegiances to Marxism and ideology critique, Mohanty wishes to lay the basis for a science of society that can identify the socioeconomic structural dynamics that cause oppression and marginalization. Somewhat surprisingly, he does not devote much time to fleshing out what he means by the category of causality in the social world, but his examples in his last chapter, as well as intermittent comments about the tasks of social science, reveal that preeminently he wishes realism to explore the ways that structures of power develop historically and enact forms of oppression. But by omitting to elaborate on this point, Mohanty not only leaves the concept of social causality somewhat empty and abstract, he also fails to give due acknowledgment to the normative dimension of human life. This dimension can be incorporated only through careful recognition—both theoretical and methodological—of the way that agent-centered reasons and structural causes both constitute the realm of the social.[8]

The derailment of the normative by the epistemological in *Literary Theory and the Claims of History* is especially disappointing insofar as the ethicopolitical considerations of Mohanty's project lead him at key points to promote a specifically dialogical model of social inquiry and interaction, one that appears to privilege communicative reason as a process rather than a socially situated project that is driven above all by the need to further objective knowledge about the laws that structure the natural and social world. In mounting a critique on the side of postpositivism and against essentialist versions of truth and objectivity, in other words, Mohanty not only appeals to the contextual and situated nature of all knowledge, but also specifically accentuates the dialogical, communicative nature of human inquiry. This perspective appears most dramatically in Mohanty's discussion of an "instructive exchange" in anthropology between Ernest Gellner and Talal Asad.[9] Gellner's essay develops a critique of anthropological relativism, specifically the notion that all aspects of another culture should be explicated in terms relative to their own belief systems, with the accompanying assumption that such belief systems necessarily have internal coherence. Over and against what he calls a problematic approach of "charity," Gellner argues that we need to and cannot help but make strong evaluative interpretations of other cultures. The basis for such interpretations, moreover, is the specifically logical assessment of those ideas, assessments that isolate and examine ideas from the other culture apart from any assumed unity and coherence of the overall culture.

---

[8] Influential versions of this point have been made, of course, by both Habermas, in *On the Logic of the Social Sciences*, and Giddens, "Hermeneutics and Social Theory."

[9] The term "exchange" is a bit misleading. Ernest Gellner's classic essay was first published in 1951 and Asad's critique was published in a 1986 collection.

Drawing on Asad, Mohanty trenchantly criticizes Gellner's argument. Insofar as Gellner makes an appeal to logical structures that can be translated or derived automatically from other cultures, he fundamentally ignores "the existence of institutionally sanctioned power relations between interpreter and interpreted which determine the politics of meaning in the first place" (126). Further, and equally important, Gellner's account does not take into consideration the possibility that the anthropologist's own evaluations and assessments might be radically challenged (and even changed) by the material and subjects he or she is studying. Mohanty suggests that we not aim to get beyond relativism by positing a pristine conception of logical assessment enacted by universal reason; rather, we should acknowledge that common communicative practices enable us to engage in mutually enriching and transforming exchanges with other cultures. Mohanty will, in the end, insist that we press beyond the potential relativism embodied in this communicative model, but this important moment in his argument stresses the need for respectful engagement with the belief systems of others, something foreclosed in the "indifferent" relativism that Mohanty repeatedly attacks.

The communicative practice evoked here does acknowledge the important defining feature of the social sciences that I raised earlier, the fact that the object of study is capable of "talking back." Indeed, this specific condition of interpretive practice introduces self-reflexive practice into social scientific study, in a sense forcing the interpreter to interrogate his own assumptions and methods for their blindness to institutionalized power relations, and for their blindness to unexamined intellectual and cultural values. In addition to practicing self-criticism, the interpreter must also remain open to transformation based on reflexive consideration of the dialogical responses of the other culture.

The problem, of course, is that it becomes difficult to see how this refined notion of anthropological practice can itself escape a higher-order relativism, in its notion of competing and mutually transforming rationalities and systems of value. This is the question that universalism is always trying to grapple with. Contemporary neo-Kantians resolve the problem by privileging the values embedded in the very practices of communicative exchange (as, for example, in Habermas's conception of communicative rationality and the ideal speech situation) and in the principles of respect and reciprocal recognition that are derived from those communicative practices. That is, if communicative action underwrites the possibility for mutually transforming reciprocal exchanges, then any cultural practices that fundamentally deny the principles of open dialogue and exchange can be judged without anxious fear that the interpreter has him- or herself failed to properly respect the other.

Mohanty does not, however, take this route to solve the reemergent relativism of his argument against Gellner. Instead, he makes a somewhat different point, one deriving from his fundamental privileging of realism over universalism:

> A basic question to ask about particular disagreements is whether—and to what extent—they refer to the same things, the same features of the world. This question cannot be settled a priori; it must be part of the "actual study" of cultures, the evolving empirical inquiry that should accompany and inform any theoretical cross-cultural negotiation. . . . Vital cross-cultural interchange depends on the belief that there is a "world" that we share (no matter how partially) with the other culture, a world whose causal relevance is not purely intracultural. (146–47)

Even though he repeatedly stresses that justifying any claims we make about the "causal relevance" of the world is a complex dialogical process, and that objectivity is ultimately a "social achievement," a shift in perspective has occurred from the earlier account about mutually transforming intercultural encounters. Now, intercultural transformations are replaced by transcultural inquiry about a third term, the "world." It becomes clearer why Mohanty has said up front that he will be advancing a model of "epistemic cooperation" across cultures. The ethical valence of "cooperation" should not distract us from what is really being advanced here, an imperative to cooperate, in the manner of a scientific community, in producing knowledge about an objective third term. Because the use of the term "world" for the object of cooperative inquiry blurs the categories of the natural and the social, it becomes possible to evade the most difficult ethical issues stemming from any rigorously self-critical science of society.

The price paid for this evasion presents itself if we examine Mohanty's extended discussion of two main examples in the final chapter of his book: Naomi Scheman's essay "Anger and the Politics of Naming" and Toni Morrison's novel *Beloved*. Mohanty introduces Scheman's essay in order to secure and elaborate a point he made when earlier discussing the limits of Althusser. Concurring with Althusser's critique of the Lukácsian idealized subject of history, Mohanty nonetheless faults Althusser for lacking a philosophical anthropology and a correlative normative position that could justify his attachment to Marxism. Insofar as Althusser neglects to pursue and privilege his own claim that Marx's political activism, and in particular his identification with the proletarian position, effected his ascension to the realm of true science, he "remains adamantly blind to the fact that some normative positions and views may be not only tolerable but also epistemically productive and illuminating" (92). Althusser thus fails to produce what Mohanty feels that he has himself arrived at, a "genuinely social and political epistemology." Without resurrecting the Lukácsian notion of the idealized subject of history, endowed with a privileged standpoint on the social totality, we can, Mohanty believes, nonetheless articulate the mutually determining relation between politics and knowledge by focusing on "the practical consciousness of situated human agents" (91).

Mohanty's claim that epistemic status can be derived from the insights of situated political agents, rather than essentialized identities, is left undeveloped until the final sections of his book, where it emerges most forcefully in the two examples around which the last chapter is organized. Mohanty uses Scheman's essay on the feminist practice of consciousness-raising to endorse and extend her claim that insightful anger, and self-understanding born of situated knowledge, can fuel an individual's achievement of political understanding and social knowledge. Such knowledge should be understood, according to Mohanty, by analogy with the naturalized epistemology being applied by philosophers to the natural sciences, where the production of beliefs is a fundamentally social process. In the feminist consciousness-raising group, experience is filtered and analyzed by a sympathetic community of knowers, and one's subject position is the precondition but never the guarantee for understanding larger social structures and systems of power. Mohanty's refurbished standpoint epistemology, which bears close relation to the articulation of achieved standpoints in the work of Alison Jaggar and Nancy Hartsock, allows that knowledge is context-dependent, but also asserts that it is demonstrably dependable, if supported by the proper conjunction of experiential insight and confirming objective analysis of the true social interests of the interpreting agent.[10] These social interests can be accurately identified only if they are linked to an empirical account of societal stratification.

This example, as with the previous discussion of Althusser, reveals the work that Mohanty is hoping that standpoint epistemology will do, and the ways in which Mohanty's claim that Althusser "shares with the positivist a distrust of all normative notions and concepts" might be symptomatic of Mohanty's own difficulties in bridging the gap between science and value (90). For there are two interesting points to be made about Mohanty's claims here. First, it is unclear whether the insight of the situated agent is securing the reliability of the knowledge, or the confirming account of objective social conditions is validating the insight of the situ-

---

[10] See Alison Jaggar, *Feminist Politics and Human Nature* (Totowa, N.J.: Rowman and Allan Held, 1983), and Nancy Hartsock, "The Feminist Standpoint: Developing the Ground for a Specifically Feminist Historical Materialism," in Sandra Harding and Merrill Hintikka, eds., *Discovering Reality* (Dordrecht: Reidel, 1983), 283–310.

ated agent. While Mohanty would doubtless reply that the two are mutually determining, that he means to identify a dialectic, the point remains that Mohanty wants to doubly secure the subordination of interpretation to explanation, first by appealing to the epistemic privilege of the oppressed, which is situated yet contains the possibility for objective reliability, for an *Aufhebung* into a form of grounded omniscience and, second, and somewhat contradictorily, by appealing to the need for an extrinsic explanatory account to ratify the standpoint in the last instance. Once again, gone are the models of transformative dialogue that fueled the critique of Gellner and laid the basis for the claims to transcended positivism. The situated perspective is legitimated not through a communicative or dialogical process but by reference to an objective account of the subject's true interests. Only if the situated epistemologist achieves an objectively determined standpoint, then, does her view of things issue in objectively reliable knowledge.

The second point to be made follows from my previous insistence on the distinction between reasons and causes in the conceptualization of human action. What Mohanty focuses on in the example of the woman whose consciousness is raised is the accuracy of her understanding of her position within a society that systematically works to exclude and oppress her—her understanding, that is, of the social causes of her oppression. What is not addressed in Mohanty's discussion, symptomatically enough, is how such achieved knowledge might become a reason or motive for action on the woman's part. In this respect, it strikes me as no accident that Mohanty uses the example of consciousness-raising, which dramatizes a moment of illumination, a sudden capacity to view one's place within a larger context. In explaining how anger can be more than merely personal and linked to the production of reliable knowledge, Mohanty writes, "her anger is the theoretical prism through which she views her world and herself in it correctly. Hers is then an objective assessment of her situation, and in this strong sense, her anger is rational and justified" (209).

Even as Mohanty stresses that political experience and activism can provide the key forms of experience that will enable the furtherance of knowledge, he does not sufficiently examine the relation between fact and value from the perspective of the self-reflective agent. The subject of his example is a woman helping to gain and advance a certain type of knowledge, a knowledge about the world and her place in it. Mohanty tries to bridge the gap between fact and value by saying that what he is calling a value-laden position (anger and the experience that fuels it) is in the service of a fact-finding practice. On this view, anger is justified because it is registering something empirically valid and structurally significant about the world, specifically that it is unjustly stratified by gender.

It is showing a moral fact about the world: its unjustness. Interestingly, Mohanty does not follow this through and say that this perception in turn becomes a reflectively endorsed *reason* for action in the world. Indeed, while Mohanty would no doubt say that of course such knowledge can and should be linked to future value-laden action, normative disposition is symptomatically adduced here only as the *basis* for knowledge about the world, not a deliberative consequence of understanding the world. Why does this distinction matter, and what does it reveal about Mohanty's realist project? It matters because from this perspective the realist perception of what is cannot be rejoined to the universalist or idealist perception of what should be. A normative stance may be compatible with understanding the world—it may even help to further knowledge and legitimate our picture of the world, which is the ultimate goal of the realist project. But the picture of the world does not in this example lead to or legitimate action. Knowledge or the achievement of objectivity validates the normative stance that produced or framed it, but normativity is superseded by objectivity, ethics by epistemology.

Before going on to Mohanty's more complicated final reading of *Beloved*, one that in large part functions as an unacknowledged compensation for the truncated dialectic of the consciousness-raising example, I would like to render Mohanty's uneasy relation between normativity and objectivity more distinct by way of a brief comparison with Nussbaum's very different use of the example of anger within the universalist project of *Cultivating Humanity*. Nussbaum advocates a broadly democratic, cosmopolitan, and educative project that involves rigorous examination of one's practices, one's culture, and one's social institutions, as well as an engaged and open-ended debate with individuals and groups whose practices, cultures, and institutions differ from one's own. In this respect, Nussbaum's vision remains trained upon the ideal that only temporarily attains prominence in Mohanty's book, during his discussions of Asad and Peter Winch. And it is importantly supplemented by an ideal arguably absent from Mohanty's book, the ideal of character, or self-fashioning in the service of cosmopolitan and civic ideals.

This is where Nussbaum's interest in anger becomes important. For Nussbaum, there are three facets to the project of cultivating humanity: the critical examination of one's way of life and one's traditions; the capacity to identify as a human being with other human beings, across and beyond local ties of region, group, culture, or nation; and the "narrative imagination," the capacity for empathetic understanding of another's point of view. The second and third facets both require emotional as well as rational forms of understanding, in their emphasis on acknowledging and extending bonds of solidarity, and through the idea that empathy is required to comprehend those situated differently from ourselves. The universal principle underlying the project is that human beings have "common needs and aims [which] are differently realized in different circumstances," and the normative dimension reveals itself through reflective questioning and justification of one's practices within the context of the broadest possible understanding of a diversely constituted world. Coming to knowledge always takes place within the context of self-examination, self-transformation, and respectful debate with others. Debate must incorporate a principle of respect because debate always involves recognition of the common humanity of the other and because communication always includes coming into contact with ways of life and understandings of identity that are implicitly or explicitly valued by one's interlocutor. Key here is the privileging of ethicopolitical practices over any project of knowledge gathering or even validation of knowledge. One is attempting to judge whether one's own way of life and other ways of life enable the development of one's own character as well as the free flourishing of others.

Nussbaum's scattered but arresting references to the emotion of anger illuminate this vision. In an initial discussion of the virtues of critical argument, Nussbaum approvingly mentions the Stoic view that critical argument fosters not only intellectual, but also ethical capacities, insofar as reason can help to dissipate anger and other irrational sentiments. For the Stoics, anger and fear often stem from adherence to unexamined social conventions. If one is angry because one feels that one has not been accorded the proper respect based on his or her place in society, then a critical challenge to outward signs of status will remove the basis for such an emotional response. More generally, if one makes a habit of always questioning and examining one's reactions to events or people—rather than simply accepting them—one will become a better-regulated and more temperate citizen. Later, in an extended discussion of the *Meditations* of Marcus Aurelius that is meant to elaborate Nussbaum's own deeply cherished ideal of world citizenship, special emphasis is laid on the way that ties of kinship and solidarity can help to lessen the most damaging aspects of political factionalism—hatred and anger. Even as we judge others to be unjust or morally wanting, we can claim our kinship with them, refuse to see them as alien, other, or monstrous. The simplest habits of thought can alter the vitiating effects of antagonism: if we refuse to reify the other as evil, if we place empathetic understanding ahead of condemnatory rhetoric of thought or speech, we will have forwarded the goal of world citizenship and remained true to the ideals that caused us to criticize our less humane adversary in the first place.

We are very far indeed from the epistemologically valorized anger of the feminist consciousness-raising group in Mohanty's text. And indeed these references to anger could be productively criticized from the perspective of

Mohanty's discussion, insofar as Nussbaum unaccountably does not ac-knowledge, in the case of her first passage on the Stoics, that passionate reactions to the injustice of social conventions can be accompanied or fueled by anger (say, by the recipient of the prideful behavior of social "superiors"). Nor does she acknowledge the ways in which ideals of tem-perance or appropriately respectful or rational critique might work, subtly and not so subtly, to blunt important forms of challenge and critique.[11] But her discussion of the individual's cultivation of critique and social un-derstanding reveals the limits of Mohanty's own normative conceptions and the way in which the privileging of the realist project produces those limitations. For Nussbaum, rational critique is not only made possible by a universal human capacity for reason (something Mohanty also asserts) but is inseparable from the normative questions that motivate and in turn issue from it. The focus is not how can we most accurately and objectively describe the world, but rather what she (like Socrates) takes to be the most basic of philosophical questions: How should we live? How do we justify the choices we make? What kind of character should I cultivate?[12]

Interestingly, and somewhat surprisingly, Mohanty's final discussion of *Beloved* does insist on the necessity of the understanding of normative questions in our approach to history and to others, but the reading of the novel exists in some tension with the focus of his project overall. In large part I view this concluding section of Mohanty's book as itself haunted by the aborted normative impulses animating his desire to know and explain the injustices of the shared histories that make up our world. The original and disproportionately emphasized claim that rela-tivism leads to indifference is pertinent here, for above all Mohanty wants to make sure that his own quest for fallible objectivity does not itself is-sue in ethical indifference. I say "disproportionately emphasized" because, Mohanty's claims notwithstanding, there is actually no necessary rela-tion between relativism and indifference. The assumption of incommen-surability among cultures, communities, and histories does not logically entail (or necessarily even tend to promote) indifference: it can just as easily issue in wonder, awe, or distant respect.

Mohanty uses his reading of *Beloved* to flesh out his claims about the ethical and political potentialities of a realist epistemology, as well as to

---

[11] Interestingly, she later implies this point of view when discussing Ralph Ellison: "Nar-rative art has the power to make us see the lives of the different with more than a casual tourist's interest—with involvement and sympathetic understanding, with anger at our so-ciety's refusals of visibility" (88).

[12] For an eloquent discussion of the divergence between the realist and more properly nor-mative approach to moral questions, see Christine M. Korsgaard, *The Sources of Normativity* (Cambridge: Cambridge University Press, 1996). I am indebted to Korsgaard's book in my treatment of these issues.

emphasize the critical concepts of community and history that have impelled his insistence on the flaws attending paradigms other than his. There are a couple of interesting points to be made about the function this reading plays within the framework of the book as a whole. First, it bears remarking that Mohanty is moved to make his final and arguably his fullest points in the context of a reading of a richly rendered historical novel, one that moreover stretches the boundaries of realist verisimilitude in a number of important ways. Does the appeal to a complexly realized literary text, with the sophisticated use of multiple voice and perspective, and the staging of complex moral dramas involving both actual and imagined encounters, undermine in any way Mohanty's insistence that we can use complicated models of knowledge gathering drawn from the natural sciences to generate a genuine and reliable human science? Is Mohanty inadvertently implying that "literary" forms of understanding, and in particular the subtle framing of hermeneutical and normative issues that the formal capacities of literary narrative allow, are necessary in order to elaborate a specifically "moral epistemology," to adopt the term that makes a dramatic appearance in this final section of his book? In other words, is Mohanty implicitly conceding one of Nussbaum's points, that narrative imagination is crucial to the universalist cosmopolitan project, and that literature, as she argues even more fully in *Poetic Justice*, should play a crucial role in the practice and cultivation of broader and more elastic forms of citizenship? If so, his attempt to undo the opposition between the natural and the human sciences—by asserting the priority of the former—might be called into question.[13]

In order to see whether these questions are pertinent to an appraisal of Mohanty's final chapter, we must first see what exactly he appears to mean by "moral epistemology," and how the reading of Morrison's novel both extends and alters the terms of his earlier discussion of a woman coming to political insight within the feminist community of the consciousness-raising group. In his reading of *Beloved*, Mohanty is most interested in the way that both Paul and Sethe achieve a better knowledge of their world and their selves through their interactions and the productive clash of perspectives that those interactions entail. Only through expansive moral imagination can each character approach a deeper understanding of the other and of their shared history and possible future. Paul's initial incomprehension and condemnation of Sethe's act of infanticide must be transformed by a deeper awareness of the situated knowledge of the mother under conditions of remembered slavery and threatened

---

[13] For a thoughtful and sophisticated discussion of the way that literary realism allows for complex renderings of situated knowledge, see Harry Shaw, *Narrating Reality: Austen, Scott, Eliot* (Ithaca: Cornell University Press, 1999).

freedom, faced with excruciating fears over the future dehumanization of her child. By grasping the context for Sethe's action, Paul will not only have attained a more complete knowledge of history, he will have advanced a more supple universalism, one that no longer subordinates the densely situated experience of historical subjects to an abstract rule. Sethe, too, has her lessons to learn, primarily that shared memory will generate a basis for the revival of trust and for the forms of cooperation that are required if she is to acknowledge her needs and desires, thereby affirming her own future as well as the future of her historical community.

Here, then, Mohanty is focused on the moral growth of the individual and the cultivation of relationships that will allow for self-examination, transformative dialogue, and reflection on fundamental normative questions concerning how we should make our own choices and judge the choices made by others, as well as how we should act toward one another in the face of shared histories, traumatic memories, and acknowledged needs and desires. But the overriding epistemological thrust of his project still makes itself felt, insofar as he tends to frame the moral achievements of the characters as a cognitive achievement, one not divorced from the affective dimensions of life but nevertheless founded on reliable and objective *knowledge*. Sethe's evolving trust is based on her ability "to appraise relevant information about her changing situation and about her needs and desires" (218); Paul is important to her self-development because "he can help create the emotional conditions in which a new kind of knowing is possible" (218–19). In the crucial instance of Paul's transformed understanding of Sethe's action toward Beloved, Mohanty insists that an acceptance of an empirical claim undergirds (and thus authenticates) his ethical recognition: "Paul's response—in fact the genuineness of his emotional and moral growth—is predicated on his acceptance of Sethe's claim about motherhood as an empirical fact about slave society" (235). Yet although this may strike some readers as an alien lexicon for the treatment of ethical experience, epistemological achievements here function more dialectically than they do in the discussion of Alice's illuminations, insofar as they become the basis for renewed understandings of self, community, and agency.[14]

I want to suggest by way of conclusion that while Mohanty's reading of the novel *Beloved* does forge an embryonic dialectic between the ethical and the epistemological, in the text as a whole, and in some ways even in

---

[14] And indeed the formulations generated here are then retroactively applied to Mohanty's reading of the woman in Scheman's essay (236), which in turn suggests a more dialectical understanding of the relation between ethics and epistemology than was indicated in his initial discussion of the example.

the reading of the novel, the primary allegiance to epistemology as both starting point and telos leaves the bridging of fact and value in this text fundamentally underdeveloped and, in key ways, misconceived. Insofar as Mohanty tries to claim epistemological authority for normative positions (which he typically construes as deriving from interested marginal cultural positions), he sees factual knowledge as enabled and illuminated by the interests of the inquirer. His goal, however, appears primarily to assure the dependability and increase of the factual knowledge rather than to pursue the normative questions of why we might pursue and value the knowledge in the first place, and what we might do with the knowledge once we have it. Indeed, a primary and scientistic allegiance to knowledge above all introduces a rather startling lapse in Mohanty's asserted fidelity to a Kantian ethics, when he comments by way of conclusion that multiculturalism is good for the advance of knowledge, insofar as the more diverse the body of (social and cultural) "researchers," the more likely that there will be healthy and productive research conditions:

> If we see moral inquiry, following Hume and Boyd, as based on observation and experimentation (in this—Boyd argues—it is no different from scientific inquiry), and we define cultures the way I have, as laboratories of moral practice and experimentation, then it would follow that without a healthy diversity of cultures, a robust multiculturalism, inquiry into the human good will be limited and parochial. Cultural diversity ensures that more of the relevant information will be available and that our questions themselves will be shaped and honed by a reasonable array of competing theoretical perspectives. (241)

This view seems to see individual moral actors and inquirers instrumentally, not as ends in themselves, but rather collectively, as a stable of competitors whose focused activity will issue in reliable knowledge that fully supersedes their individual positions or selves. The point is not to ensure their freedom and flourishing for its own sake, but rather for the sake of the greater good, the production of objective knowledge about what the world is like, and what goodness is. At this moment it seems impossible to reconcile moral realism with moral universalism, despite Mohanty's best intentions.

Mohanty's vision fails to posit ethical questions as prior to epistemological ones, insofar as the pursuit of the good is always viewed in his project as a question of objectively reliable knowledge about one's place in a mind-independent world. What I find questionable and fundamentally misguided is this privileging of epistemology over ethics and the awkward placement of normative concepts within his overall scheme, relegated as they are to an illuminating frame or an object of realist inquiry. The true site of normativity lies precisely in the anthropological capacity that Mohanty himself dwells upon—the desire for a better life and, coupled with this, the capacity for reasoned reflection on our beliefs, practices, and ongoing choices, and the ways in which our communicative rationality enables and promotes the collective examination and justification of such practices. These capacities or dispositions, and the ethical practices and convictions that spring from them, are not a form of objective knowledge, and they are not the object of epistemology. But this does not mean that we do not have good reasons for developing and extending our knowledge of the world, both social and natural. We must keep in mind that the question, How should I live? is the most basic one; the response, As a knower, is simply one modification thereof. There is no need to denigrate or foreswear scientific knowledge, whether applied to the natural or the human realms, but both the activity itself, and the forms of understanding applied to study of the human realm, must acknowledge the priority of normative questions and the fundamentally practical structure of human action and understanding.

PART III

Ethos and Argument

CHAPTER 5

Pragmatism and Character

The history of philosophy is to a great extent that of a certain clash of human temperaments. Undignified as such a treatment may seem to some of my colleagues, I shall have to take account of this clash and explain a good many of the divergencies of philosophers by it. Of whatever temperament a professional philosopher is, he tries when philosophizing to sink the fact of his temperament. Temperament is no conventionally recognized reason, so he urges impersonal reasons only for his conclusions. Yet his temperament really gives him a stronger bias than any of his more strictly objective premises. It loads the evidence for him one way or the other, making for a more sentimental or a more hard-hearted view of the universe, just as this fact or that principle would. He *trusts* his temperament. Wanting a universe that suits it, he believes in any representation of the universe that does suit it. He feels men of opposite temper to be out of key with the world's character, and in his heart considers them incompetent and "not in it," in the philosophic business, even tho they may far excel him in dialectical ability.[1]

This statement is drawn from the introductory remarks of the first of William James's eight lectures on pragmatism, delivered in 1906 at the Lowell Institute in Boston. James organizes his ensuing accounts of the two traditionally dominant modes of philosophy, rationalism and empiricism, by means of a fundamental division between what he describes as the tough-minded and the tender-minded. The alternative way of thinking that he advocates combines elements of both, and in so doing acquires a characterological distinctness of its own. Indeed, through an effortless metalepsis, pragmatism as a mode of thought not only remains inseparable from its temperamental influences, but becomes a full-fledged personality, a feminized mediator and reconciler who "'unstiffens' our theories" (43). James in fact brings his heroine to life through near-literary description: "She has in fact no prejudices whatever, no obstructive dogmas, no rigid canons of what shall count as proof. She is completely genial. She will entertain any hypothesis, she will consider any evidence." His second lecture ends with the following evocative address: "You see already how demo-

---

[1] William James, *Pragmatism: A New Name for Some Old Ways of Thinking*, in *Pragmatism and The Meaning of Truth* (Cambridge, Mass.: Harvard University Press, 1975), 11. Subsequent page number references will be cited parenthetically in the text.

cratic she is. Her manners are as various and flexible, her resources as rich and endless, and her conclusions as friendly as mother nature" (44).

This description of pragmatism's manners may not jibe particularly well with familiar images of contemporary pragmatist thinkers, many of whom, shall we say, have rather strong personalities and styles of argumentation. All the same, a persistent concern with temperament and character, with *manner* broadly construed, is a fundamental, ongoing, and relatively distinctive feature of pragmatist thought, and in this essay I consider how this concern is functioning, both explicitly and implicitly, in the work of Barbara Herrnstein Smith, Stanley Fish, and Richard Rorty. It is certainly the case, and worthy of remark, that pragmatism's detractors themselves often feel moved to use characterological terms when expressing their negative reactions to pragmatist claims. Pragmatists are accused of being, among other things, smug, complacent, cynical, blithe, and dismissive.[2] It is equally worthy of remark that detractors seldom seem to evince any self-consciousness or scruples about such forms of attack, such as the possibility that they may be lapsing into ad hominem modes or turning away from a substantive engagement with primary claims. Pragmatism is of course not the only intellectual terrain where such forms of critique occur. Many lines of thought have been assigned characterological excesses or distinctive pathologies: hermeneuts of suspicion are paranoid; feminists are, as we well know, angry and humorless; rationalists are uptight purists; and multiculturalism has introduced a particularly onerous version of piety in the form of the politically correct person. Like the charges leveled against the pragmatists, these charges stem in large part from deeply felt political and moral differences. It is my hypothesis, however, that there is something of theoretical significance going on in the characterological rhetoric of the pragmatists themselves, something that the terms of abuse leveled by others only obliquely illuminate. Analyzing the ways in which the pragmatists themselves negotiate the question of character will, I believe, shed light not only on their own views, but also on some of the features and lacunae of contemporary intellectual argument in the humanities.

At the outset, it is important to distinguish between pragmatism's psychology, which tends to be explicitly avowed and theorized, and its characterology, which remains gestural, descriptive, and implicit, typically not fully integrated into the logic of the argument. To take the psychology first: from its inception, pragmatism has incorporated a psychological

---

[2] For a particularly rich example of characterological rhetoric on the side of both pragmatism and its critics, see Simon Critchley, Jacques Derrida, Ernesto Laclau, and Richard Rorty, *Deconstruction and Pragmatism*, ed. Chantal Mouffe (New York: Routledge, 1996).

dimension into its understanding of truth. By this I mean it has had something to say about how the mind works. James, for example, defined truth at least in part by its relation to a psychological feeling of satisfaction. This facet of pragmatism drew fire immediately. In his 1908 essay, "The Thirteen Pragmatisms," a painstaking critique of the ambiguities and confusions he saw proliferating in the then-very-new school of American pragmatism, A. O. Lovejoy argues that this particular pragmatist claim blurs psychology and epistemology, and in fact props the epistemological on the psychological in dubious ways. Lovejoy indicts the pragmatist use of the vague and unspecified term "satisfactory," arguing that one cannot tell whether it means an experience of certitude or conviction, a desire for consistency or empirical verification, a charm for the imagination, or a general cheerfulness in the face of whatever is being propounded. Instead of using this term, Lovejoy suggests, the pragmatist should simply admit that theoretic satisfactions must meet specific intellectual demands—for clarity, consistency, and evidence. Yet once one has made such an admission, he adds, the pragmatist's criterion of truth has been emptied of any distinctive character, since it "is simply the old, intellectualist criterion supplemented by the psychologically indisputable, but the logically functionless, remark that, after all, a 'theoretic' satisfaction is a kind of satisfaction."[3]

But pragmatism has not been willing to admit the notion that the psychological and the logical can be separated with such easy surgical precision. Indeed, Barbara Herrnstein Smith has recently pursued a project based on the conviction that the specifically psychological dimensions of cognitive life are centrally important to understanding intellectual practices. In her 1997 book, *Belief and Resistance*, she offers an account of the ways in which cognitive stabilization and destabilization—which might be glossed as theoretic satisfaction and dissatisfaction—structure epistemic life and shape the dynamics of intellectual inquiry, development, and debate.[4] Smith appeals to cognitive science both to describe how we go about our intellectual practices generally and to account for those hypertrophied conservative mental tendencies that thwart the genial projects of postmodernism, pragmatism, and constructivism. Explaining the recalcitrance of one's opponents through appeal to psychology appears in Stanley Fish's work, as well. In an ostensibly offhand remark at the conclusion of his essay "Critical Self-Consciousness, Or Can We Know What We're Doing?" Fish attempts to fold in the rather startling

[3] A. O. Lovejoy, *The Thirteen Pragmatisms and Other Essays* (Baltimore: Johns Hopkins University Press, 1963), 20.

[4] Barbara Herrnstein Smith, *Belief and Resistance: Dynamics of Contemporary Intellectual Controversy* (Cambridge, Mass.: Harvard University Press, 1997). Page number references will be cited parenthetically in the text.

point that, despite his assertions that critical self-consciousness does not even exist, its "appeal . . . will certainly survive any argument I . . . make against it."[5] He attributes this to the nature of convictions: one always experiences them as universally true. Thus, "even though the self-reflective clarity of critical consciousness cannot be achieved, the experience of having achieved it is inseparable from the experience of conviction" (467). Fish thus brings in a general psychology to account for the fact that others seem so sure of their capacity for reflective distance, just as Smith brings in the tendency toward cognitive conservatism to account for the persistence of traditional investments in truth and reason.

A generalized psychology is typically brought in to account for relations toward belief and, as happens in both these cases, to explain the difficulty of converting people to the pragmatist worldview. But at certain moments, more expansive characterologies make their appearance. By "characterology" I mean something other than those general observations about epistemic practices that appear in psychological analyses. When pragmatists make appeal to character, they sketch a more elaborate, individualized way of life, evoking settled dispositions, habits, and temperament. Although these character sketches are generally not contextualized temporally or spatially, remaining at some level atomic and individualist, they move toward a descriptive thickness that evokes the literary, and often they can be situated with regard to generic literary modes, such as irony or comedy. These unusual descriptive moments, and the pragmatists' relatively unexamined and untheorized relation to them, are what I would like to explore.

Apart from anything else, these characterological appeals help to focus what drives the persistent moral critique of pragmatism, a critique that typically responds to something more elusive and attitudinal than discernible characterology. The facet of pragmatism that most annoys those detractors moved to moralizing terms of disdain—smugness, complacency, cynicism, and so on—is not so much a specifically outrageous constative claim as the persistent performative enactment of a casual attitude toward the fact that truth and belief cannot be grounded in anything greater than the working vocabularies in which we express them, or in their own contingent and situated effectiveness. The critics are ultimately responding, that is, to an attitude toward contingency and situatedness that they find inappropriately weightless and unbothered. If in the end we are fully responsible for constructing our own webs of belief, if we are not simply discovering a priori principles or hard facts or a real world, then at

[5] Stanley Fish, "Critical Self-Consciousness, Or Can We Know What We're Doing?" *Doing What Comes Naturally: Change, Rhetoric, and the Practice of Theory in Literary and Legal Studies* (Durham: Duke University Press, 1989), 465.

the very least, such criticisms imply, this human condition should be described and faced with a certain gravitas, or attitude of dignity—say, tragic heroism, stoicism, defiance, or pathos. Unlike the more appropriately serious hermeneut who humbly submits to the authority of tradition or the standpoint epistemologist who respectfully honors the illuminations of particular perspectives, the pragmatist seems far too comfortable in his or her own horizon of meaning or community of belief, unmoved to much except the game of persuading others that there is no truth outside of persuasion.

The more full-fledged characterologies often make this temperamental clash more evident; they also invite a deeper analysis than the occasional epithet-hurling would seem to allow. Rorty has written extensive descriptions of "the ironist" (whom he opposes to "the metaphysician"); likewise, Smith provides a portrait of "the postmodern skeptic" (whom she opposes to "the traditionalist"). These figures might be classed along with other contemporary intellectual ideals that are crafted in response to intellectual modes or traditions conceived as outdated or falsely universalist. I have in mind here Foucault's specific intellectual and the new cosmopolitanism espoused by writers such as Martha C. Nussbaum, Anthony Appiah, and Bruce Robbins. Cosmopolitanism, in particular, exhibits the same investment in a cultivated stance that appears less explicitly in the pragmatists.

Smith's *Belief and Resistance* stands as one of the more striking examples of the appeal to character in contemporary pragmatism. As I have indicated, her book analyzes cultures of controversy and debate by focusing on cognitive features of epistemic life. The two main intellectual conditions that Smith analyzes—cognitive stabilization (trying to protect and reinforce what you believe to be true) and cognitive destabilization (being open to conversions and transformations of various kinds)—exist in a kind of uneasy tension with the more partisan aspect of her book: its strong-minded promotion of postmodern, pragmatist, and constructivist points of view (three terms that are persistently linked in Smith's account). Smith is nothing if not explicit and self-reflective about both her desire to maintain symmetry in analyzing the cognitive features of all forms of belief and the inevitable asymmetries generated by her own predilections and cognitive tastes. She also clearly wants to enliven her subject matter by dramatizing debates; there is a distinctly literary feel to the book as she elaborates the generic conventions that come into play when thinkers present their opponents' views. For example, she redescribes as "theaters of instruction" those forms of argument by means of which traditionalists cast their skeptical opponents as tragically caught in their own performative contradictions (80–82).

Such theaters of instruction represent for Smith a pervasive tendency on the part of traditionalists to criticize not only the arguments but also the moral characters of antifoundationalists. She unambiguously presents this move as one that can and should be discredited, one that is clearly illegitimate and distasteful, like a baldly ad hominem argument. Yet it is not as though she entirely manages to avoid a version of this strategy herself, though it is one she pursues indirectly, through intermittent indications of the kind of attitude, stance, or temperament that marks the postmodern skeptic. A more elaborate and distinctly characterological instance appears, however, at the end of "Unloading the Self-Refutation Charge," the chapter in which Smith defends antifoundationalists against the charge of self-contradiction. Smith's defense is to a large extent a multipronged offense; she exposes the literary ruses of her opponents (their theaters of instruction) and dismantles the suppressions, distortions, and identifiable fallacies of their arguments. But her final move is itself characterological rather than directly logical, as she simply allows a sketch of the postmodern skeptic to speak for itself:

> The postmodern skeptic thinks that the interest and utility of all theoretical formulations are contingent. She is not disturbed, however, by the idea that, in order to be self-consistent, she must "concede" the "merely" contingent interest and utility of her own theoretical formulations. Nor is she embarrassed by her similar "obligation" to "concede" the historicity—and thus instability and eventual replacement—of the systems and idioms that she finds preferable to traditional epistemology and that she would, and does, recommend to other people. She is not disturbed or embarrassed,—or to her own way of thinking, self-refuted—by these things because she believes, in comfortable accord with the conceptual systems and idioms she prefers, that that's the way all disciplinary knowledge—science, philosophy, literary studies, and so forth—evolves. And she also believes that, all told (as she tallies such matters), that's not a bad way for it to happen. (86–87)

In many ways this reads as a move of exasperation, especially given its odd function as the chapter's breakaway conclusion, its disconnection from the prior argument typographically enforced by a break on the page. Yet, in a way, this argument from character is fully continuous with Smith's prevailing argumentative posture, a seeming anomaly that is actually recognizable as the outgrowth of a series of comments dropped along the way about the wild card of individual differences of cognitive taste and preference. In many ways, of course, character would appear to be the ideal pragmatic category. As opposed to identities conceived in terms of essence or nature, character is antifoundational, open-ended, and in process, the site of self-crafting and mediation between the individual actor and the wider social world. But in this passage—as elsewhere in pragmatist works—an ideal of character represents the perfect coincidence between philosophy and psychology. When this occurs, a narrowly conceived character is set forth, effectively foreclosing any idea of character as a work in progress. Only certain virtues are stressed. Here, for example, the postmodern skeptic is defined as precisely immune to any friction generated by opposition or defiance. It is moments like these, of course, that prompt the charges of smugness or complacency. The postmodern skeptic is in comfortable accord with her preferences; she believes that all is for the best in this most contingent world. She's fine, thank you very much, and refuses her opponent's idea that her arguments have any shortcomings or weaknesses. She knows that her arguments are fine because she feels so very comfortable about her beliefs. She rests easily on this plush sofa. How too very bad that you can't feel this comfortable. The fact that you don't feel comfortable must mean that you are still in thrall to the seductions of rationality and metaphysics— defensive, haughty, and intent upon crushing this threatening opponent who galls you with her infuriating equanimity. If only you could see that it's like trying to fight with mother nature.

What is the status of Smith's argument from character? Is it an informal fallacy that we can easily dismiss? Can we say that Smith has stopped making real arguments and is trying to persuade simply by saying that postmodernism is legitimized by its own attitude of self-satisfaction? Is this Lovejoy's psychologism taken to a new level, a fourteenth pragmatism where not some vaguely defined satisfaction but rather some all too self-knowing self-satisfaction provides the warrant for truth? And am I performing a similar style of fallacious argument when I cast aspersions on the kind of character that Smith flaunts?

This is a tempting way to dispense with things but one I think we should reject. It would leave us with a very pared-down intellectualism, when in fact what I think is most interesting in Smith's approach is the incorporation of the dimension of character into the discussion of intellectual practice. The introduction of the characterological is, I suggest, potentially a deep and important move, reorienting us toward the question of whether and how certain ideas can be expressed as a way of life or, less encompassingly, as forms of practice vitally significant to any larger conception of the good. Such a question, as Alexander Nehamas reminds us in *The Art of Living*, stretches back to Aristotle's *Nicomachean Ethics* and exercised Foucault's thought in its latest stages.[6] Nehamas might also have adduced the recent interest in cosmopolitanism, which is precisely the attempt to imagine a lived universality or, to put it in the terms of my present analysis, to embody and *characterize* universalism.

---

[6] Alexander Nehamas, *The Art of Living: Socratic Reflections from Plato to Foucault* (Berkeley and Los Angeles: University of California Press, 2000). Page number references will be cited parenthetically in the text.

It is certainly true that variously conceived arts of living can accommodate or even promote tendencies toward a stifling piety or the privileging of a narrowly individualized ideal. The merit of an attention to characterology, however, lies in the way it brings theory and practice into relation, vivifying and testing theory through embodiment and enactment. Indeed, a heightened attention to the distinctly characterological dimension of various bodies of theory might provide a new perspective on debates in which identity politics, performativity, and confessionalism have exercised a certain dominance over the subjective dimension of theory. In certain key ways, characterological analysis would be on the side of such identity-based modes, insofar as it explores practice at the level of the individual. But, beyond this formal similarity, it is as foreign to such identity-based modes as ethics is to sociology. This is especially true of those conceptions of character that stress not only habituation and learning but self-cultivation, as in Aristotle, Mill, and the tradition of moral perfectionism defined through the work of Stanley Cavell. Assuming a human capacity and propensity for the self-authorization of beliefs and values, this tradition provides resources for an incorporation of characterology into the analysis of theories whose domain is in no sense strictly or primarily ethical. In my view, characterology potentially enriches antifoundationalist theory when it prompts such theory to imagine the self-conscious cultivation of those virtues that will help to promote whatever theoretical and practical goods it envisions. Such an exercise can (and, in my view, ideally should) include a recognition of the historical conditions out of which beliefs and values emerge, as well as the possibility for the ongoing recognition of the many forces (psychological, social, and political) that can thwart, undermine, or delay the achievement of such virtues and goods.

The understanding of both agency and ethics in the identity-based approaches, by contrast, is relatively impoverished. Such approaches typically envision enactment or practice as a simple choice between (or, at best, taut combination of) espousal and subversion of various ascriptive and power-laden identities (gender, race, ethnicity, class, sexuality); such enactments are imagined, moreover, as directly and predominantly political in meaning and consequence. Reflexivity is limited to one's relation to generalized social and cultural categories, whether that relation expresses itself as affirmation, affiliation, subversion, or disidentification; and what Nancy Fraser calls "recognition politics" dominate the landscape of political practice and debate.[7] Ultimately, a whole range of possible dimensions of individuality and personality, temperament and character, is bracketed, as

---

[7] See Nancy Fraser, "From Redistribution to Recognition: Dilemmas of Justice in a 'Postsocialist' Age," in *Justice Interruptus: Critical Reflections on the "Postsocialist" Condition* (New York: Routledge, 1997), 11–39.

is the capacity to discuss what might count as intellectual or political virtue or, just as importantly, to ever distinguish between the two.[8]

It still remains, however, to specify the kinds of questions, assumptions, and procedures that might define a project that seeks to preserve rather than discount the pertinence of character, or *ethos*, to argument and practice. For the purposes of the present essay, I propose that we can distinguish two forms of characterological critique. First, in the mode of analysis and diagnosis, a characterological approach can describe and examine the relation between argument and ethos in any given body of thought, establishing what implicit or explicit characterological ideals are in play, and whether those characterological ideals are actually consistent with the arc of the argument or the set of beliefs being promoted. Second, as a significant subset of this broader question, we might consider how different bodies of thought construe the relation between intellectual (theoretical, epistemological, professional) virtue and ethicopolitical virtue. As I shall argue, the pragmatists under consideration here model their characterological ideals too narrowly on more abstract epistemological claims; Rorty's division between the private ironist and the public democrat is at once a symptom and revision of this trend in its recognition that politics may demand a set of virtues that would cramp the ironist's style. In its Smithian form, the narrow derivation of characterology might be viewed as a misguided symbolization of the pragmatist refusal of a distinction between theory and practice, and it shares affinities with those identity-based projects that seek to weld individual enactment too tightly to theoretical premises, as though, for example, one should dedicate one's personality to the proposition that identity is a construction.

Before getting to these larger claims, however, it is important to return to Smith's characterological moments and subject them to a more detailed analysis and diagnostic critique. As formulated, her endorsement of the postmodern skeptic evinces two basic problems. First, Smith elevates a specific kind of attitudinal stance as the recognizable, even ideal, stance of the postmodern skeptic. In doing so, she becomes narrowly normative in a way not warranted by the claims of pragmatism, whose recognition of contingency, one would think, should produce a tolerant, pluralistic, and open-minded approach to the cultivation of character. The second problem is internal to the type of character that Smith sketches for us. While some people may well feel relaxed in the face of contingency, or may even

---

[8] It is the occlusion of individuality in much contemporary literary and cultural theory that produced Eve Kosofsky Sedgwick's compensatory Axiom 1 in *Epistemology of the Closet*, which reads simply, "People are different from each other," and is followed by the immediate observation: "It is astonishing how few respectable conceptual tools we have for dealing with this self-evident fact." See Eve Kosofsky Sedgwick, *Epistemology of the Closet* (Berkeley and Los Angeles: University of California Press, 1990), 22.

think that a relaxed attitude should be cultivated toward contingency, a symptomatic strain marks the idea that the skeptic can so conclusively inhabit the frictionless stance that Smith here attributes to her. For despite a claim in a subsequent paragraph that no orthodoxy or skepticism can be stable, Smith's characterology is nothing if not impenetrable in its calm assurance and irrefutability. In other words, it seems to rely upon models of selfhood that have hardly learned the lesson of contingency. The postmodern skeptic does not lose control; she is not disturbed or embarrassed; nor, it would seem, is she angry, passionate, or irrational. How did we get to such an unexamined, pre-Freudian conception of selfhood? Why isn't the contingency that we hear about on every page disrupting and subverting the self's relation to the self? This character seems more premodern than postmodern, more complacent than skeptical. The pathologies—rigidity, purism, and a hypertrophied need for cognitive conservatism—are all allotted to the traditionalist. The pragmatist, by contrast, is a postpathological subject: hysteria, neurosis, and anxiety have all been transcended.

One might imagine that Smith is not so much presenting a fully endorsed character as indulging in an imaginative moment, trying to make vivid to critics the manner in which postmodern convictions can be held. The investment in this character's reality, robustness, and staying power is made clear in Smith's next chapter, however, when she actually contrasts Habermas's hypothetical skeptic with "the real-enough postmodern skeptic evoked at the conclusion of Chapter 5" (101). It is no accident that Smith reinforces this sketch in her critique of Habermas, for it is there that the characterological dramas become most heightened. What Smith views as Habermas's illegitimate and moralizing attempts to discredit his opponents provoke her considerable ire—and the characterological stakes of the argument make themselves more fully felt as she repeatedly represents his arguments as not only wrong, but distasteful, especially insofar as they remain inattentive to the specific character of postmodern belief.[9] She singles out for special attention Habermas's remarks on Rorty:

> While I find myself in agreement with much of what Rorty says, I have trouble accepting his conclusion, which is that . . . [philosophy] must also surrender the function of being the "guardian of rationality." If I understand Rorty, he is saying that the new modesty of philosophy involves the abandonment of any claim to reason. . . . [H]e also unflinchingly accepts the end of the belief that ideas like truth or the unconditional *with their transcending power* are a necessary condition of humane forms of collective life. (quoted in Smith, 107; Smith's emphasis)

[9] It must be acknowledged, however, that Smith presents an unusually attentive and detailed critique of Habermas, in a landscape of debate in which references to this important theorist are often glancing and dismissive.

Smith rightly points out that Habermas slips in a certain characterization of truth and the unconditional, casually referring to "their transcending power," and thereby does not adequately acknowledge a profound disparity of belief between himself and Rorty. Turning to the dimension of affective disposition, Smith adds that insofar as Rorty does not share Habermas's views, it cannot make sense to call his attitude "unflinching," because for Rorty, there is nothing to flinch about. This point is a cogent one; yet it also raises the question of Smith's persistent privileging of manner, attitude, and stance despite her own dismissals of any attempts to discredit the character of one's opponent. Because Smith herself is interested in showing forth the characterological dispositions that distinguish the postmodern skeptic, she inevitably betrays subtle and not-so-subtle judgments against those who do not attain the proper insouciance. For example, Smith, in a mirror version of Habermas's portrayal of Rorty, refers to Habermas's "strenuous affirmation" of transcendental criteria. But if Habermas simply believes that such criteria exist, why would his affirmations be called "strenuous"? Smith also criticizes Habermas's claim that without some sort of "justificatory discourse," Rorty and other postmodern critics "will not be able to find a resting place." Smith comments: "That may be true, but Habermas himself, even with such a discourse, seems unable to find one; and 'a resting place' may not be what postmodernists seek, or what any of us will find this side of the moon or short of the grave" (114). And yet, if we recall the earlier description of the postmodern skeptic, what is a "comfortable accord" with one's own preferences, what is characterological immunity to the arguments of one's opponents, if not a "resting place"? Why, in other words, is Smith's "comfortable accord" a legitimating calm, while Habermas's convictions are self-indicting?

Smith's analysis of Habermas relies upon the impulse to preserve a recognizable distinction between two different stances toward the shifting sands of modernity. For beneath the claim that Rorty isn't suppressing any flinches lies the implication that such stoicism, were it to exist, would bespeak an inauthentic relation to contingency. Smith seems to suggest that where the conditions of contingency are experienced not as weightless freedom but as a fateful caprice that must be faced down we are in the deluded realm of frustrated idealism. One is led to wonder how Smith would respond to those who interpret the absence of foundations as a far-reaching and deeply felt effect of historical disenchantment, an experience of loss that must be endured, or to those who consider the search for foundations as a recurrent human aspiration or need, one for which there is no cure, however much the fact of contingency is recognized. We think here, variously, of figures such as Matthew Arnold, Max Weber, Paul de Man.

Smith's mood is comic; it asserts a consciousness cheerfully reconciled to its contingent formulations, doing what comes naturally. But there is

no relation to contingency—no characterological attitude or stance—
that follows naturally or necessarily from a general belief about contingency. One can imagine any number of attitudes beyond those I have
mentioned. For that reason, there is something actually jarring in the dis-
cordance between the sensibility Smith elevates and the sets of beliefs it
purports to express. The postmodern skeptic seems to display a limited
relation to contingency, one dictated in no small part by the need or desire to trump the opponent characterologically. It may be helpful here to
recall the critique of pragmatist complacency adduced earlier: that critique is formally similar in that it, too, imagines that a stance of gravitas
is superior to the carefree attitude of the pragmatist. But why would we
need or want to choose between the two? Nor does it make sense to me
to imagine futures in which certain stances have been eliminated or cease
to matter, a point tellingly made by Rorty:

> It is tempting to suggest that in a culture in which poetry had publicly and
> explicitly triumphed over philosophy, a culture in which recognition of con-
> tingency rather than necessity was the accepted definition of freedom . . .
> there would be no pathos in finitude. But there probably cannot be such a cul-
> ture. Such pathos is probably ineliminable. It is as hard to imagine a culture
> dominated by exuberant Nietzschean playfulness as to imagine a reign of the
> philosopher-kings, or the withering away of the state. It is equally hard to
> imagine a human life which felt itself complete, a human being who dies
> happy because all that he or she ever wanted has been attained.[10]

In a sense, I am leveling a version of the charge of performative contradiction against Smith. I am saying that the very character that she
sketches as the embodied enactment of her pragmatist views is at odds
with the views professed. Again, a comparison with the cosmopolitan reframing of universalism is in order. As I have argued in chapter 3, the
cosmopolitan ideal can be distinguished from neo-Kantian universalism
by its deliberately casual or informal relation to normative universalist
principles. For the cosmopolitan, a too-bald or rigorous universalism is
at odds with the ethical task of developing a capacious intersubjective
competence within a culturally diverse horizon. Normative explicitness
is felt, somehow, to violate the cosmopolitan spirit, even as that very
spirit is animated by the conviction of human commonality. Here, a
characterology refines the philosophy; it is precisely the imagining of
lived universality that causes a reframing of the doctrine of universalism.

The odd thing about the pragmatist characterology in Smith, however,
is that it has paradoxically rendered the casual absolute. It is simply the

---

[10] Richard Rorty, *Contingency, Irony, and Solidarity* (Cambridge: Cambridge University
Press, 1989), 40.

flip side of the traditionalist assumption that one does and should care about justificatory discourse. It says that one *should not* and *need not* care about justificatory discourse. But why should the pragmatist care whether others care?

It is not the appeal to character itself that is problematic. My position is simply that the pragmatist view cannot coherently elevate one temperament above all others, one contingent subjective vocabulary that is somehow more authentic than the rest. Fish seems to register and indeed insist on this point, in his claim that there is no one style that attaches to pragmatism. As he argues in the introduction to *Doing What Comes Naturally*,

> Of course there are distinctions between the ways in which the objective knowledge that flows from one's beliefs might be urged on others, styles of self-presentation that are often thought of wrongly as styles of knowing. I might say to you, for example, "what you have just said is obviously false for the following indisputable reasons" (this is, in fact, my style), or I might say, "I see your point, and it is certainly an important one, but I wonder if we might make room for this other perspective," and, depending on your sense of decorum and on the conventions in place in the arena of our discussion, the conversation between us would unfold differently. But whichever style of discussion I adopt, that style will always be grounded firmly in the beliefs that ground me.[11]

The final sentence notwithstanding, Fish attempts to cleanly separate belief and style, what one knows and how one displays that knowledge. He is a style pluralist; there is no necessary connection between the beliefs, which are grounding, and the style, which gives expression to those beliefs, but could easily do so in any number of ways. While this is preferable to the imposition of a normative characterology, Fish nonetheless does try to enforce a blanket casualness in his notion that we are always already "doing what comes naturally." Further, in claiming that we cannot help but know what we are doing, he fails to acknowledge any form of self-questioning or self-criticism that could stand apart from the practices that we always so naturally inhabit. Fish identifies a certain kind of knowingness—hard to distinguish from simple human consciousness—as a universal fact of human practice and belief and allows no place for an ongoing process of self-cultivation. In this sense, psychology is paramount while character is impertinent and irrelevant, simply a set of clothes that we happen to have put on, and might easily exchange, as we go about our business. In fact, the category of character is not one that he recognizes; we don styles, which are as evanescent and superficial as fashion.

[11] Stanley Fish, "Introduction: Going Down the Anti-Formalist Road," *Doing What Comes Naturally*, 21.

In *Anxious Intellects*, John Michael finds fault with the disjunction between Fish's claims and his style, thereby refusing Fish's attempt to enforce a non-necessary relation between the two. "Fish's rhetorical performances," writes Michael, "enact a style of self-presentation that does not, I think, flow easily from Fish's belief that the world is a rhetorical place."[12] For Michael, the rhetorical condition that defines our world, along with the fractured and contentious nature of our cultural life, necessarily condemns us to forms of uncertainty, uneasiness, and anxiety. Michael does not so much offer an opposing characterology as insist on a fuller psychology, one that acknowledges the conditions that intellectuals face in our current culture, conditions that dismissive, casual pragmatists seek to disavow. Fish's conviction and sureness of argument are to Michael's mind symptoms of a desire to master contingency through rhetoric itself. This critique parallels to a certain extent my critique of the tensions internal to Smith's conception of a calm relation to an uncontrolled and uncontrollable world. In contrast to Michael, however, my point is not that such attitudes toward contingency cannot coherently exist or be actively valorized and cultivated; my point is rather that such stances cannot be inhabited in the seamless way imagined by both Smith and Fish, nor is there any warrant for elevating them above other stances toward contingency.

Fish's refusal of the notion that one might experiment with doing things that come unnaturally, or actively cultivate a style that might in turn affect or differently enact belief, limits his account of both intellectual and ethical life. He, in effect, shuts out those forms of thought that understand philosophy as a practice of the self. Smith, on the other hand, *is* drawn to a characterological ideal, but she cannot quite conceive of it as the expression of an ongoing project of self-cultivation; her book allows for individual temperament, but typically as a pregiven taste or preference.[13] Rorty's ironist, by contrast, is neither free of anxiety nor defined by it.[14] Rorty offers the ironist as a figure who enacts antifoundationalism as a way of life or even, one might say, an art of living. Rejecting the idea of intrinsic human nature or essential truth, the ironist always cultivates a certain distance from those "final vocabularies" that at any given time most prominently structure her world and her sense of self. Open to vocabularies that differ from her own, the ironist is involved in an endless process of questioning and self-creation, one that recognizes the fact of contingency

---

[12] John Michael, *Anxious Intellects: Academic Professionals, Public Intellectuals, and Enlightenment Values* (Durham: Duke University Press, 2000), 73.

[13] This happens, I believe, because at one level Smith wants to see the warrant for the pragmatist view of things as simply evident in temperament. Her characterology would appear less peremptory if it were actually cast as an ongoing achievement. As it stands, it functions as just the type of empirical evidence that her own constructivism rejects.

[14] For Rorty's description of the ironist, see *Contingency, Irony, and Solidarity*, 73–95.

rather than attempting to attain universality. The practice of irony, as Rorty conceives it, constitutes the triumph of poetry over philosophy. It involves simultaneously the project of selfhood and the project of describing and redescribing our world. In Rorty's view, the ironist is troubled by a productive and incessant concern that his or her vocabulary could be faulty and attempts to correct for this, if never fully successfully, by the use of terms that light up contingency.

The ironist is opposed to the metaphysician, who prides himself on common sense and does not question his final vocabulary. Rorty presents the metaphysician as disdainful of what he construes as the ironist's disabling relativism; this disdain in turn provokes disdain on Rorty's part: the metaphysician is at once complacent and desperate, satisfied with his platitudes yet "clinging" to the idea that he can be saved from contingency by the anchor of reality. Metaphysicians have a need for clear categories, boundaries, and grids, through which they filter all the influences with which they come into contact. The ironist favors the thick description characteristic of ethnography and literary criticism and is endlessly seeking to enlarge his circle of acquaintance and his powers of redescription. The metaphysician uses abstract and thin terms and seeks to stabilize his conceptions.

Rorty's ironist engages in an art of living that is defined more formally than substantively; one might say that it is a practice devoted to self-cultivation broadly conceived rather than the insistence on a particular character. Thus it integrates practice and theory, the characterological and the intellectual, but in tending toward a formal definition, it is elastic and pluralist. Rorty does not entirely avoid the suggestion of a superior indifference to the foibles of metaphysicians, a sureness that accompanies the constant questioning, and his very use of the clear label *ironist* can seem to reify the character's singularity. But there is a very relevant difference here, insofar as ongoing self-cultivation comes to the fore, and the casual self-assurance that otherwise marks pragmatist characterology is not as prominent. Rorty's pragmatism thus becomes a version of the art of living, as distinguished by Nehamas from more impersonal forms of philosophy:

Some philosophers want to find the answers to general and important questions, including questions about ethics and the nature of the good life, without believing that their answers have much to do with the kind of person they themselves turn out to be. Others believe that general views, when organized in the right manner and adhered to in everyday life, create a right sort of person—perhaps really good, perhaps simply unforgettable and, to that extent, admirable. In the case of pure theory, the only issue that matters is whether the answers to one's questions are or are not correct. In the case of theory that affects life, the truth of one's views is still an issue, but what also matters is the kind of person, the sort of self, one manages to construct as a result of accepting them. (2)

If this latter form of philosophy plausibly applies to Rorty, it cannot be said to apply to Smith, who is not so much interested in a project of the self that would emerge from her constructivist views as she is in using characterology to underwrite and even immunize her views. As I have established, what happens in the pragmatist valorization of the casual relation to contingency—and such moments do occur to some degree in Rorty, as well—is that concern with character is narrowed down to what might be called the "character" of the theory. At such moments, these writers are confining themselves simply to an attitude toward contingency itself rather than considering the practical enactment of any contingently affirmed institutions or goods. To focus on the stance toward contingency—the casual relation to doing what comes naturally, the unbothered relation to historicity and contingency, the ironist's interest in simply keeping the engine of redescription going—limits discussions of character to a strictly conceived model of enacting the fundamental claims of the theory, of reproducing attitudinally the seamless relation between belief and truth. The result is an oddly hypertrophied form of intellectualism transmuted into characterology, an ironic outcome for the pragmatist, who here seems unaware that what is being projected as personality is actually personification.

The alternative suggested by Nehamas and represented at least intermittently by Rorty is a less compressed understanding of the relation between theory and practice, more in keeping with the traditional pragmatist understanding of inquiry as rooted in problem solving and the resolution of practical difficulties (variously represented in the work of James, John Dewey, and Ludwig Wittgenstein). But this alternative still remains open to the charge of individualism, raising the larger question of whether conceptual, practical, and political limits might be introduced by any approach that accords centrality and value to the cultivation of character. Doesn't an emphasis on character, whether compressed or elastic, substantive or formal, evade precisely the forms of social and collective practice that are generally gathered under the rubric of the political? If identity-based theories are too exclusively political in conception, isn't a characterological approach itself ideologically mystified? Doesn't Pierre Bourdieu's sociological category of *habitus* and mapping of forms of distinction show rather definitively that characterological ideals help to structure hierarchies of social and cultural power?[15] Even if we refuse Bourdieu's premises, there still

---

[15] Pierre Bourdieu, *Distinction: A Social Critique of the Judgement of Taste*, trans. Richard Nice (Cambridge, Mass.: Harvard University Press, 1984). Bourdieu draws on the equally relevant work of Norbert Elias, whose *The Civilizing Process* examines the ways in which concepts of civilization, culture, and manners supported the formation of states and the increasing monopolization of power in Western culture. Norbert Elias, *The Civilizing Process: Sociogenetic and Psychogenetic Investigations*, rev. ed., trans. Edmund Jephcott (Oxford: Blackwell, 2000).

remains the question of whether an emphasis on character simply diverts attention from the political, operating in Arnoldian fashion to elevate self-cultivation above participation in public politics.

These are significant questions, to which I can offer only preliminary responses. Any geneaology of character should, of course, acknowledge the ways in which the concept functions to create and enforce social distinctions. But like other complex cultural forms, the category of character is neither exhausted nor fully defined by its complicity, in various writings or historical transformations, with exclusivity and power. On the separate question of whether a privileging of character constitutes an evasion of politics, Rorty is especially pertinent, since he has been the pragmatist thinker to consider most extensively the relation between cultivation of ethos or character and larger political goals, although his thinking has taken different forms. In "Private Irony and Liberal Hope," he simply asserts a division between the private personal journey of the ironist, which I sketched earlier, and the public role of reason in democracies.[16] For this reason, he disagrees with Habermas's claim that ironic and postmodern thinkers have been destructive of social hope and instead advances a public-private split in which one could conceivably be Nietzschean in private and Millian in public. Rorty refuses the idea that political goals must be underwritten by a metaphysics and, in particular, by an idea of human nature. He defines the liberal ironist as one who wishes to diminish cruelty and suffering but does not have the same philosophical aspirations as the metaphysician:

> The liberal metaphysician wants our *wish to be kind* to be bolstered by an argument, one which entails a self-redescription which will highlight a common human essence, an essence which is something more than our shared ability to suffer humiliation. The liberal ironist just wants our *chances of being kind*, of avoiding the humiliation of others, to be expanded by redescription. She thinks that recognition of a common susceptibility to humiliation is the *only* social bond that is needed. (91)

For Rorty, nothing limits the uses of redescription in the private sphere, since humiliation of others is not an issue in that sphere. In the public sphere, by contrast, the ironist needs to be acutely aware of as many other vocabularies as possible so as to avoid the potential for humiliation. This point begins to shade into a point that Rorty espouses elsewhere, but has explicitly relinquished in this essay; the practices of the ironist, insofar as they involve a salutary disenchantment that promotes openness to other vocabularies, are actually conducive to the interests of democracy. In any event, Rorty does advance a pluralism when it comes

---

[16] Rorty, *Contingency, Irony, and Solidarity*, 73–95. Page number references will be cited parenthetically in the text.

to private experience and expression, while showing at least a compatibility, if not a necessary connection, between irony and democracy.

Rorty's division between public and private can be criticized on several grounds. Nancy Fraser, for example, argues that it fails to register the politics of culture—the fact that forms of self-expression, the use of vocabularies to describe the self's journey, themselves participate in the production and framing of our political and social world. Hence they cannot be cordoned off in this way as though they are unproductive of political effects. Fraser also levels the familiar criticism that the view of the private ironist is overwhelmingly individualistic and neither accounts for nor promotes collective self-understandings and practices.[17] Another point that could be made against Rorty, as well, is that there are highly public and political deployments of irony and disenchantment, which contribute powerfully to democratic goals of greater inclusion; one thinks in particular of the more theatrical tactics of the feminist and queer movements.

I suggest that it is ultimately a failure of specific conceptual schemes rather than any inherent opposition that leads to the too readily expressed notion that there is something narrowly individualistic, indulgent, or apolitically aesthetic about character. Such an approach neglects the considerable tradition of civic virtue, and the potential for a creative rethinking of the categories of civility, tolerance, and liberal-mindedness. The deployment of the category of character in the contemporary political arena is symptomatic here. It is a term that has been effectively manipulated and appropriated by the right, even though in many ways it remains a commonly acknowledged category of judgment, one that is often seen as ideally beyond spin.[18] The right's significant appropriation and narrowing of this category results in large part, I would argue, from the severing of the term's historical links to liberalism and the liberal temperament and the left's abandonment of the term "liberal."[19] This informal linguistic policy merits reconsideration.

A similar consequence attends the narrowing of the characterological tradition in these recent pragmatist theories, insofar as they focus on the

[17] See Nancy Fraser, "Solidarity or Singularity? Richard Rorty Between Romanticism and Technocracy," in *Unruly Practices: Power, Discourse, and Gender in Contemporary Social Theory* (Minneapolis: University of Minnesota Press, 1989), 93–110. Fraser's essay contains a useful map of Rorty's changing thought about the relation between irony and democracy.

[18] For example, Marjorie Williams, in an op-ed piece for the *Washington Post*, laments the treatment of character as a strategic element of campaign theater. She calls the coverage of political character as something that we manufacture and frame "a malign bastard sired by the horse-race school of political reporting from the legitimate form of journalism that examines character itself." Marjorie Williams, "Theater of Character," *Washington Post*, June 23, 2000.

[19] For the related question of the left's abandonment of the realm of micropolitics more generally, see Bill Connolly, *Why I am Not a Secularist* (Minneapolis: University of Minnesota Press, 1999).

epistemic attitude toward abstract contingency rather than the potential pertinence of characterology to more practical matters such as the political and social institutions of democracy and education, a key element of early American pragmatism (particularly in its Deweyan form) and its close ally, liberal political theory. In general terms, I have been arguing that the attitude toward abstract contingency adopted and promoted by the pragmatists is too singular in conception: not only are there are any number of intellectually coherent attitudes one might adopt toward contingency but the pragmatist viewpoint does not sufficiently recognize the array of experiential moods and stances that can express a lived relation to contingency. Similarly lost to view is any distinction between epistemological and ethicopolitical understandings of virtue, the latter of which tend to articulate those practices that advance specific ethical and political goods. Rorty acknowledges the distinction but assigns dullness and banality to public character in liberal democracies, so as to sharpen the contrast with his flamboyant, romantic, frenetic, but utterly private ironist. His approach, however, plays into the idea that public, political characterology must be a site of restraint, self-effacement, and procedure; it narrowly reads character out of the liberal principle of tolerance, and it consequently forecloses the characterological dimensions of liberalism's dedication to individual flourishing, ongoing critique, and openness to difference (rather than mere toleration of it). Procedures may be impersonal, but the individuals who follow them should not be required to reproduce impersonality in countenance, expression, and action, though, of course, one might imagine instances or institutional sites in which one would actively seek to model such neutralizing behavior. In other words, ethicopolitical virtue can certainly include deliberately featureless forms of impartiality, justice, and tolerance; yet it also might include, less familiarly, defiance, righteous indignation, theatricality, irony, or pathos. Just as the acknowledgment of contingency does not require a casual attitude, then, proceduralism does not require impersonality.[20] It is only when it is imagined in such a way that any introduction of a more pronounced attention to characterology is seen as compensatory, private, individualistic, or mere stylistic accessory.

---

[20] The point I am making here has been made, from a different perspective, within communitarian critiques of Rawls. See, in particular, Michael Sandel, *Liberalism and the Limits of Justice* (Cambridge: Cambridge University Press, 1982), 179–83, and "The Procedural Republic and the Unencumbered Self," *Political Theory* 12, no. 1 (1984): 81–96. For a related debate on the relative merits of impersonality in democratic debate, see Iris Marion Young, "Communication and the Other: Beyond Deliberative Democracy," and Seyla Benhabib, "Toward a Deliberative Model of Democratic Legitimacy," in Seyla Benhabib, ed., *Democracy and Difference: Contesting the Boundaries of the Political* (Princeton: Princeton University Press, 1996), 67–94, 120–35.

CHAPTER 6

Argument and Ethos

AN INSISTENCE on the subjective, psychological, or irreducibly human elements of ostensibly impersonal or objective theories informs much of contemporary scholarship in the humanities. Yet at the same time a key dimension of subjectivity in the tradition of ethics and in the practical criticism of many literary genres—character or ethos—has suffered a kind of exile from theoretical work in the field of literary and cultural studies. Indeed, the theoretical terms of art used to denote subjective experience in contemporary literary and cultural studies—identity, hybridity, performativity, disidentification, embodiment—simply fail to capture key features of character and ethos. To be sure, characterological terms appear with a kind of regularity across many debates in theory; at the least, they form part of the adjectival and adverbial arsenal that enlivens any richly descriptive analytical critique. We have become accustomed to hearing pragmatists called smug, or rationalists depicted as defensive and uptight. The hermeneut of suspicion is paranoid; the p.c. brigade oppressively pious. But in part because of established disciplinary protocols, such ascriptions often seem not to be an integral part of the formal argument; indeed, it typically remains unclear, when they appear, whether they are gratuitous or crucially significant, descriptive flourish or evaluative death blow. On the one hand, as terms of critique, such statements seem to dismiss without examining, to imply deficient psychology rather than misguided argument. On the other hand, such judgments are assumed to matter, to need saying, to carry some vital explanatory force. And indeed, appeals to character appear not only at moments of negative judgment; theorists sometimes feel impelled to flesh out their accounts through appeal to characterological enactment. What the critic of pragmatism sees as smugness, for example, the practitioner occasionally elaborates as an admirable characterological achievement. In the case of Richard Rorty's "ironist" or Barbara Herrnstein Smith's "postmodern skeptic," in fact, a properly casual and unbothered relation to the postfoundational world is offered up precisely as exemplary character.[1]

As the example of pragmatism shows, the concept of character is not always fated to outright exile, though it is salient that both Rorty and

---

[1] I address the particular itinerary of appeals to character in pragmatism in chapter 5.

Smith work across the fields of philosophy and literature. Within the philosophical field more generally, the concepts of character and ethos have enjoyed something of a resurgence, not only within the subfield of "virtue ethics," but also across a range of writings in political philosophy that might be seen as affiliated with this larger development.[2] Yet even as there are multiple lines of influence extending from political philosophy to literary studies, the concepts of character and ethos have tended to undergo strange transformations and suppressions in the literary field, despite widespread claims of a "turn to ethics."[3] It is worth exploring when and how such transformations and suppressions occur, especially given the persistent refusal to avow categories of thought that nonetheless make themselves felt with such persistence.

The odd status of character and ethos in contemporary literary and cultural studies in some ways might be viewed as the effect of a more general skepticism toward the self-authorizing subject. But as concepts allied above all with habitual practice and self-cultivation, character and ethos need not evoke or consolidate mystified notions of autonomy or individuality. Indeed, these concepts might be seen as fully pertinent to a theoretical field obsessively occupied with naming and delineating the subjective effects and potentialities of its more general, transsubjective claims. The subjective forms that currently prevail in literary and cultural studies—identity, hybridity, performativity, and so on—all imagine various ways in which one might enact, own, or modify one's relation to the impersonal determinants of individual identity. As such, they involve a high level of attentiveness to the experiential and practical dimensions of theory. But these understandings of subjective experience typically do not assign importance to, or even recognize, characterological concepts or rhetoric, stressing instead forms of self-understanding that revolve around sociological, ascribed understandings of group identity: gender, race, class, nationality, sexuality. Certainly ethical language may be employed to suggest better or worse ways of dealing with the dynamics of identity and with others. But the notion that those practices that constitute our various intellectual and political spheres, whether actively cultivated

---

[2] For an interesting overview of the field of virtue ethics, as well as a critique of its label, see Martha C. Nussbaum, "Virtue Ethics: A Misleading Category?" *Journal of Ethics* 3 (1999): 163–201. Nussbaum argues that although virtue ethics is usually distinguished from Kantianism and utilitarianism, the taxonomy is a confusion insofar as both Kantianism and utilitarianism contain elements of virtue. Nussbaum then goes on to analyze two divergent strands of so-called virtue ethics, the anti-Kantian and the antiutilitarian.

[3] For a representative collection, see Marjorie Garber et al., eds., *The Turn to Ethics* (New York: Routledge, 2000). For a useful map of different approaches within literary studies, see especially Lawrence Buell's essay in the collection, "What We Talk About When We Talk About Ethics."

or less reflectively routinized, carry ethical significance in part because they tend to become inscribed as character and ethos, seems incompatible with the popular notion that dramas of identity are staged as a performance or subversion of multiple and variously experienced social identities. The latter framework for understanding selfhood and practice equates inscribed or fixed identities with hegemonic force, while it imagines subversion as a practice that negates identity rather than builds anything like character, which in its eyes would be an anachronistic, ideological term associated with individualism and moralism.

The present essay proposes to examine what at first blush might look like the strongest counterexample that could be drawn from the theoretical field influencing literary and cultural studies: the later work of Foucault, which very much foregrounds an ethos of self-cultivation. My analysis will comprise two parts. First, I will argue that the appeal to ethos in Foucault's late work—and more importantly in the reception of that work by the Anglo-American academy—actually functions to cloud the ways that character and ethos might redress the underdeveloped normative and practical dimensions of much current theory. The prominence accorded to ethos by many of Foucault's admiring commentators has taken place within a specific polemical field: it has been introduced as a key element in the response to charges of normative incoherence leveled by Habermas and like-minded critics. Consequently, a misleading and unfortunate opposition between ethos and rational argument has become entrenched. To pursue and amplify this claim, I will in the final portion of the essay turn to Habermas's writings, including his critique of Foucault, so as to show where we might begin more fully to acknowledge the role played by ethos in Habermas's own theories. While I shall identify the ways that Habermas himself plays into the tendency to oppose reason and ethos, I will be trying to tease out the important and overlooked ways in which he also relies upon ethos in his own conceptions of intellectual attitude and democratic practice. This particular strand of his work suggests compelling ways in which reason and ethos might be configured dialectically, rather than oppositionally. More generally, by exploring the category of ethos in the work of both thinkers, this essay hopes to illuminate the ways in which the analysis of intellectual fields of debate might be advanced by a fuller acknowledgment of the insistent presence of ideals of character and ethos in our practical philosophies.

My yoking of the terms "character" and "ethos" requires preliminary comment, especially insofar as the term "ethos" does enjoy some privilege in certain dimensions of current theory, and insofar as it functions prominently in the Foucauldian literature, whereas "character" tends not to appear at all. As I will show, the term "ethos" can allow for pronounced mystification: as a term that can loosely mean habit, custom, practice, or

manner, "ethos" often allows one to assign honorific status or moral resonance without seeming to specify virtue or value in any bald, vulgar way.
Precisely because "ethos" cannot be reduced to the explicitness of a rule or
code, it is open to slippery usage, and seems especially useful to theorists
who seek to avoid direct avowal of norms and principles yet nonetheless
want to affirm their commitment to practical ethics and politics. On the
Foucault side of the Foucault/Habermas literature, as I will show, it functions in this way.

In this essay, I will favor the word "ethos" over "character," not only
because "ethos" is the operative word in the Foucault literature I am examining, but also because across the Foucault/Habermas debate, the term
tends to cover both individual and collective understandings of practice,
thereby making a distinction between individual character and collective
ethos less necessary. But I introduce the terms as a pair in this prefatory
discussion so as to amplify the cluster of meanings and the complex genealogy I mean to invoke. To some extent, by using the terms together I
mean to evoke the Aristotelian conception of ethos *as* character, which
stresses the elements of self-cultivation and confirmed habit that can be
said to shape and define any successfully realized ethical practice. But
I also intend for the modern-day gap between the terms to allow each to
perform a useful connotative correction on the other. It is not simply that
the solidity of the term "character" helps to give shape to the otherwise
simply positive yet somewhat indeterminate "ethos." In its designation of
cultivated ethical practices that have become settled and that can inform
collective as well as individual practice, "ethos" serves as an important
corrective to the individualist focus of "character."

There are objections that might be raised against foregrounding the
term "character" at all, I realize. Not least is the sense that it can be
taken to announce, or at least entail, an alliance with the political right
in contemporary U.S. culture. The conservative rhetoric of character persistently peddles the view that the solution to larger social and political
problems lies within the (potentially heroic) individual rather than in
larger forms of restructuring that result from political projects, institutional changes, and the systemic analyses that make them possible. For
many who would opt to avoid the term, "character" is fatally shadowed
by its long ideological history in the service of mystified notions of distinction, nobility, and worthiness. Such a concern motivates the critiques
of republican virtue by Habermas and Rawls, who precisely want to
avoid heroic and elitist implications in their proceduralist theories.

The criticism of character and virtue is pertinent and should promote
vigilance in the usage of the word. But it is also the case that the history
of the term is not limited to its ideological uses by governing classes: there
is another tradition that allies notions of character and self-crafting to the

progressive projects of liberalism and socialism. Moreover, if one simply cedes terms such as "character" and "virtue" to the right, one pays a considerable political price, especially insofar as such terms appear to resonate so powerfully with such considerable segments of the population. Beyond such political concerns, there is the more basic issue of how integral the concept of self-cultivation is to *any* practical philosophy. If, as my analyses suggest, some version of the characterological haunts all forms of contemporary practical philosophy, then the character issue, broadly conceived, is not simply to be evaded or rejected. A more direct avowal of ideals of character and ethos, in my view, will extend our resources for talking about ethics and politics, at the same time correcting for some of the more narrow understandings of the "personal" and of "identity."

I.

If we take even a modest historical perspective on the genealogy of characterological thought, it becomes clear that the narrowing of the "personal" to exclude or at least significantly downplay characterological dimensions is a rather distinctive feature of contemporary literary and cultural studies. In nineteenth-century European thought, for example, character functioned in large measure as the site where threateningly impersonal practices might be given meaningful enactment, might take form as embodied virtue. As I have argued elsewhere, part of what defines the peculiarly Victorian response to the disenchantments of modernity is the attempt to imagine the methods of modern science, critical reason, and cosmopolitan detachment in terms of exemplary or heroic characterology: in this way, what we might call early antifoundationalism was underwritten by ethos, and thereby imbued with value, achieved or earned through practices that could successfully take on a human face.[4] Prominent examples include Arnoldian disinterestedness; those forms of "moralized objectivity" in scientific practice charted by historian of science Lorraine Daston; and the imbrication of character formation and epistemological advance in the thought of John Stuart Mill, where the quality of a particular truth takes its coloring from the dialogical process by which it was attained. For Mill, truth held in the absence of such a process may be accidentally true, but the individual who holds it will not own it properly and, as a consequence, will fail to attain to the epistemological virtue that safeguards intellectual practice as well as the characters of its practitioners.

---

[4] Amanda Anderson, *The Powers of Distance: Cosmopolitanism and the Cultivation of Detachment* (Princeton: Princeton University Press, 2001).

What has become, one might well ask, of this interarticulation of method and ethos that so defined the precarious modernity of the nineteenth-century, where the manner of enactment was seen to legitimate or effectively moralize those practices constructed on the scaffolding of the post-Kantian dispensation? One can certainly trace how the emphasis on manner—initially fused with the impersonal methods of modern aesthetic and disciplinary practice—breaks away from the yoke of its service to variously defined transsubjective or objective projects: the glorification of the subjective in Wilde; the will to power and the heroic characterology of Nietzsche (becoming who one is); the more general aggrandizement of the individual in early modernism. But what happens to the dialectic of subjectivity and impersonality in the major paradigmatic transformations of the twentieth century—throughout the complex development of modernism, in the movement from modernism to postmodernism, or in the line of development from structuralism to poststructuralism to cultural studies?

Foucault merits reconsideration in the context of this large question because his own trajectory—his famous turn somewhere between volume I and volume II of the *History of Sexuality*—dramatizes the dialectic I refer to, and his work as a whole, taking into account the distance it travels from its structuralist beginnings, helps to focus the paradigmatic shifts referred to above, as well. But I in no way intend a comprehensive discussion of Foucault; rather I am interested in approaching his work, and his famous so-called debate with Habermas, from an oblique angle, one that brings the submerged or at least underexplored category of ethos to light.

I refer to this as a "so-called debate" to highlight two points. First, and most basically, although both thinkers discussed each other's work on various occasions, there was never any formal debate between Foucault and Habermas.[5] A conference scheduled for Berkeley, California, in November 1984, which promised a fruitful exchange, never took place due to the untimely death of Foucault.[6] Second, and more importantly, from within the context of literary and cultural studies, what has since the early to mid-1980s passed as an understanding of the differences between Habermas

[5] Habermas, of course, devoted two chapters of *The Philosophical Discourse of Modernity* to Foucault, whereas Foucault's comments about Habermas were restricted to occasional moments. In this sense the debate is "uneven" since there is a more extensive treatment/critique of Foucault on Habermas's part.

[6] According to Habermas, Foucault delivered the lecture "What is Enlightenment?" just prior to suggesting the conference idea to Habermas in March 1983. The conference was to include as participants not only Foucault and Habermas, but also Richard Rorty, Charles Taylor, and Hubert Dreyfus. In his memorial address for Foucault, Habermas discusses the proposed conference and this lecture's surprising turn back toward the Enlightenment. See Jürgen Habermas, "Taking Aim at the Heart of the Present: On Foucault's Lecture on Kant's *What is Enlightenment?*" in *The New Conservatism: Cultural Criticism and the Historians' Debate*, trans. Shierry Weber Nicholsen (Cambridge, Mass.: MIT Press, 1989), 173–79.

and Foucault has often served to foreclose rather than foster debate. Indeed, what occurred in this arena would better be described as a bloodless coup on the part of the Foucauldians. In the years that saw routine contrasts between the two thinkers, a time when Foucault's work was pervasively influencing the literary field, Habermas was more often glancingly invoked than seriously discussed, typically serving to exemplify or condense a rationalist or utopian position that could help negatively to define the favored Foucauldian approach. Habermas's position was caricatured, as was his complex relation to the Frankfurt School: he was alleged to be simply on the side of reason and enlightenment, a promulgator of the deluded and dangerous belief that communication has the capacity to be "transparent." The complexity of Habermas's systems-theory was left to the side, as was his careful differentiation between forms of reason and his insistence that enlightenment is an unfinished project. To be sure, the historical argument about the public sphere fared better. There are several reasons why this was the case: it was seen as more acceptably historical in nature; it was amenable to being treated separately from the rest of his theory; and it was productively revised to accommodate more plurality and contestation than the original theory seemed to house.[7] The critiques here were immanent, in the interest of retaining an extremely serviceable concept, whereas the theory of communicative action and the discourse ethics seemed to require outright rejection insofar as they were seen to be irretrievably marred by transcendental, developmental, universalist, and utopian assumptions. Leaving aside the more capacious uses of the public sphere work, however, in general the name Habermas was used economically to signify any number of denigrated practices, from the mere distastefulness of rationalist modes to the inevitable oppressiveness of normative thinking to the dangers of a totalized Reason seeking to disavow its drive to power.[8]

I pause to make this point because I want to stress at the outset that this analysis returns to Foucault/Habermas material in order to explore the particular way in which an appeal to ethos functioned within it dur-

---

[7] Perhaps the most influential essay within scholarship on the public sphere, one that influenced the fields of literature, history, and political theory, was Nancy Fraser's "Rethinking the Public Sphere: A Contribution to the Critique of Actually Existing Democracy," which originally appeared in *Habermas and the Public Sphere*, ed. Craig Calhoun (Cambridge, Mass.: MIT Press, 1991), 109–42.

[8] To provide an example of how the invocation of Habermas often played out in the theoretical field, I point to the first page of Ernesto Laclau's *New Reflections on the Revolution of Our Time*. Here, and nowhere else in the text, Laclau invokes the name of Habermas. But it is clear that the invocation is carrying a lot of weight. The text reads:

An initial reaction to this new intellectual climate has been to become entrenched in the defence of "reason" and attempt to relaunch the project of "modernity" in opposition to those tendencies considered "nihilistic." The work of Habermas is perhaps the most representative of this attitude. Our position, however, is exactly the opposite: far from perceiving in the "crisis of reason" a nihilism

ing its late stages. I am not returning to the "debate" in its original form, when it focused centrally on the question of the relation between power and communication. But the history is salient insofar as habitual contrasts between the two thinkers retain a hold over the discursive community, occluding the specific issues I wish to bring to the fore and prompting resistance to the attempt to give Habermas a fuller hearing. As it did in the earliest days of the "debate," the name "Habermas" often continues to provoke a knowing weariness in the literary field, one that defines a certain consensus about what Habermas signifies—plodding style, an embarrassing optimism of the intellect, and dangerous complicity with the Enlightenment. This entrenched view is all the more striking in view of the fact that Habermas's work has developed in complex and historically sensitive ways, and continues to hold the potential for productive dialogue with literary and cultural studies, particularly in the arena of cosmopolitanism.[9] In any event, I want to stress at the outset that to the extent that I do reinvoke the terms and texts of the original debate, it is to shift and reframe them, so as to acknowledge the polemical contours of the Foucault/Habermas literature as a founding instance of key elements in our current habits of argumentation. This claim requires rethinking what has been at stake in the reception of Foucault's "turn," and returning to a late stage in the debate with Habermas as a key moment where ethos played an utterly central—if consistently misrecognized—role.[10]

---

which leads to the abandonment of any emancipatory project, we see the former as opening unprecedented opportunities for radical critique of all forms of domination, as well as for the formulation of liberation projects hitherto restrained by the rationalist "dictatorship" of the Enlightenment. (Ernesto Laclau, *New Reflections on the Revolution of Our Time* [London: Verso, 1990], 3–4)

[9] See Jürgen Habermas, *The Inclusion of the Other: Studies in Political Theory*, ed. Ciaran Cronin and Pablo de Greif (Cambridge, Mass.: MIT Press, 1998). Another irony among several is the fact that Habermas is a profoundly engaged public intellectual in Germany and Europe: his work in this sphere considerably complicates his profile, and unsettles the ease with which he can be described as hopelessly idealist. See especially Jürgen Habermas, *The Past as Future: Interviews by Michael Haller*, ed. and trans. Max Pensky (Lincoln: University of Nebraska Press, 1994). See also Max Pensky, "Jürgen Habermas and the Antinomies of the Intellectual," in *Habermas: A Critical Reader*, ed. Peter Dews (London: Blackwell, 1995), 211–37.

[10] There are important disciplinary distinctions to be made here. While Habermas "lost" in the arena of literary and cultural studies, the nature of the battle as well as the range of positions was quite different in political philosophy, where the Foucauldians felt disadvantaged precisely because the Habermasian camp was using strong forms of philosophical argumentation. Some of the anthologies on the debate emanating from philosophy are trying to reframe the terms so as to give Foucault a better hearing: the appeal to ethos that I will discuss is at the heart of this reframing, and has been advanced by political theorists who are in alliance with certain trends in the literary and cultural studies field. See Michael Kelly, ed., *Critique and Power: Recasting the Foucault/Habermas Debate* (Cambridge, Mass.: MIT Press, 1994); Samantha Ashenden and David Owen, eds., *Foucault Contra Habermas* (London: Sage, 1999).

Foucault's "turn" constitutes a movement away from the monistic theory of power dominating *Discipline and Punish* and the *History of Sexuality, Volume I*, toward an art of living—what he variously calls "practices of the self" or an "aesthetics of existence." As such, it shares affinities with those elaborations of subjective enactment or practice that were formed in reaction, as I earlier noted, to the impersonality of structuralist and poststructuralist paradigms of thought. Deliberately myopic, restricting its gaze to the middle distance at best, Foucault's aesthetics of existence affirms agency by circumscribing its venue, like those modest Dickensian endings, where the glare of omniscience is relinquished and the perspective descends to meld with the participant's view. Highly individualized, the aesthetics of existence also imagines itself as an achievement of certain forms of ethical practice; it carries an echo of the Nietzschean ideal of self-becoming; in this it is distinct from those poststructuralist forms of individual enactment that focus the self's relation to self predominantly within the terms of sociologically ascribed identities: gender, race, class, nationality. It is in this sense that Foucault's "aesthetics of existence" constitutes a theoretical event that could be said to reintroduce the exiled categories of ethos and character.

Yet, as a rule-proving exception, the Foucauldian turn to ethos also manages to emphasize the constraints of the defining intellectual terrain, in a symptomatic and even exacerbating way. This is above all the case to the extent that Foucault is seen, as a thinker, to instantiate a certain philosophic ethos. Partly with his own help and reflective endorsement, the dramatization of Foucault as enacting a model of intellectual practice parallels and draws energy from the late Foucault, where ethos becomes important conceptually across a range of classical topics, culminating in his last course at the Collège de France on the *parrhesiast*, or the philosopher as truth-teller.[11] The topical attention to ethos in the later Foucault is construed as continuous with his more encompassing *style* of negative

---

[11] "In his last years, Foucault became more comfortable than he had been in the past with the profession of philosophy, and he proposed that his entire work be approached in terms of its ambition to be a philosophical ethos, a philosophy as life, a way of acting in the contemporary world which manifests both a way of belonging to it as well as a task within it. This ethos is exhibited most prominently in the philosopher's mode of thinking and one of the most striking features about Foucault's last period is the amount of attention which he gives to meditation on thought itself." James M. Bernauer, "Michel Foucault's Ecstatic Thinking," in James Bernauer and David Rasmussen, eds., *The Final Foucault* (Cambridge, Mass.: MIT Press, 1988), 66. For a fuller discussion of Foucault's lectures on the *parrhesiast*, as well as an example of the investment in a clear continuity between Foucault and his subject matter, see Thomas Flynn, "Foucault as Parrhesiast: His Last Course at the Collège de France (1984)," in Bernauer and Rasmussen, eds., *The Final Foucault*, 102–18.

critique, what Paul Bové has described, at least in part, as "ironic integrity."[12] Beyond the methodological investment in genealogical detachment, a provocative posture of deliberate evasion and negation is certainly intermittently in evidence throughout the interviews, which are themselves often treated as privileged moments by those commentators who are invested in what we might call "the ethos-bearing Foucault." Most readers of Foucault's work are familiar with the form of response that acts as a refusal of the very terms of the question, a refusal of certain characterizations of his thought, and, it might even be said, a kind of studied refusal to engage the terms that shape debate. Thus Foucault will act bemused in the face of terms like postmodernity—"What are we calling postmodernity? I'm not up to date"—or emphasize the inapplicability of any labels to him or his work—"It's true that I prefer not to identify myself and that I'm amused by the diversity of the ways I've been judged and classified."[13] This tendency toward refusal of terms is allied, by Foucault's admiring commentators, with exemplary ethos, associated to varying degrees with rhetoric, style, dialogue, and artful disruption, and placed in ennobling contrast to the constraints of rationality, doctrine, and formal argument. In fact, in some sense—and this is displayed most strikingly in the so-called debate with Habermas—the aversion to formal argument in Foucault becomes, for many of his admiring commentators, ethos-defining.[14]

[12] This phrase is drawn from Bové's foreword to the English translation of Deleuze's book on Foucault. The immediate context is a discussion of Foucault that compares him with R. P. Blackmur, and that stresses Blackmur's "marked effort to resist the possible commodification of even the most ironic stance into a critical program." Paul Bové, "The Foucault Phenomenon: The Problematics of Style," foreword to Gilles Deleuze, *Foucault*, trans. Sean Hand (Minneapolis: The University of Minnesota Press, 1988), xxxv.

[13] Michel Foucault, "Critical Theory/Intellectual History," in Kelly, ed., *Critique and Power*, 124; Michel Foucault, "Polemics, Politics, and Problematizations," in *The Foucault Reader*, ed. Paul Rabinow (New York: Pantheon, 1984), 384. Also see Michel Foucault, "Politics and Ethics: An Interview," in Rabinow, ed., *The Foucault Reader*, 375: "If you like, what strikes me is the fact that from the beginning I have been considered an enemy by the Marxists, an enemy by the right wing, an enemy by the people in the center. I think that if my work were essentially political, it would end up finding its place somewhere in the long run." This comment interestingly comes shortly after Foucault states that "the key to the personal poetic attitude of a philosopher is not to be sought in his ideas, as if it could be deduced from them, but rather in his philosophy-as-life, in his philosophical life, his ethos" (374). "Ethos" for Foucault becomes associated with a kind of singularity and ineffability.

[14] I do not mean to suggest that the feature of Foucault's intellectual style described here—and often most strikingly in evidence in the interview format—encompasses the whole of his repertoire or manner of being. There is great variety within the interviews, which also include moments of self-conscious fallibility and marked openness. I am interested here in the ways that the specific polemical field has shaped the emphasis on ethos as negation, ethos as aversion to formal argument.

This approach to Foucault encompasses those scholars in both the literary and philosophical fields who are particularly concerned to defend him against rationalist and political critique, with Habermas as the central, though not only, opponent. In his foreword to Deleuze's book on Foucault, for example, Bové advocates an attention to style over and against "position," faulting the philosopher Charles Taylor for imagining that paraphrase is adequate to Foucault, and charging that the literary critic Fredric Jameson makes hermeneutic demands that similarly miss the prevailing significance of style. Critical of thinkers who base their readings of Foucault on predetermined philosophical or political criteria, Bové makes appeal to sensibility, style, and ironic negation, placing Foucault in a line of thinkers that includes Socrates, Montaigne, and Nietzsche. Among political theorists, both William Connolly and Richard Bernstein present Foucault as a canny rhetorical strategist aiming to play upon and thwart our presuppositions, to disrupt and dislodge our comfortable ways of thinking—in this view he deliberately eschews formal coherence in argument, which would only reinforce our settled habits.[15] Both of these critics see Foucault's project as the enactment of an ethos that cannot be reduced to doctrine or theory. Assumed here is also Foucault's commitment to a tutelary, Socratic mode that schools the reader in negative critique, that prompts the reader to "critique" as an attitude of questioning. As with Foucault's own characterization of the philosopher as one who cares about the care of others, these readings position Foucault's philosophic ethos as simultaneously an ethical and intellectual model.[16]

The context for these defenses of Foucault are the charges of incoherence and self-contradiction that have been leveled against his work, and that are associated above all with Habermas's critique. The argument that Foucault is self-refuting is based on the claim that Foucault cannot really account for his account: if critique is itself a form of power, then it cannot be used coherently to criticize power. This argument rests on a prior assumption of the existence of communicative reason itself, one that challenges Foucault's own refusal to distinguish communicative reason

---

[15] William Connolly, "Taylor, Foucault, and Otherness," *Political Theory* 13 (August 1985); Richard Bernstein, "Foucault: Critique as a Philosophic Ethos," in Kelly, ed., *Critique and Power*, 211–41.

[16] Connolly and Bernstein are just two prominent examples. See also Niko Kolodny, "The Ethics of Cryptonormativism: A Defense of Foucault's Evasions," *Philosophy and Social Criticism* 22, no. 5 (1996): 63–84; David Owen, "Genealogy as Exemplary Critique," *Economy and Society* 24, no. 4 (1995): 489–506; David Owen, "Orientation and Enlightenment: An Essay on Critique and Enlightenment," in Ashenden and Owen, eds., *Foucault Contra Habermas*, 21–44; Bernauer, "Michel Foucault's Ecstatic Thinking"; Flynn, "Foucault as Parrhesiast."

sufficiently from instrumental or disciplinary reason.[17] For Habermas, there are assumptions entailed in the very act of rational argumentation, assumptions about possibilities for rational critique, and it constitutes a performative contradiction to deny those assumptions at the level of theory, when the very act of communicating the theory must presuppose them. The reason this is a performative contradiction and not simply a contradiction is because the contradiction is not internal or locatable at the level of the theory but instead a result of the incoherent gap between the very nature of human communication and the content of the theory proffered. In some sense, then, while Habermas is insisting on rational criteria, he is also insisting, more deeply and existentially, on the unlivability of Foucault's theory, in the same manner that theorists like Cavell speak to the unlivability of skepticism. I point to this aspect of Habermas's critique to provide context for the appeal to ethos in the defenses of Foucault, which proposes an art of living based on conditions Habermas fundamentally contests, and to lay the groundwork for a later discussion of Habermas's own views on practice, enactment, and ethos. For the purposes of the present discussion, what is central to note is that the significance invested in the notion of ethos is conditioned, and ultimately limited, by the terms of the Habermasian critique: the investment in ethos is cast above all as a refusal of the insistence on rational coherence, and often justifies itself in these terms. The forms of restless and negative critique that the genealogist manifests, it is stressed, are themselves a *practice*. To try to force them into a rationalist framework is wrongheaded not only because the genealogist is engaged in a critique of rationality, but also because such a criticism fails to recognize the way in which negative critique is inseparable from its manner of enactment: it is not a performative contradiction but rather a form of critique dependent upon its performance as a refusal of the logic of contradiction.[18]

One of Foucault's own statements about Habermas illuminates this dynamic and indicates the extent to which ethos specifically challenges

[17] For a discussion of Foucault's engagement with such a distinction in "The Subject and Power" (1982), see David Ingram, *Reason, History, and Politics: The Communitarian Grounds of Legitimation in the Modern Age* (Albany: SUNY Press, 1995), 188–97. Despite Foucault's somewhat shifting position on this issue, the question of whether and to what extent power saturates all communicative contexts remains the key locus of difference between the two thinkers, both in the primary and the secondary literature that can be said to constitute the "debate."

[18] For a discussion of the explicit embrace of performative contradiction in poststructuralist thought, as well as a general discussion of the intellectual historical context of this Frankfurt School category, see Martin Jay, "The Debate Over Performative Contradiction: Habermas vs. the Poststructuralists," in Axel Honneth et al., eds., *Philosophical Interventions in the Unfinished Project of Enlightenment* (Cambridge, Mass.: MIT Press, 1992), 261–79.

rational argument. This statement occurs in the 1984 interview, "The Ethic of Care for the Self as a Practice of Freedom." In response to a question about how games of truth might become, in certain societal conditions, relatively independent of structures of power, Foucault replies,

> This is indeed an important problem; I imagine you are thinking a little about Habermas when you say that. I am quite interested in what Habermas is doing. I know that he does not at all agree with what I say—I for my part tend to be a little more in agreement with what he says. But there is something which always causes me a problem: it is when he assigns such an important place to relations of communication and, above all, a function that I would call "utopian." [19]

Of especial interest here is Foucault's assertion that while Habermas does not agree at all with what he says, he (Foucault) is a little more in agreement with what Habermas says. This is a provocative and complicated utterance. First and most strikingly, it refuses the strictures of logic, insisting that ethos—attitude or stance—is utterly crucial to determining the relation of one person's thought to another. By essentially saying, "I am a little more in agreement with him than he is with me," rather than, "I think we are more in agreement than he acknowledges," Foucault implies that there is no external perspective from which one might adjudicate their differences or agreements, precisely because one essential element of agreement stems from the attitude of the thinker toward the other's work. Second, this utterance constitutes a pause in which Foucault congratulates himself upon his own good manner. Foucault is capacious enough to see through to and acknowledge an affinity or coincidence between Habermas and himself, while Habermas has fully rejected Foucault's views: Foucault displays higher communicative delicacy than the theorist of communicative action. By extension, there is the suggestion that Habermas is rigidly defending his position against those who do not conform utterly to its governing principles and claims. There is the suggestion, in other words, that Habermas is ethos-challenged. This dimension of Foucault's comment is continuous with much stronger remarks he makes elsewhere about his dislike of polemic:

> The polemicist . . . proceeds encased in privileges that he possesses in advance and will never agree to question. On principle, he possesses rights authorizing

[19] Michel Foucault, "The Ethic of Care for the Self as a Practice of Freedom," trans. J. D. Gauthier, S. J., in Bernauer, *The Final Foucault*, 18. I have emended the translation somewhat. For the original transcription of the interview, see Michel Foucault, "L'éthique du souci de soi comme pratique de la liberté," *Dits et écrits* IV (Paris: Gallimard, 1994), 726–27.

him to wage war and making that struggle a just undertaking; the person he confronts is not a partner in the search for truth but an adversary, an enemy who is wrong, who is harmful, and whose very existence constitutes a threat. For him, then, the game consists not of recognizing this person as a subject having the right to speak but of abolishing him, as interlocutor, from any possible dialogue.[20]

What interests me here is a certain inversion or doubling back that occurs, in both the statement on Habermas and the minidiatribe against polemic: the thinkers who are most wedded to reason and to strong versions of argument are revealed to be ungenerous and even violent in relation to those they oppose, so much so that they discredit the purity of their arguments. Formal or strong argument is itself necessarily an ethos, and a not-very-appealing one at that. So is Foucault a little more in agreement with Habermas than Habermas is with him? How exactly can he be, when there is no agreement without attunement, and attunement here is demonstrated to be the element that divides them?

We might call the appeal to ethos, on the part of Foucault and his admiring commentators, an attempt to evade or trump the moves of the rationalist. Above all, this move opposes a valorized ethos to reason, exacerbating an inverse tendency in Habermas and his followers. But there are further criticisms that can be lodged against this appeal to ethos, especially as it appears in the secondary literature. It disavows its own polemical status in imagining itself beyond or to the side of polemic. And it relies very heavily upon the charismatic force of Foucault as a figure, in its positioning of his statements in interviews—whether evasive or revisionist—as somehow oracular. Thus, critics of Foucault are wrong because Foucault's own accounts of what he was always up to constitute the last word on the matter. For example, Michael Kelly, offering a synopsis and commentary on Foucault in his interesting anthology, *Critique and Power: Recasting the Foucault/Habermas Debate*, takes as his starting point for a response to the Habermasian critique Foucault's statements in the interview "Critical Theory/Intellectual History," because, in his view, it offers Foucault's "most complete account of his intellectual development from *Madness and Civilization* to the *History of Sexuality*."[21] But an approach that credits Foucault's own assertions about the

---

[20] Foucault, "Polemics, Politics, and Problematizations," 112. For a fascinating reading of Foucault's approach to polemic, see Jonathan Crewe's contribution to Jane Gallop, ed. *Polemic: Critical and Uncritical* (New York: Routledge, 2005). It is interesting to note that Foucault's ire about polemics was primarily focused on Marxism, and that Habermas of course is partly associated with this tradition.

[21] Michael Kelly, "Foucault, Habermas, and the Self-Referentiality of Critique," in Kelly, ed., *Critique and Power*, 371.

guiding questions of his work, assertions clearly tilted toward his most recent interests and orientations, is highly questionable methodologically. Foucault was a famous self-revisionist, going so far as to disavow or rewrite some of his already published works: this seems a tendency to be analyzed, not simply accorded hermeneutic privilege.[22] Kelly's statement is strange also because such questionable methodology sits right next to more traditional ones in his analysis, as when he assesses critiques of *Discipline and Punish* by culling only evidence internal to the text, and weighing different passages against one another.

An example that distills the moves involved in this approach to Foucault can be found in Richard Bernstein's essay, "Foucault: Critique as a Philosophic Ethos." Bernstein suggests that we can account for the stronger agency-denying claims in middle Foucault by understanding them rhetorically rather than literally. In these instances we can

> even grasp Foucault's use of that favored rhetorical device of Nietzsche, hyperbole. One might think, for example, that Foucault is heralding the death of the subject, that he is claiming that the subject itself is *only* the result of the effects of power/knowledge regimes, that he completely undermines and ridicules any and all talk of human agency. There is plenty of textual evidence to support such claims. But it is also clear, especially in his late writings when he deals with the question of the self's relation to itself and the possibility of "the man who tries to invent himself," that he is not abandoning the idea that "we constitute ourselves as subjects acting on others."[23]

On the one hand, we are told that a strict adherence to logical argument will cause us to miss the rhetorical strategy of hyperbole, though we are not told what the reason for hyberbole is in this instance. It simply stands in as a trope for rhetoric itself. On the other hand, Bernstein admits that there's plenty of "textual evidence" for a denial of agency—here now limiting himself to the explicit argument, and to formal criteria for assessing logical coherence—but then adds that it "is also clear" "in the late writings" that he has not abandoned agency. How do we answer such a flexible defense? Initially, we are presented with an almost esoteric appeal to rhetoric, then we are expected to simply accede to the notion that Foucault's later utterances have a corrective power over prior utterances, as though early and middle Foucault were simply early and middle drafts, interesting but needing to give way to the aggrandized intentionality legible in the decisive revision.

---

[22] See Didier Eribon, *Michel Foucault*, trans. Betsy Wing (Cambridge, Mass.: Harvard University Press, 1991), 185, 323–24.

[23] Bernstein, "Foucault: Critique as a Philosophic Ethos," in Kelly, ed., *Critique and Power*, 223.

The appeal to Foucault himself, the elevation of his own artful rhetoric and self-representation, partakes ultimately of what we might call "charismatic fallacy," a version of positive ad hominem. The appearance of this form of argument is instructive, revealing the ways an appeal to ethos here merges with a cult of the theorist's personality, shifting the criteria of argumentation so as effectively to thwart the charges of incoherence. This move confuses the turn to ethos with the elevation of the theorist's personality, the effect of which is to narrow the significance and resources of the former. Rather than understanding Foucault's geneaological project as crucially mediated through forms of cultivated characterology (understood both intellectually and ethically), this framing of Foucault invokes the aura and mystique associated with his person so as to forestall a moment of critique and potential dialogue. A glamorized notion of personality eclipses the more complex mediations involved in articulating the relation between theory and enactment, mediations that Foucault's work itself often works hard to promote. Thus, although Foucault's late work does in key ways constitute a promising, exceptional turn to ethos, both the defining opposition to the Habermasian position and the cult of personality have warped its development.

It should also be noted that the charismatic fallacy, or the cult of the theorist's personality, functions in Foucault's case not only to disable the charges of incoherence associated with the Habermasian critique, but also to absorb what is after all a rather dramatic theoretical turn in the late work. It is not simply the case, as in the Bernstein example, that the turn is used to answer critiques of the earlier theories. The late work is accepted and heralded precisely because it is a self-correction by a charismatic figure whose legitimacy derives from his earlier embrace of suspicious reading. Indeed, if anyone else had published the second and third volumes of the *History of Sexuality*, they would have had little to no impact on the theoretical domains of literary and cultural theory in the U.S. academy.[24] More generally, one might say, the enduring identity of the theorist allows the legitimating aura to extend backward as well as forward, so that both orientations at once correct for one another and remain somehow untouchable on their own terms. Under such conditions, we do not have far to travel to a work like David Halperin's *Saint Foucault*, which confidently yokes Foucault's later work to the agenda of politically minded theory in the United States, an alliance that would not be easily achieved without the (very much avowed) hagiography driving

[24] I would hazard a similar claim about the influential Eve Kosofsky Sedgwick essay, "Paranoid and Reparative Reading; or, You're So Paranoid, You Probably Think This Introduction is About You," in *Novel Gazing: Queer Readings in Fiction*, ed. Eve Kosofsky Sedgwick (Durham: Duke University Press, 1997), 1–37.

the study. Indeed, if the work from the two phases of Foucault's career had been done by different individuals, we would never encounter a statement like the following of Halperin's: "Queer politics itself, finally, is a kind of spiritual exercise, a modern practice of the self."[25] Nor would we see a trend of literary scholarship informed by Foucault's late work on "practices of the self" or the "aesthetics of existence."[26]

II.

Within the context of the Habermas/Foucault "debate," the appropriation of ethos on the part of Foucault and his admiring commentators, buttressed as it is by a cult of personality, works above all to promote the view that Habermas and his followers are somehow locked into a rigid and abstract rationalism that fails to understand not only the workings of power (the abiding focus of the Habermas/Foucault literature), but also the subtle demands of intellectual and political practice. As Foucault himself says when distinguishing his views from those of Habermas, "The problem, then, is not to try to dissolve [power relations] in the utopia of a perfectly transparent communication, but to give one's self the rules of law, the techniques of management, and also the ethics, the *ethos*, the practice of self, which will allow these games of domination to be played with a minimum of domination."[27] There is a kind of characterological or ethical piety here, an attempt to trump Habermasian criticisms by casting the investment in rational argument or democratic procedure as not simply deluded about the nature of power, but also vulgar and misguided from the standpoint of practice, which requires subtle adjustments, tact, and phronesis precisely because of the ubiquity of power. There is the suggestion, both in Foucault and in the

---

[25] David Halperin, *Saint Foucault: Towards a Gay Hagiography* (New York: Oxford University Press, 1995), 101. This book appropriates the turn to ethos but in a particular way that subordinates it to, and legitimates it via, politics (see esp. 106).

[26] See James Eli Adams, *Dandies and Desert Saints: Styles of Victorian Masculinity* (Ithaca: Cornell University Press, 1995); Jeff Nunokawa, *Tame Passions of Wilde: The Styles of Manageable Desire* (Princeton: Princeton University Press, 2003); John Guillory, "The Ethical Practice of Modernity: The Example of Reading," in Garber et al., eds., *The Turn to Ethics*, 29–46. For the purposes of this argument, however, I am far more interested in the work directly on Foucault in this arena, such as Halperin's. The practical criticism is often to be distinguished from the more theory-identified work insofar as it often cites the need to correct for the disciplinary Foucault by turning to the late Foucault. From a longer perspective, I see this phenomenon as related to the claims about legitimating aura that I am making here. But this does not mean that the individual studies enact the same blur that one sees in more strictly theoretical analyses and discussions.

[27] Foucault, "The Ethic of Care for the Self as a Practice of Freedom," 18.

secondary literature, that Habermas just does not "get" ethos, and therefore does not "get" Foucault. As a consequence, everything that might have seemed inappropriately personal in the earliest poststructuralist reactions to Habermas—the complaints about his "style" or the unreadability of his work—in this context emerges as suddenly salient.

But Habermas's critique of Foucault is by no means reductively limited to the sphere of logos, and it is fundamentally misguided to think that Foucault is somehow the guardian of ethos while Habermas is locked in logos. Admittedly, Habermas holds Foucault's work to standards of coherence, and is critical of the offhand or gestural remark that Foucault's followers would be more likely to treat as living philosophy. After approvingly citing Nancy Fraser's well-known critique of Foucault's failure to give any positive elaboration of the grounds for opposition to the modern power/knowledge regime, for example, Habermas writes, "Once, in a lecture, Foucault addressed this question in passing and gave a vague suggestion of postmodern criteria of justification."[28] Should we infer from Habermas's frustration here that he adheres rigidly to protocols of formal argumentation and is deaf to the art of negative critique, whose informing commitments will ever remain elusive of outright exposition, appearing, leprechaun-like, in transient forms like the lecture or interview? Habermas's understanding of ethos is far more developed than such an inference would have it—though fraught with ambivalence, as well. Habermas's neo-Kantianism defines itself via an intersubjective turn: his notion of communicative reason, the ground on which he mounts the charge of performative contradiction, requires an understanding of the individual speaker as embedded in social relations. But there is a tension in Habermas's conception of sociality. On the one hand, he stresses the value of, and need for, embedded sociality in his emphasis on primary socialization processes and their centrality to moral development, individual autonomy, and the cohesion of cultural groups. On the other hand, Habermas emphasizes the preeminent value of reason's capacity to break free of tradition and custom: reflective distance defines the crowning achievement of modernity. It is true that he to some extent characterizes this achievement as a social and historical development. Valorized forms of communicative rationality derive from specific cultural forms: the public sphere in Enlightenment culture, the conditions of multiculturalism within the democratic state, the pressing current challenges of globalism. Indeed, in a sense one could say that Habermas's insistence on the reflective institutionalization of communicative and demo-

---

[28] Jürgen Habermas, *The Philosophical Discourse of Modernity*, trans. Frederick G. Lawrence (Cambridge, Mass.: MIT Press, 1987), 284. Subsequent page number references will be cited parenthetically in the text.

cratic principles promotes a practical philosophy that operates, unlike the Foucauldian art of living, at the collective and institutional levels of political life. This is ethos as an emergent democratic culture, not ethos as individual cultivation or charismatic critique. But it also must be acknowledged that in persistently figuring modern reason as an abstractive ascent out of embeddedness, Habermas seems to deny what he otherwise acknowledges as the primacy of the social and historical, insisting more absolutely on reason's transcending power. Reason's capacity to break the bounds of context is, moreover, what for Habermas defines the moral as opposed to the ethical, the universal as opposed to the particular. In sum, Habermas oscillates between wanting to redefine universalism as a new ethos, and wanting to assert universalism over and against ethos, insofar as the latter always seems to fall into some form of blinkered adherence to custom. His detractors tend to emphasize only the latter move, which they see as misguided and off-putting in its deindividuating and decontextualizing drive toward the procedural and the impersonal.[29]

The shape of the received Foucault/Habermas opposition shifts, however, if one explores more fully the positive pole of Habermas's ambivalence toward ethos. In this section I will therefore examine a few important moments where Habermas's own thinking displays attentiveness to the significance of ethos—as a critical tool, as a philosophical stance, and as an integral element of democratic culture. My analysis will continue to acknowledge the limits of Habermas's conception of ethos—the persistent pressure of his ambivalence—while still trying to allow as much space as possible for these more capaciously imagined understandings of ethos. The entrenched opposition between Foucauldian ethos and Habermasian rationality, partly enforced by Habermas's own patterns of expression, has hitherto left these suggestive aspects of Habermas's thought largely in shadow. They are of interest in their own right, as a dimension of his thought, but also insofar as they suggest a dialectical relation of theory to practice, or argument to ethos, that reflectively encompasses individual, collective, and institutional domains. This involves, above all, a demystification of the move that distributes ethos exclusively to negative critique.

---

[29] Portions of this discussion are indebted to Richard J. Bernstein, "The Retrieval of the Democratic Ethos," in *Habermas on Law and Democracy*, ed. Michel Rosenfeld and Andrew Arato (Berkeley and Los Angeles: University of California Press, 1998), 287–305. Bernstein's evenhanded appraisal of Habermas yields a more balanced, and ultimately illuminating, analysis of ethos in this case than it does in his essay on Foucault. I found it very helpful in thinking through the dual stance Habermas takes toward this concept. I take up the issue of ethos in Habermasian proceduralism, and discuss the particulars of Bernstein's position on Habermas more fully in chapter 7.

Habermas employs ethos as a critical tool in his discussion of Foucault in *The Philosophical Discourse of Modernity*. It is noteworthy that in this text, his most sustained engagement with the critique of modernity stemming from the Frankfurt School through poststructuralism, Habermas's analyses are centered almost exclusively on individual figures; somehow the notion of an individual's life and history is absolutely vital to his sense of how one should understand his or her thought. To be sure, in addition to tracing intellectual genealogy Habermas tends to accord privilege to historical psychology and ideological forces rather than characterology: there is in fact a leitmotif of historical crisis and political disappointment in the text, which is meant to explain the dark mood of the theorists he criticizes. Thus, Stalinism and fascism are seen to provoke the bleak cynicism of Adorno and Horkheimer, while the disappointment of May 1968 is alleged as key in the development of Foucault's work, as well as in the emergence of the general mood that allowed the success of the postmodernists in France.[30] But Habermas does not restrict his discussion to this form of historical psychology, and indeed implies a far more nuanced understanding of how we might analyze the character of theory when he registers certain excesses or tensions internal to the writing of specific thinkers.

This is strikingly the case in his discussion of what he calls Foucault's "cryptonormativism," a form of internal tension that needs to be distinguished from performative contradiction. Indeed, these two charges—performative contradiction and cryptonormativism—are crucially different. The charge of performative contradiction rests upon a prior assumption about communicative rationality, a claim about certain presuppositions built into linguistic use itself: if one does not buy into these transcendental claims, one can quite justifiably reject the notion of performative contradiction, as well as the appeal to the arguably loaded notion of livability that accompanies it. But the charge of cryptonormativism takes on a different hue. Less insistent on the underlying transcendental assumptions of the theory of communicative action, it points rather to internal tension and strain in Foucault, a strain evident precisely in the gap between tone and assertion. It reads Foucault more in the manner that we are instructed to read Victorian dramatic monologue. The charge of cryptonormativism *can be* distilled into a form of logical contradiction or paradox: Foucault's critique of normalization, which gets extended into a critique of normativity tout court, is incoherent insofar as it has to implicitly make appeal to certain norms that it is unwilling to acknowledge or avow. But the *elaboration* of the criticism typically finds the cryptic appeal to norms evident in tone or stance. That is what the

---

[30] See Habermas, *The Philosophical Discourse of Modernity*, 257.

"crypto-" in cryptonormativism is: an implicit appeal felt most vividly at the level of tone or rhetorical gesture. For example, Habermas notes the extreme difficulties that arise as Foucault aims to maintain second-order value-freeness in his critique of the false pretense to value-freeness in the human sciences:

> Now this grounding of a second-order value-freeness is already by no means value-free. Foucault understands himself as a dissident who offers resistance to modern thought and humanistically disguised disciplinary power. Engagement marks his learned essays right down to the style and choice of words; the critical tenor dominates the theory no less than the self-definition of the entire work. Foucault thereby distinguishes himself, on the one hand, from the engaged positivism of a Max Weber, who wanted to separate a decisionistically chosen and openly declared value basis from an analysis carried out in a value-free way. Foucault's criticism is based more on the postmodern rhetoric of his presentation than on the postmodern assumptions of his theory. (94)

In building itself out of a recognition of the tension between ethos and explicit claim, Habermas's critique of Foucault in some crucial sense honors the way in which ethos inhabits argument, rather than insisting on a suppression of ethos and the absolute purity of the argument.[31] One might be tempted to read Habermas's critique, reliant as it is on noting the investments of furtive tone and rhetorical shading, as a dedication above all to explicitness and rule-governed coherence. But the attention to the disjunction between tone and assertion seems better understood, within the context of Habermas's larger investment in democratic dialogue, as continuous with those principles of openness and transparency that forward the practices of deliberative debate. Dialogue is stymied or at best asymmetrical when one party to the debate is accorded an exclusive charismatic privilege. If the polemicist "proceeds encased in privileges that he possesses in advance and will never agree to question," the construct that I have called "the ethos-bearing Foucault" proceeds suffused with an aura that he, too, is seen to possess in advance, one that seems to elude entirely the realm of open questioning.

If Habermas shows an attentiveness to ethos in the critique of Foucault, his tendency to criticize the views of his philosophical opponents partly by appeal to the moods (*die Stimmungen*) they express or provoke reveals, I think, the limits of his capacity to accord the dimension of ethos any positive centrality within the project of communicative reason.

---

[31] Similarly, a respectful attention to, and even recuperation of, "instructive contradiction" is palpably evident in Habermas's memorial address to Foucault, "Taking Aim at the Heart of the Present: On Foucault's Lecture on Kant's *What is Enlightenment?*" in Habermas, *The New Conservatism*, 173–79.

This is a habit of thought that extends beyond the recourse to historical psychology that I noted earlier, one that issues from his enduring ambivalence toward anything that seems to attenuate reason's distancing powers. A distinctly negative quality, ethos in the guise of mood appears only as that which undermines or overwhelms moral and intellectual clarity. "Under the sign of a Nietzsche revitalized by poststructuralism, moods and attitudes are spreading that are confusingly like those of Adorno and Horkheimer. I would like to forestall this confusion." Or: "In interviews of the early 1970s, Foucault revealed the vehemence of his break with earlier convictions. At that time, he joined the choir of disappointed Maoists of 1968 and was taken by the moods to which one must look if one wants to explain the remarkable success of the New Philosophers in France."[32]

This pattern mirrors the very opposition that we saw in the Foucault material, where the appeal to ethos involved a rejection of formal argument. Moreover, the discourse of mood plays into—and in part derives from—the ideal of mature moral development as it appears in Habermas's writings on communicative action, reflecting his persistent tendency to apply an evaluative contrast between youth and maturity. In this sense, Habermas might be said to psychologize the contest between philosophical positions.[33] But it is also the case that mood functions in a deliberate contrast with a form of maturity that seems to supersede an investment in psychological depth: the deliberate nongrandiosity of proceduralism. Relevant here would be a discernible continuity between the critique of republican virtue and the refusal of the grand gestures and self-indulgence connoted by moods. Particularly revealing is a statement from an interview with Michael Haller, in which Habermas responds to a question about whether his views on political and social

[32] Habermas, *The Philosophical Discourse of Modernity*, 107, 257.

[33] Two examples are salient here. When discussing what for him is the unappealing moral stance of strategic rather than principled postconventionalism—what Kohlberg designated as stage $4\frac{1}{2}$ in his overall schema of moral development—Habermas notes that this arrested stage has its own philosophical counterparts in the value-skepticism of thinkers in a line from Weber to Popper. See Jürgen Habermas, *Moral Consciousness and Communicative Action*, trans. Christian Lenhardt and Shierry Weber Nicholsen (Cambridge, Mass.: MIT Press, 1990), 184. And the relative values assigned by Habermas in his use of the concepts of youth and maturity assert themselves somewhat strangely in an acrobatic moment in his analysis of Hegel in *The Philosophical Discourse of Modernity*. Habermas has been showing that Hegel's youthful insights (as manifest in his critique of the one-sidedness of the principle of subjectivity) are replaced, as he gets older, with the misguided notion of the Absolute. But as though unable to distinguish between the literal and the metaphorical in the case of this governing conceptual contrast, Habermas manages to recast the youthful insight as maturity relative to the later ideas: "With this concept of the absolute, Hegel regresses back behind the intuitions of his youthful period" (22).

changes in Europe have failed to take into account the profound material inequities between Europe and the third world:

> But *we* can overcome Eurocentrism only out of the better spirit of Europe.
> Only if we are able to do this will the wounds inflicted on the world by Euro-
> centrism, and the material world culture that grew from it, become if not
> healed, then at least treatable.
>
> These are somewhat too grand turns of phrase for characterizing the com-
> pletely profane, piecemeal kind of perspectives that we need to work from.
> I've got a tin ear for Heideggerian melodies. "Only a god can save us"—that's
> the kind of noble tone in philosophy that already got on Kant's nerves. Philoso-
> phers don't change the world. What we need is to practice a little more soli-
> darity: without that, intelligent action will remain permanently foundationless
> and inconsequential. Such practice, certainly, requires rational institutions; it
> needs rules and communicative forms that don't morally overtax the citizens,
> but rather exact the virtue of an orientation toward the common good in
> small change.
>
> If there is any small remnant of utopia that I've preserved, then it is surely
> the idea that democracy—and the public struggle for its best form—is capable
> of hacking through the Gordian knots of otherwise insoluble problems. I'm
> not saying that we're going to succeed in this; we don't even know whether
> success is possible. But because we don't know, we at least have to try. Apoca-
> lyptic moods sap the energies that nourish these initiatives. Optimism and pes-
> simism aren't really relevant categories here.[34]

We might call Habermas's modest program an appeal not so much to
the spirit of Europe as to the spirit of proceduralism, here construed as
forms of institutionally bound collective practice that are best advanced
through modes of interaction that downplay extreme affect or, presumably, strong investments in personal style. This conception, too, is an
ethos, of course, and the negative charisma that marks the response necessarily exists in tension with the appeal to modest procedure. Habermas
here lights up the ways in which romantic notions of opposition and critique have tended to minimize the hard work of institution building and
collective practice: one might distill the point down to the observation
that the valorization of individual ethos has undermined the advance of
collective ethos precisely by romanticizing politics. This zero-sum conception, whereby affect is conceived as a limited resource whose overspend-
ing depletes the reserves of political energy, is surely itself too defended,
narrowing ideas of political practice and expression in unwarranted
ways. Where it is suggestive, however, is in the challenge it poses to the

---

[34] Jürgen Habermas, "Europe's Second Chance," in *The Past as Future*, ed. and trans.
Max Pensky, 96–97.

valorization of individual ethos, and in its willingness to dwell on the more mundane, pragmatic task of promoting simple acts of citizenship.

In addition to the attention to collective ethos, one finds the occasional attempt within Habermas's writings to conceive of his own theoretical stance as *askesis*, as a refusal of various seductions to which others fall prey: the desire to absolutize reason by conflating it with power, for example, or to imagine one could engage in a "final unmasking." The end of the chapter on Adorno and Horkheimer is one such moment and, placed next to the attentive analyses of ethos in his critique of individual theorists, suggests a possible attention to philosophic ethos that might complement his already strongly developed conception of political culture:

> In one respect, ideology critique had in fact continued the undialectical enlightenment proper to ontological thinking. It remained caught up in the purist notion that the devil needing exorcism was hiding in the internal relationships between genesis and validity, so that theory, purified of all empirical connotations, could operate in its own element. Totalized critique did not discharge this legacy. The intention of a "final unmasking," which was supposed to draw away with one fell swoop the veil covering the confusion between power and reason, reveals a purist intent—similar to the intent of ontology to separate being and illusion categorially (that is, with one stroke). However, just as in a communication community the researcher, the context of discovery, and the context of justification are so entwined with one another that they have to be separated procedurally, by a *mediating* kind of thinking—which is to say, continuously—the same holds for the two spheres of being and illusion. In argumentation, critique is constantly entwined with theory, enlightenment with grounding, even though discourse participants always *have to suppose* that only the unforced force of the better argument comes into play under the unavoidable communication presuppositions of argumentative discourse. But they know, or they can know, that even this idealization is only necessary because convictions are formed and confirmed in a medium that is not "pure" and not removed from the world of appearances in the style of Platonic ideas. Only a discourse that admits this might break the spell of mythic thinking without incurring a loss of the light radiating from the semantic potentials also preserved in myth.[35] (130)

In this dense and difficult passage, Habermas goes a considerable way toward answering the charge that his theory is itself caught up in a blind idealization of reason. And he does so, interestingly, by insisting that it is the rigorously suspicious ideological critics—here, Adorno and Horkheimer—who necessarily assume or project a form of theoretical

[35] Translation emended to correct for what was probably a printer's error in the penultimate sentence.

purism, insofar as they imagine that theory can itself cleanly unmask the workings of ideology. In a complex reframing of the conditions of communicative reason—a form of reason that Adorno and Horkheimer fundamentally did not recognize in their totalizing conception of reason as instrumental—Habermas builds to the notion that participants in communicative reason have the capacity for a self-conscious relation to their own idealizing presuppositions about the reciprocity of dialogue and the communicative telos of mutual understanding. What is striking about this passage is that the discourse participants are reminded not simply of the cornerstone of communicative ethics—that is, the kinds of validity claims that they *have to suppose* when they engage in any form of communicative action—but also of what they *can know* about their own necessarily idealizing presuppositions. Thus, rather than simply reiterating that speech participants implicitly raise and recognize validity claims about their utterances—elsewhere specified as claims of comprehensibility, truth, truthfulness, and appropriateness—Habermas here invokes a higher-level awareness of the import of these presuppositions. He therefore does not simply impose a transcendental claim about the conditions of communicative reason, but rather imagines that the significance and effects of speech conditions are bound up in the attitude one cultivates toward them, the way in which one makes sense of them. Specifically, discourse participants are here encouraged to affirm their idealizing presuppositions in full recognition of the impurity—or profound embeddedness—of all linguistic practice, the impossibility of theory ever operating apart from mediated and embedded practice. This is thus an important moment where Habermas is effectively situating the ethos that animates what others see as his own unthinking purism.

Habermas's stress on the realization and institutionalization of practices of communicative reason, as well as his ethos-infused notion of cryptonormativism and his gestures toward a kind of enabling theoretical *attitude* (in the passage just cited), both interrogate and advance the relation between theory and practice, and they significantly do so at the individual, collective, and institutional levels. But, as I have shown, other elements of Habermas's thought direct attention away from these potentialities, primarily by opposing mature reason to ethos (conceived as either embedded custom or emotional excess). This narrow conception of reason jars with the otherwise firmly held differentiation between the right and the good, and it in part drives the unforgiving charges of mood-driven thought that appear in Habermas's critique of the anti-Enlightenment positions of postmodernism and earlier Frankfurt School theorists. There is no need to understand communicative reason so narrowly, when it can very much encompass a plurality of styles and modes, including, as Habermas seems to suggest, a kind of second-order ability to reflect on the reasons for its own "inescapable" idealizing attitudes. The formal reduction evident in such limiting moments is a problem that recurs in proceduralism more generally: it tends to restrictively imagine the character of public debate, reading it narrowly out of the liberal principle of tolerance, and thereby strangely foreclosing liberalism's dedication to individual flourishing, ongoing critique, and openness to difference (rather than mere toleration of it).

Practical philosophy is always engaged, to one degree or another, in one manner or another, in imagining how it might be lived, imagining its relation to enactment. We have our own versions, that is, of the Victorian attempt to weld character to method. No matter how disavowed the category of ethos or character may be in many philosophies of the present, it tends to come back in shadow forms, haunting the debate through strange displaced appearances, as when a pragmatist is called smug. Or it may make its presence felt more forcefully, as in the case of the charismatic fallacy or the narrow understanding of reason, where a certain style is elevated to endorse, express, or underwrite the theory. These suppressions and displacements emanate from different sources, depending on the theory to which they are tethered, and they clearly have a complex relation to the genealogy of thought on subjectivity, as the case of Foucault is intended to illustrate. It is my contention here that such suppressions and displacements merit scrutiny on a number of levels, and more generally can be said to reflect a failure sufficiently to think through questions of enactment or practice, especially in their relation to value and concrete political realization. My own intellectual affiliations and commitments aside, the most general aim of this essay is to promote an attention to characterology in the analysis of the practical dimensions of much recent theory.

The problem that emerges most pronouncedly in the Foucault/Habermas debate is the tendency to play upon and reinscribe an unnecessary opposition between reason and ethos. I concluded the previous section by summarizing the way this occurs in Habermas; on the Foucault side, by contrast, the appeal to ethos is used to lend an aura or sheen to Foucault, one loosely associated with rhetoric, art, and dissidence, and intended to render moot, even vulgar, the problem of formal coherence in the theory, while at the same time magically claiming ethicopolitical effectivity.[36] In this way ethos is used to trump or eclipse certain forms of reasoned argument, rather than to imagine more productively the ways in which

[36] For a more considered attempt to link Foucault's writings on the parrhesiast with the demands of political practice in the present age, see Paul Rabinow, "Modern and Countermodern: Ethos and Epoch in Heidegger and Foucault," in *The Cambridge Companion to Foucault*, ed. Gary Gutting (Cambridge: Cambridge University Press, 1994), 197–214.

theory might deliberate upon its relation to practice. Both sides of the debate, and certainly the understanding of the work of both thinkers, suffer from the distorting postures wrought by the defining polemical situation, itself in turn exacerbated by disciplinary and political contests. The form of practical philosophy that is most lost to view in this particular debate is one that would seek to promote a highly deliberative, reason-infused cultivation of ethos, one that, as in one of the more interesting strands of recent virtue ethics, might wed the insights of Aristotle with those of Kant.[37] Such a practical philosophy promotes reflection and deliberation in the cultivation of habit; it also has the potential to accommodate ideals of self-cultivation alongside ideals of collective deliberation. Above all recognizable in the seemingly outmoded "liberal temperament," this dialectical conception attempts to hold to a pluralism while not imagining that it can itself rise above the demands of enactment, which includes an attention to the ways we might actively guide the inevitable layering of character. By foreclosing even the recognition of such a synthesis, the loyal inheritors of the entrenched Foucault/Habermas opposition imagine themselves to be promoting "ethos," when in fact they are cornering it.

[37] See Nussbaum, "Virtue Ethics: A Misleading Category," for a discussion of the strand of virtue ethics that retains a privileged place for reason.

CHAPTER 7

Beyond Sincerity and Authenticity

THE ETHOS OF PROCEDURALISM

IN THIS ESSAY, I interpret the political theory known as "proceduralism" as an alternative to the paradigms of thought that dominate within poststructuralism. Proceduralism is a normative model for the justification of specific political practices and institutions: in the case of the forms of democracy favored by Rawls and Habermas, the aim is to elaborate those processes, rules, and procedures that will determine legitimate or justifiable outcomes. Historically associated with liberalism and legal formalism, proceduralism contrasts itself with moral and political theories that make appeal to substantive guiding concepts such as human nature or a pregiven notion of the good. In Habermas's case, ongoing intersubjective argument conducted within conditions of fairness and reciprocity, and animated by a moral point of view committed to the enlargement of perspective that argument itself promotes and demands, is the privileged procedural component of liberal and internationalist democratic institutions. Only those outcomes that have been accepted by all those concerned—whether by consensus or reasoned compromise—can be considered legitimate from a moral point of view.

In its Habermasian version, I will argue, proceduralism harbors a challenging conception of ethos, one that effectively displaces the antinomy between reason and ethos that I examined in the previous essay. The very idea of a proceduralist ethos will, I realize, be viewed by some readers as counterintuitive, insofar as proceduralism is often seen as fundamentally impersonal in its emphasis on processes, rules, and institutional practices that exceed the level of individual actors. But I will excavate proceduralism's own interest in ethos at both the individual and collective levels, and in order to set the stage for my analysis, I will revisit Lionel Trilling's genealogy of the modern concepts of sincerity and authenticity, arguing that proceduralism constitutes an extension of the sincerity paradigm, while poststructuralism remains the inheritor of the authenticity paradigm. The essays in the final section of this volume have identified ways in which a certain exiling of the categories of character and ethos has impoverished the theoretical resources of contemporary literary and cultural studies. My central presupposition has been that sociological conceptions of identity—ascriptions of race, class, sexuality, ethnicity, nationality—have so dominated the understanding of subjective experience that we do not tend to reflect sufficiently on the complex relations among ascribed identity, cultivated ethos, and practice. Even in much work influenced by poststructuralism, where identity is of course a complex affair, there is no coherent analysis of the relation between implied ideals of intellectual or ethical or political virtue, and the insistence that identities are fundamentally multiple and unstable because shot through with various group identifications. Ethical rhetoric certainly appears when theorists discuss the desirable or undesirable consequences of various stances toward identity and social relations. But the conceptual gulf between stance and identity typically remains unacknowledged—the former implies capacities for reflective distance, self-cultivation, and situated judgment, while the latter remains either extrinsic or imposed (even when unstable or precarious). The idea that intellectual and political practices carry ethical significance precisely insofar as they become a part of one's character or contribute toward the formation of a developed ethos seems foreign to the view of identity as imposed, subverted, unstable, or even performed (precisely because the notion of performance is fundamentally elaborated in relation to conditions of imposition and opportunities for subversion). In the end, the current frameworks for understanding selfhood and practice tend to imagine action as a negation or negotiation of identity, rather than something that might develop a character or foster an ethos.

Habermas's proceduralism departs from prevailing paradigms of identity—and their consequent theoretical impasses—by addressing two questions whose fates are deeply intertwined. First, his proceduralism interestingly reframes the poststructuralist attempt to trouble, subvert, or denaturalize identity, both at the level of individual practice and in relation to the collective dimensions of identity. It very much subordinates group identity to the moral framework of a universalist procedure that can subtend diverse forms of self-understanding: in this sense it mounts a critique of identity politics and discloses certain limits or problems in recent attempts to promote pluralist accommodation of disparate cultural practices and self-understandings. But in doing so, I will argue, it in no way fails to conceptualize an ethos that meets the demands of a pluralistic democracy. Indeed, its ability to mediate among the individual, intersubjective, and collective levels of practice constitute, I will suggest, one of the strongest claims of this tradition upon our attention.

The second achievement of Habermasian proceduralism that I isolate lies in its manner of addressing a core problem that has emerged within those pockets of theory, analyzed in previous chapters, in which ethos emerges as conceptually significant, but remains oppositional or mystified insofar as it is invoked as that which exceeds, escapes, or resists either rational argument or abstract universalism. Proceduralism departs dramatically from this theoretical predisposition by suggesting that argument informed by universalistic principles might itself become an ethos. In doing so, it pushes beyond not only the impasses of identity paradigms (in either their affirmative or deconstructive guise), but also certain entrenched excesses of the critique of enlightenment. The account that I will offer will refuse the prevalent tendency to offer ethos—whether understood as individual style or group culture—as the corrective to reason.

I.

Lionel Trilling's *Sincerity and Authenticity* (1971; originally delivered as the Charles Eliot Norton lectures in 1970) undertakes a modest genealogy of two key concepts in the understanding of modern social and moral life. To the extent that the book can be said to have an organizing argument or claim, it is that over the course of the modern era authenticity as a concept came to triumph over sincerity, whose appearance in the language and as a discernible moral value Trilling first dates to the sixteenth century, and finds preeminently at play in *Hamlet*. While "sincerity," by Trilling's account, is most broadly linked to the emergence of that which we designate as society and the public—the term testifies above all to the importance of one's self-presentation in public—it comes to carry particular force as that which cannot be achieved: it is construed either as inherently artificial, because the mere product of societal demand, or impossible, because denied by the forces of convention.

In the face of sincerity's ineluctable interpenetration by the social, an alternative ideal emerges, which in Trilling's book goes by the name of "authenticity." From Rousseau's natural man, free of the constraints of society, to Rameau's Nephew, to Hegel's insistence on the superiority of the Spirit in Self-Estrangement, to the transgressive personalities associated with Wilde and Nietzsche, authenticity refuses to accept the social as a final limit on human development and self-expression. Allying itself with the aesthetic—and in particular with irony and the sublime—authenticity seeks a way beyond both social and moral convention. Indeed, the initial critique of what Trilling at one point calls "the principle of insincerity upon which society is based" fuels an impulse to transcend the very categories that structure the critique, to get beyond virtue and vice, good and evil, sincerity and insincerity.[1] A rejection of the customary

---

[1] Lionel Trilling, *Sincerity and Authenticity* (Cambridge Mass.: Harvard University Press, 1971), 31. Further page number references will be cited parenthetically in the text.

and conventional, authenticity is at heart an oppositional concept, built up out of negations. Or, as Trilling puts it, authenticity is "implicitly a polemical concept, fulfilling its nature by dealing aggressively with received and habitual opinion, aesthetic opinion in the first instance, social and political opinion in the next. One topic of its polemic, which has reference to both aesthetic and social opinion, is the error of the view that beauty is the highest quality to which art may aspire" (93).

Despite Trilling's legible sympathies with authenticity's conceptual force and scope, and with those works and thinkers that are seen to transcend the limitations imposed by the moral category of sincerity, his study can hardly be said to trace a simple triumphal story. *Sincerity and Authenticity* is more subtle than that, in both its analytic and its evaluative dimensions. Trilling registers ambiguities and exhibits ambivalence with respect to both concepts, and the book in fact concludes with a particularly strong warning against the glamorization of madness and schizophrenia as authenticity (he attributes this view above all to R. D. Laing). At moments such as this, Trilling is keen to point out the kinds of evaluative missteps that can occur if one blindly celebrates the idea of authenticity as a refusal of social inscription tout court.

A further complexity is introduced with Trilling's identification of certain achievements of intellectual and political life that accompanied the rise of society and its concomitant principle of sincerity. In recognizing these achievements, Trilling sets aside the negative aspects of demand and constraint that figure so prominently in his initial discussion. And while it must be admitted that Trilling's strongest forms of attention do not settle on these aspects of sincerity, his brief discussion of them does suggest what might get diminished or laid aside in any emphatic rejection of sincerity in favor of authenticity. In this context, Trilling's insistence on the relation between the rise of society and the rise of opinion and critique is of crucial importance:

> A salient trait of society, I have suggested, and what differentiates it from the realm or the kingdom and even from the commonwealth, is that it is available to critical examination by individual persons, especially by those who make it their business to scrutinize the polity, the class of men we now call intellectuals. The purpose of their examination is not understanding alone but understanding as it may lead to action: the idea of society includes the assumption that a given society can be changed if the judgment passed upon it is adverse. In the framing of such judgements the ideal of sincerity is of substantial importance. It is adduced as a criterion in three considerations: 1) Of the sincerity of the person making the judgment. This must be beyond question and fully manifest. 2) Of the degree of correspondence between the principles avowed

by a society and its actual content. 3) Of the extent to which a society fosters, or corrupts, the sincerity of its citizens. (26–27)

In its recognition of principles of social transformation, moral integrity, and civic virtue, Trilling's sincerity principle would appear to cover significant terrain, to importantly undergird what we might broadly designate as "critique." Authenticity as a form of experience not encompassed by the social helps to displace the constraints imposed by conventional life. The tradition of sincerity, by contrast, interrogates society on its own terms, with a view toward possible reformist action, and it is conceptually linked to a notion of integrity through critical reflection at both the individual and societal levels. This is why the charge of something like *insincerity* remains so important: it allows one to charge a political system or its rulers with forms of hypocrisy, bad faith, or bald ideological maneuvering. It keeps alive the notion of accountability to social forms and practices that, from the authenticity perspective, may be seen as merely constraining, but from the sincerity perspective have been granted legitimacy through consent, accreted custom, and/or reflective endorsement.

Trilling here participates in the recognition of what Habermas has identified as the emergence of the public sphere in Enlightenment Europe, a historical condition in which critique, argument, and debate inform developing political practices and institutions.[2] For Habermas, the development of a distinctive culture of public debate in civil society, originally in the sphere of letters but later transferred to politics, provides the conditions for new forms of communicative practice in which the force of any given argument is given precedence over the status of the speaker. Those thinkers—such as Kant, Mill, Tocqueville—who theorized and also helped to consolidate the emerging public sphere developed a considered defense of the legitimating force of public opinion and the rule of law, the successor to now delegitimated forms of absolute sovereignty. Importantly, Habermas traces the way in which an earlier denigrated notion of opinion was replaced with a more ennobling conception of public opinion as a critical form of deliberative reasoning. To be sure, Habermas notes that this achievement later devolves into forms of ideology, conformity, mass opinion, and special interest politics—but the truly lasting contribution of his project lies in its attempt to salvage the tradition of vital critical debate within the public sphere, to give it its due and to foster its survival and further growth in the face of the many forces working against its full realization. Trilling's emphases fall elsewhere,

[2] Jürgen Habermas, *The Structural Transformation of the Public Sphere: An Inquiry into a Category of Bourgeois Society*, trans. Thomas Burger and Fred Lawrence (Cambridge, Mass.: MIT Press, 1989).

but he includes, as we have seen, a crucial recognition of what Habermas more fully defends and elaborates.[3]

In Trilling's account of individual works, moreover, authenticity's polemical relation to sincerity-as-constraint often appears alongside, or even seems to collaborate with, sincerity's own internal forms of critique. Indeed, those works of art that most facilitate Trilling's exposition of sincerity and authenticity—and therefore are held to reflect a heightened form of aesthetic insight into this defining conceptual duo—manifest a dialectic between the movement of social and political critique (underwritten by the informing ideal of sincerity) and a transgressive authenticity (which seeks to go beyond sincerity and insincerity). This is true preeminently for *Rameau's Nephew* and Conrad's *Heart of Darkness*; it is true also for Hegel's *Phenomenology of Spirit*, with its opposition between the honest soul and the higher, disintegrated consciousness. Trilling in fact relies on Hegel's opposition in his own reading of Conrad, where Marlow stands as the honest soul, Kurtz as the more authentic, disintegrated consciousness. Through these contrasting characters, *Heart of Darkness* comprehends both a critique of European political and social life as profoundly compromised in its avowed principles, and an exploration of a regression to savagery that illuminates "the irreducible truth of man, the innermost core of his nature, his heart of darkness" (109). The two movements of critique and transgression are profoundly intertwined: "It is of the essence of his fate that Kurtz is implicated in one of the most brazen political insincerities ever perpetrated" (107). The reference here is to the Belgian possession of the Congo in 1885, as an outright imperial coercion justified through the ideological ruse of the civilizing mission. Interestingly, this passage on Conrad constitutes one of the few moments in Trilling's text where the word "insincerity" appears, and it underscores the critical force it carries, a force that authenticity trades on. The richest relation between sincerity and authenticity is shown to be a dialectical one, with authenticity overcoming but also being generated out of the opposing terms of sincerity and insincerity. This emphasis on the dual stance of critique and transgressive displacement thus necessarily preserves the importance of the sincerity topos: it is not a simple rejection or eclipsing or replacement.

If we recognize this informing dialectic, and then also recall Trilling's caveat against simple celebrations of asocial authenticity (in his critique of Laing), what emerges is a subtle range of ambiguities attending both the logic of sincerity and the logic of authenticity. Sincerity is linked to

---

[3] It should also be noted that Trilling follows out an aesthetic trajectory whereas Habermas is interested in the aesthetic only to the extent that literary critical practices were themselves a kind of template for the political public sphere.

the positive values of critique, transparency, and civic virtue yet seems inescapably tied to the negative values of social conformity and disciplinarity. Authenticity looks beneath or beyond the surface of convention to access meaningful funds of human experience—nature, the unconscious, creative transgressive possibilities—yet from another perspective risks glamorizing forms of negative freedom that are ultimately impotent to answer to "the most brazen political insincerities," not to mention dangerously allied with painful and crippling forms of asociality.

I revisit Trilling's study because his historical and thematic treatment of a certain denigration of sincerity illuminates the more recent denigration of proceduralism within the fields of literary and cultural studies. For it is arguably the case that the one intellectual site where the tradition of sincerity still significantly endures precisely is within theories of proceduralism in political theory, particularly those of Habermas and Rawls. Whether construed as one of the four "validity claims" of communicative action (Habermas)—in this case it goes by the name of "truthfulness"—or simply presupposed as a necessary condition of the public use of reason (Rawls), sincerity is a central value of proceduralism. In full accord with Trilling's schema, moreover, theories of proceduralism also make appeal to the importance of the public sphere, the value of critique as a transformative social force, and the desirability of fostering a democratic culture of debate.

This is not to say that proceduralism does not itself register the consequences of the embattled position of sincerity within modern thought. Indeed, one of the reasons to consider the case of proceduralism is because it so interestingly raises the question of sincerity's fate within modernity and postmodernity. In Trilling's study, sincerity functions as an understanding of selfhood that is linked to a cluster of moral, social, and political values. Authenticity then intervenes to contest sincerity's ability to capture the truth of human existence: in doing so it displaces the normative understanding of stable selfhood and transparent self-presentation that sincerity seems to presuppose. But what gets most consequentially left aside in this challenge are the transpersonal dimensions of the sincerity paradigm, those forms of transparency and moral integrity that undergird critique and interarticulate with larger social and political practices and institutions. At this level, it becomes harder to simply reduce the sincerity paradigm to a mistake founded upon an illusory and outmoded form of agency or identity, since sincerity here operates more as a form of critical integrity rather than an absolute achievement of selfhood.

Sincerity in its transpersonal dimensions becomes not only pronounced, but explicitly thematized, in versions of contemporary proceduralism. This is most dramatically the case in Habermas, who actually recasts sincerity as the transcendental criterion of truthfulness. For Rawls, on the other hand, the term "sincerity" is retained and continues to function in the guise of an assumed virtue. Sincerity in Rawls is nonetheless explicitly not a feature of any metaphysical understanding of selfhood but rather the basic political virtue required for the use of public reason, which itself underwrites the possibility for a stable and just pluralistic society. If citizens do not undertake to present their views sincerely, and if those in power do not sincerely believe in the reasons they themselves offer for their actions, then the entire project of political liberalism founders.[4] Here, therefore, sincerity is an integral feature of the constitutive practice of a particular political form and, while not intended to function in a metaphysical way, still plays into older traditions of the sincerity paradigm.[5]

Habermas's transcendental approach is more radical in its abandonment of the characterological residue of the term "sincerity." In Habermas's conception of communicative action—which serves as the foundation for his discourse ethics as well as his democratic proceduralism—speech is immanently oriented toward reaching understanding, and as such, implicitly makes a series of validity claims.

> In the attitude oriented toward reaching understanding, the speaker raises with every intelligible utterance the claim that the utterance in question is true (or that the existential presuppositions of the propositional content hold true), that the speech act is right in terms of a given normative context (or that the normative context that it satisfies is itself legitimate), and that the speaker's manifest intentions are meant in the way they are expressed.[6]

In this recasting of sincerity as a communicative presupposition, Habermas moves away from the idea of sincerity as anything approaching a substantive virtue, or even an attribute of persons.[7]

---

[4] "Our exercise of political power is proper only when we sincerely believe that the reasons we offer for our political actions—were we to state them as government officials—are sufficient, and we also reasonably think that other citizens might also reasonably accept those reasons." John Rawls, "The Idea of Public Reason Revisited," *University of Chicago Law Review* 64 (Summer): 771. Also see John Rawls, *Political Liberalism* (New York: Columbia University Press, 1993, 1996), 241–42.

[5] In his critique of Rawls, Habermas claims that Rawls does not actually succeed in bracketing out certain philosophical considerations in the way that he hopes. See Jürgen Habermas, "'Reasonable' versus 'True,' or the Morality of Worldviews," trans. Ciaran Cronin, in *The Inclusion of the Other*, ed. Ciaran Cronin and Pablo de Greiff (Cambridge, Mass.: MIT Press, 1998), 75–101.

[6] Jürgen Habermas, *Moral Consciousness and Communicative Action*, trans. Christian Lenhardt and Shierry Weber Nicholsen (Cambridge, Mass.: MIT Press, 1990), 137.

[7] Indeed, Habermas's critique of Rawls focuses at a key point on the confusion introduced by the use of the term "reasonable," which tends to indicate "a reflective attitude of enlightened tolerance" rather than serving as a predicate for "the validity of moral judgments." By personalizing public reason in this way, Rawls fails to do the important work of philosophical justification. See Habermas, "'Reasonable' versus 'True,'" 60.

There are far-reaching ramifications of this depersonalizing approach to sincerity, ramifications that extend into the theory of proceduralism as well as into Habermas's treatment of identity and ethos at both the individual and collective levels. As I hope to show, Habermas's commitment to the transpersonal dimensions of the sincerity paradigm does not translate into an abandonment of practical philosophy's traditional interest in the relation between practice and theory. To put this another way: if Habermas abandons the idea of sincerity as a substantive virtue, this does not mean that he does not himself conceive of proceduralism as a cultivated practice. While this aspect of his thought is not systematically elaborated in his writings, I hope to continue the analysis of the previous essay by suggesting ways in which Habermasian proceduralism recaptures the sincerity paradigm even as it radically recasts it, just as his discourse ethics redeems the Kantian tradition while reframing it in intersubjective and collective terms.

The rejection of proceduralism by poststructuralism has made it impossible to recognize the most interesting elements of the former, elements that in fact might speak productively to some of the more intractable theoretical issues within poststructuralism's treatment of ethical and political issues. This rejection stems in part from an anachronistic association of proceduralism with the older sincerity paradigms. And this makes a certain amount of sense: if proceduralism is a successor to the earlier paradigms of sincerity, then it should not come as a particular surprise to note the vehemence with which it has been rejected by those thinkers who might themselves be seen as descendants of the modernist champions of authenticity. If Wilde and Nietzsche stand for Trilling as the clearest representatives of authenticity's triumph, then their poststructuralist successors might be expected to react strongly when faced with any representatives of sincerity's enduring relevance, however transformed, however ambivalent. It is certainly the case that proceduralism has functioned largely as a bête noire in poststructuralist debate. A pronounced instance of its status is evident in *Contingency, Hegemony, Universality: Contemporary Dialogues on the Left* (2000), which stages a debate between Ernesto Laclau, Slavoj Žižek, and Judith Butler. Although the authors assert sharp differences among themselves in terms of theoretical assumptions and claims, one thing they find to collectively define themselves against is proceduralism, viewed as indissolubly linked to reason and false universalism in its presumption that "the political field is constituted by rational actors."[8]

[8] The full passage is as follows:

Along the way, we each consider different ideological deployments of universality and caution against both substantial and procedural approaches to the question. We thus differentiate ourselves (already internally differentiated) from the Habermasian effort to discover or conjure a

If we view poststructuralism's attitude toward proceduralism in light of Trilling's schema, we can discern more fully how the authenticity topos continues to inform theoretical practice. Certainly poststructuralism is "beyond" sincerity in the sense that it would reject any concept that appears to rely on a logic of discernible truth and stable moral selfhood underwriting transparency of speech. But does it make sense to associate poststructuralism with authenticity, which would appear to be an equally mystified notion? I would argue that it does make sense to do so, and that authenticity functions throughout many poststructuralist writings as an unacknowledged informing ideal. An appeal to authenticity not only underlies the insistent poststructuralist refusal of various illusions and constraints—of metaphysics, of normativity, and of conventionality—it also fuels a whole range of appeals to valorized forms of practice and identity, however unstable or complex—however parodic, performative, or hybrid—they might imagine themselves to be.[9] Moreover, and perhaps most tellingly, the same dialectical pattern at play in the works that capture Trilling's imagination is at play in many versions of poststructuralist critique, where there is both a registering of social or structural constraint (represented variously as language, power, or the law) and a concomitant appeal to acknowledging an authentic substratum (materiality, the body and its pleasures, undecidability, the unconscious). In key instances, in fact, special attention is given to the manner in which one might actively recognize or even artfully cultivate an experience of such conditions of existence, as for example in the case of performative enactment (Butler), or the politics of the gesture (Agamben).

II.

For a cluster of reasons, proceduralism has been viewed as lacking what we might call, adapting Trilling, an authenticating ethos. First, as an extension of the sincerity paradigm, proceduralism is seen to enforce a normative selfhood, one constituted through conventional rules of self-presentation and action and therefore coterminous with the social. This

---

pre-established universality as the presupposition of the speech act, a universality which is said to pertain to a rational feature of "man", and a substantive conception of universality which equates it with a knowable and predictable determination, and a procedural form which presumes that the political field is constituted by rational actors." (Judith Butler, Ernesto Laclau, and Slavoj Žižek, *Contingency, Hegemony, Universality: Contemporary Dialogues on the Left* [London and New York: Verso, 2000], 3)

[9] For a discussion of the cryptic ideal of authenticity underlying many putatively constructionist accounts of identity, see James Buzard, "On Auto-Ethnographic Authority," *Yale Journal of Criticism* 16:1 (2003): 61–91.

is why, even when appeal is made to an ethos of sincerity—as that which underpins and generates a more broadly conceived form of civic virtue—proceduralism can be viewed as concerned with what we might call a narrowly social form of virtue. I will, however, be suggesting that in its Habermasian version, proceduralism itself generates a dialectic between sincerity and authenticity. This dialectic does not, it should be stressed, take the shape that we saw in Trilling's privileged works of modernity. The polemical relation to received opinion that Trilling assigns to authenticity, which in his account always insists on that which exceeds the social (nature, fate, the unconscious), operates in proceduralism as the progressive expansion of horizons and enlargement of perspective that defines universalist argument. The "excess" here is a spirit of critique that cannot rest within any embedded practice, nor can it ever be simply conventionalized (though procedure ideally acts as a facilitating spring). Because it so fully understands itself as an ongoing enactment, I will characterize this procedural dynamic as an ethos. In doing so I want to suggest that proceduralism recasts the sincerity paradigm in ways that render the critique of proceduralism by means of the authenticity perspective misguided.

Before laying out my own argument more specifically, I must make one terminological clarification. "Ethos" in the following discussion will migrate between two different meanings: on the one hand, the word will denote individual manner, attitude, or stance, and, on the other hand, it will indicate forms of collective ethical life (Hegelian *Sittlichkeit*, cultural identity). The surrounding context should make the meaning clear in any particular instance, but an awareness of the divergent uses is crucial to bear in mind. One key difference between the two meanings is that the former is actively cultivated by the reflecting individual, while the latter is a form of embeddedness that can become self-aware, but that is fundamentally prereflective and given. One key context for the discussion is the fact that both forms of ethos have been invoked as a counterposing force to the universalist project. At first glance, Habermas may appear allergic to most of the more familiar versions of ethos as manner and suspicious of those forms of theory (communitarian, pragmatist, and multiculturalist) that invoke *Sittlichkeit* as a court of last appeal. And yet I hope to establish that a closer look at his proceduralism allows us to refute the notion that individual and collective ethos cannot survive in the rarefied air of rational universalism. In the end, I will suggest, Habermas fundamentally reconceives, and sets into dynamic interrelation, both forms of ethos.

In the preceding essay, I explored a late stage in the so-called debate between Foucault and Habermas. There, I examined an unnecessarily stark opposition between ethos as manner, on the one hand, and reason as formal argument, on the other. In the later work of Foucault, which holds a privileged place among scholars in literary and cultural studies, ethos stands as an exemplar of negative critique, the charismatic reply to those forms of reason associated with Habermasian critical theory. Viewed from a somewhat longer perspective, this admiration for Foucauldian ethos might be read as an extension or refinement of the poststructuralist critique of reason, a kind of rapprochement between that critique and what we might call the "postpoststructuralist turn to subjectivity." And if the reception of the work of later Foucault is paradigmatic of this move, an appeal to ethos as manner is also manifest elsewhere in the theoretical field, as for example in cosmopolitanism's "answer" to universalism. But there is an important difference to be noted. In the case of Foucault and his admirers, the appeal to ethos functions to trump, eclipse, or subordinate the claims or value of rational or impersonal argument. In the case of cosmopolitanism, the approach is more synthetic. Cosmopolitanism presents itself as a deliberately mannered transformation of universalism; refined by tact, phronesis, sensibility, cosmopolitanism infuses universalism with an authenticating ethos. Both approaches, however, artfully avoid any overly explicit avowal of norms, which they associate negatively with rationalism and universalism. By this logic, to render a norm explicit is also always to impose a norm; it also reveals a dangerously naive commitment to rational justification. By contrast, by remaining on the side of the negative, the restless, or the tacit, valorizations of ethos imagine that they can avoid the dangers of reinstating a locatable norm. They thereby find some resonance with, are in part a response to, the poststructuralist critique of reason.

Proceduralism's adaptation of the sincerity paradigm provocatively reconfigures the relation between reason and ethos, and it does so by refusing the assumptions that fuel the reductive opposition of the terms. In the previous essay, I pointed to those aspects of Habermas's thinking that displayed an attentiveness to ethos as a critical tool, as a philosophical stance, and as an integral element of democratic culture. While acknowledging that Habermas is ambivalent toward ethos understood as constitutive ethical life—this carries for him a certain stigma of blinkered embeddedness—I argued that it is distorting to interpret him as dedicated uniformly or exclusively to postures of abstract, universal rationality that transcend all situated, partial, or embedded forms of life. In this essay, I want to advance the reframing of Habermas by considering his specific defense of proceduralism against theorists in the field of political theory who imagine that they, and not Habermas, are appropriately acknowledging the primacy of an authenticating ethos in either its attitudinal or collective cultural form. In doing so, I hope to establish two crucial claims. First, proceduralism as Habermas conceives it requires a specific ethos: the cultivated habit of refusing the comfort of a claimed collective identity (cultural, national, sexual, and so forth). Second—and here I return to a point I introduced earlier—proceduralism offers one way of refusing the false option between reason and ethos precisely insofar as it affirms the possibility of argument as ethos. One consequence of this alternative, I shall argue, is an understanding of practice that more fully instantiates those democratic and cosmopolitical principles of recognition and respect that many theorists believe can rightfully be claimed only by those who champion ethos (again, whether conceived as authenticating identity or charismatic critique) over reason.

Because proceduralism can invite different characterizations with respect to the concepts of reason and ethos, it poses a particular challenge to any approach that focuses on them. On the one hand, as I suggested earlier, proceduralism can seem to make appeal to ethos or virtue, both through its emphasis on the ways in which sincerity and truthfulness are presupposed in communicative interaction, and through its at least implicit reliance on forms of civic virtue in its elaboration of democratic procedure. On the other hand, in sharp contrast to much of the work in cultural criticism on the determinants of particular subject-positions, proceduralism emphasizes the productive effects of its own transsubjective impartiality, presenting itself as a way to move beyond specific interests and values and achieve the common good. In this sense it is anti-ethos, where ethos is conceived as being always already too embedded or partial. It can also appear antisubjective, one might say, as it shifts from the perspective of the individual subject and aims to locate virtue and agency in objective institutions, practices, and procedures. As I indicated when distinguishing Habermas's adaptation of the sincerity concept from Rawls's, Habermas has already imported this depersonalizing move into the description of communicative action. But institutional procedure is all about moving away from the personal, as is evident even in Rawls. As the first sentence of *A Theory of Justice* famously puts it, "Justice is the first virtue of social institutions, as truth is of systems of thought."[10] Rawls later in the book goes on to extend his discussion to the realm of moral goodness in persons, but this only lights up further the initial displacement of virtue onto institutions.

Because of this deliberate impersonality, proceduralism has been seen as lacking a spirit of authenticity in two regards. First, like the domain of the social in Trilling's study, it is seen to constrain public expression and force conformity. This aspect of proceduralism, along with its perceived misguided faith in rationality, is what provokes the poststructuralist

[10] John Rawls, *A Theory of Justice* (Cambridge, Mass.: Harvard University Press, 1971), 3.

critique. Second, from the perspective of communitarian-style political theorists, proceduralism is seen as overly thin, arid, and abstract, unable to register the interpenetration of the right and the good, of reason and ethos. It is further asserted that people *need* affective attachments and meaningful affiliations, that attachment to impersonal procedures and universal principles cannot provide the glue that holds communities of various scales together. It is important to register that these are separable critiques: on the one hand, it is asserted that there is no such thing as pure procedure, that any conception of proceduralism necessarily is saturated with specific values—hence the idea of proceduralism simply does not capture the reality of political culture—and, on the other hand, it is asserted that proceduralism is not a desirable ideal, insofar as it endorses detachment from those affiliations that constitute the meaningfulness of who we are and what we want. Proceduralism is thus deficient as both fact and value.

Historically, the idea that participants in modern democratic life might fundamentally aspire to the forming of an attachment to abstract or universal principles has been a key issue in the debate over the possibilities for a nationalism defined in civic rather than ethnic terms (stretching back at least as far as J. S. Mill), and it has also informed discussions about cosmopolitan attachment (can one experience solidarity as a world citizen?) and about proceduralism of the type that Habermas espouses (not only through his concept of "constitutional patriotism," but also through the idea of commitment to postnational institutions like the European Union and to international law). Habermas has to some degree accepted the terms of the communitarian critique, acknowledging that crucial forms of thick cultural affiliation must provide the basis for higher-order commitment to abstract principle and democratic procedure. He gathers this enabling condition under the rubric of cultural identity, which is essentially identified as an authenticating ethical life: cultural identity constitutes a holistic, bounded, shared form of life that helps to solidify one's self-understanding and autonomy.[11] In vivid contrast to the dangers of ethnic nationalism (bad identity), cultural identity in Habermas's theory remains linked to the crucial processes of socialization that undergird the possibilities for higher moral life. In this way, Habermas combines a politics of recognition with a politics of rights and democratic procedure.

In a departure from this rapprochement with the communitarian view, whereby proceduralism needs to be supplemented by ethos understood as *Sittlichkeit*, I am interested in pressing harder on the possibility of

---

[11] See Jürgen Habermas, "Struggles for Recognition in the Democratic Constitutional State," in *The Inclusion of the Other*, esp. 220–26.

understanding proceduralism as itself an ethos and therefore not simply dependent upon ethical life as a prior enabling condition. Such an understanding, moreover, would comprehend both individual stance and collective practice. I am above all interested in drawing out the ways in which Habermas may be seen as pointing toward this alternative approach himself, even despite his seeming capitulation to the importance of authenticating ethical life.

Some recent interpretive approaches have sought, at least in part, to address these issues. Richard Bernstein, for example, has argued forcefully that Habermas presupposes a democratic ethos that he does not adequately or consistently acknowledge. On this account, Habermas is faulted for failing to elaborate and own the ethos that must define any proceduralist conception of democracy, for lacking a properly dialectical conception of the relation between substance and procedure, the right and the good. Bernstein goes so far as to charge Habermas with "self-misunderstanding." That is, Habermas wrongly imagines he is elaborating a discourse theory that does not make any substantial-ethical presuppositions:

> There is no adequate discourse theory of democratic procedure that avoids presupposing a democratic ethos—an ethos that conditions and affects how discussion, debate, and argumentation are practiced. . . . There cannot be any discourse theory that does the work that Habermas claims for it unless it presupposes the existence of determinate ethical dispositions and virtues. Democratic debate, ideally, requires a *willingness* to listen and *evaluate* the opinions of one's opponents, *respecting* the views of minorities, advancing arguments *in good faith* to support one's convictions, and having the *courage* to change one's mind when confronted with new evidence or better arguments. There is an ethos involved in the practice of democratic debate. If such an ethos is violated or disregarded, then debate can become hollow and meaningless. We might even say that democratic polity requires the transformation and appropriation of classic virtues: practical wisdom, justice, courage, and moderation. Democratic versions of these virtues are required for democratic debate.[12]

Bernstein admits that sometimes Habermas comes close to admitting this point; more frequently, however, he is held to deny it, to insist that a discourse-theoretical understanding of democracy is superior to its alternatives precisely because it does not make any presuppositions about the democratic virtues of citizens. This strand in Habermas comes out most sharply when he is criticizing what he calls the "communitarian" and

---

[12] Richard Bernstein, "The Retrieval of the Democratic Ethos," in Michel Rosenfeld and Andrew Arato, eds., *Habermas on Law and Democracy* (Berkeley: University of California Press, 1998), 291.

"republican" defenders of democracy, such as Frank Michelman. In defining his proceduralism against civic republicanism, Habermas insists that "discourse theory employs a structuralist argument that relieves citizens of the Rousseauian expectation of virtue—the orientation to the common good only needs to be exacted in small increments insofar as practical reason withdraws from the hearts and heads of collective or individual actors into the procedures and forms of communication of political opinion and will formation."[13]

There is a crucial tension in Habermas's reply to the type of critique that Bernstein makes. On the one hand, Habermas readily and almost impatiently admits that his theory presupposes the existence of an "open political culture" and therefore does not deny that proceduralism itself may lay claim to a certain ethos.[14] On the other hand, Habermas continually resists the assumption, at the heart of communitarianism and of Bernstein-style critiques, that we can raise and answer moral questions only within the horizon of our own ethically articulated, and thus particular, world view and self-interpretation. Habermas insists that we can expand our interpretive horizon by taking the moral point of view, indeed so radically that, to use Gadamer's terms, our horizon "fuses" with the horizons of all other persons. In this case it is not a matter of what is good for us as belonging to a collectivity distinguished by its own ethos but rather a matter of what is right for all. Against approaches to pluralism that insist that we cannot escape our particular horizons, or that at best we can hope for an overlapping consensus (Rawls), Habermas espouses the progressive expansion of horizons. This continual aspiration to the moral point of view, and the dedication to those forms of argument and procedure that will most conduce to promote such expansion, is, it seems to me, itself an ethos, as Habermas admits when he acknowledges the possibility of a postconventional *Sittlichkeit*. But it cannot be properly viewed as the same "democratic ethos" to which Bernstein refers, and it is not captured by the explicit naming of adapted classical virtues that Bernstein engages in.

First, let me establish in what way I think that Habermas's conception of the progressive expansion of horizons seems to invoke or rely upon something that we can designate as ethos. In his critique of civic republicanism, as we saw, Habermas shifts the perspective to that of political institutions and collective practice, explicitly refusing the notion that individuals carry the burden of cultivating the virtue required for a well-ordered polis. But in his assumption that individuals can be motivated

---

[13] Jürgen Habermas, "Reply to Symposium Participants, Benjamin N. Cardozo School of Law," in *Habermas on Law and Democracy*, 385.

[14] Ibid., 386.

to progressively expand their horizon—that is, in his assumption that individuals can and should assign to themselves the task of rigorous impartiality in acting in the name of the right—Habermas necessarily renders the normative aspirational, and as such, collapses the moral into the ethical, or, I am suggesting, arguably assigns it an ethos. Moreover, while the democratic and proceduralist elements of his argument seek to relieve the burden of constant moral wakefulness, the ethos of impartiality and self-transcendence seems nothing if not a stringent ascetic imperative, requiring an ongoing self-assessment and striving that shares affinities with the Aristotelian understanding of virtue, which by a certain reading is far more exacting and ambitious than the tolerant expectation, in the Kantian tradition, that wayward inclinations simply will continue to oppose duty.[15] Habermas would, on this reading, actually oscillate back and forth between this compartmentalizing Kantian tolerance—displacing civic duty onto law and procedure with the expectation that the petty passions will rule in the personal life and the marketplace—and an Aristotelian exactingness—a demand for stringent self-reflexivity and post-conventionality.

Therefore, while Habermas's reply to Bernstein seems to dispatch with the ethos issue by immediately admitting that his theory presupposes a culture of open political debate, I want to suggest that the real intimation of ethos comes with Habermas's own discussions of the stance that one takes toward the proceduralist-universalist project: the aspiration to impartiality, the constant attempt to break free of the horizon(s) of one's ethical life, and the dedication to the right over the good. This will always necessarily exist in a tension with any affirmation of substantive ethos, the kind of affirmation that Bernstein elaborates with such rhetorical ease.

Bernstein interestingly remarks that there is a seeming paradox in Habermas's attempt to rigorously evacuate proceduralism of any substantive ethical content, especially given his ongoing insistence that other theories own up to their own normative assumptions. By contrast, I am

---

[15] For a reading of Aristotle along these lines, see Martha C. Nussbaum, "Virtue Ethics: A Misleading Category?" *Journal of Ethics* 3 (1999): 163–201.

> The Aristotelian view, so understood, gives reason an extremely ambitious role—far more ambitious, in some salient respects, than its role in Kant's moral philosophy. For reason not only sets ultimate ends and determines practical choices, it also is responsible for forming the motivational and passional character. If we do the right thing with reluctance, or perform our duty with little sympathy, Kant will not think the less of us, so long as we were using every means in our power to do the right. For Kant thinks that some things just can't be helped, and he is inclined to be merciful to the deficiencies of the passional personality. Aristotle, however, is less tolerant: he asks us to bring every motive, every wish, every passion into line with reason's commitments to ends. (187)

going to suggest that this is a moment of sublime rigor in the Habermasian position. Habermas's austere refusal of virtue talk, coupled with his critique of civic republicanism and his near-trivialization of Bernstein's objection, might be viewed as a kind of stoicism: a rigorous ethos that aims to avoid any sense that we should rest comfortably within our visible horizons. To name and enumerate democratic virtues, to hold them up as the ideal ethos of democratic culture, is perhaps not so much a problem because it implies that procedures thereby would appear to depend upon the virtues of citizens—this is Habermas's stated objection—but because it collapses the right into the good, releasing the pressure of the regulative ideal of the right, or the farther horizon of the universal. The rigorous impersonality of Habermas's rhetoric of the right, the moral, or the universal might therefore be viewed not as some deluded and dangerous investment in universal reason, or a failure to understand the embedded nature of our practices, but rather as a requirement that we not easily own as our ethical life, our achieved virtue, the aim to disembed. It is, paradoxically then, a kind of anti-ethos ethos. It functions effectively to disallow a kind of assured sense, most commonly associated with the more thoroughgoing pragmatism that Bernstein wishes Habermas would avow, that we are left only with our defining practices: that they are, in some deep sense, self-legitimating.

This understanding of an aspiration to universality spans Habermas's understanding of individual and collective practice. In this regard, it begins to join the individual conception of ethos with a collective culture that, paradoxically, embeds the practice of disembedding. (This is of course just another way of describing postconventional *Sittlichkeit*.) It is not always easy to see this double aspect of Habermas's thinking, since his consistent dedication to the intersubjective turn makes his own implied ideals of individual ethos harder to excavate. On the collective level, however, there is much evidence of his views. Habermas has emphasized the ways in which citizens can form solidarities and affiliations based on a common struggle to install abstract principles and procedures at the heart of their national political institutions. Sharing a common history in which there were collective efforts to overcome the damning effects of ethnic nationalism—as is certainly the case in Germany—can have the effect of what we might call "thickifying the thin." In these instances, a shared dedication to principled democratic procedure itself promotes those forms of affective solidarity that Habermas elsewhere assigned exclusively to preexisting ethical life. "The political culture of a country crystallizes around its constitution. Each national culture develops a distinctive interpretation of those constitutional principles that are equally embodied in other republican constitutions—such as popular sovereignty and human rights—in light of its own national history.

A 'constitutional patriotism' based on these interpretations can take the place originally occupied by nationalism."[16] Just as the individual aspiration to impersonality is itself more an art of living than an evacuation of embodiedness or affect, so, too, the collective attempt to resist forms of patriotism that attempt to subordinate or sidestep the rigorous demands of law, principle, and right—at either the national or the international level—can themselves promote productive forms of patriotic and cosmopolitan affiliation. Such a possibility was made evident in the public protests against the invasion of Iraq, which for some took shape as an articulated demand for a respectful attitude toward the protocols of international adjudication as laid out in the U.N. Charter. It has also emerged in concerned activism over voter transparency in U.S. elections, where nonverifiable electronic voting seems to threaten democracy at its most basic level.

The presuppositions underlying Trilling's discussion of sincerity and authenticy endure in the form of a persistent skepticism that a cultivated attachment to procedures and principles, or an aspiration to impersonality, can be seen as an authentic ethos. It would appear from the genealogy provided us by Trilling, as well as by the logic of many discussions of proceduralism, that authenticity always has to alter or disrupt the explicit, articulate claims of universality in order to count as authenticity. Even though proceduralism's sincerity is less a virtue than a presupposition that claims of truthfulness inform communicative action, the enactment of proceduralism by individual actors still seems to emblematize the interpenetration of the social and the conventional that dogged and diminished the ideal of sincerity from the start. Insofar as it both imagines and enforces a kind of fully public self, it is seen to thwart authenticity.

Even theorists sympathetic to Habermas tend to recuperate him by insisting that there is a possibility for redeeming his theory by *incorporating*

---

[16] Jürgen Habermas, "The European Nation-State: On the Past and Future of Sovereignty and Citizenship," in *The Inclusion of the Other*, 118. Habermas produces an equally suggestive description of the possibilities for the formation of a European citizenry, a citizenry capable of identifying beyond the limits of national feeling. Against the skepticism expressed toward the possibility of a successfully integrated European Union, Habermas writes:

> one could point to the decisive historical experiences that undeniably unite the European peoples. For the catastrophes of two world wars have taught Europeans that they must abandon the mind-sets on which nationalistic, exclusionary mechanisms feed. Why should a sense of belonging together culturally and politically not grow out of these experiences—especially against the rich background of shared traditions which have long since achieved world-historical significance, as well as on the basis of the overlapping interests and dense networks of communication which have more recently developed in the decades of economic success of the European Community? (Jürgen Habermas, "On the Relation Between the Nation, the Rule of Law, and Democracy," in *The Inclusion of the Other*, 152)

an authenticating affect. Seyla Benhabib's feminist critique of Habermas stresses the importance of integrating feeling and sympathy into discourse ethics.[17] Max Pensky has argued that group affiliation should be viewed not as the result of prior authenticating cultures but rather as the result of shared melancholia in the face of modernity's disenchantments: we identify as groups precisely because we have had to demand rights and thereby disenchant any sense of ourselves as a holistic integrated culture. Moreover, the recognition that we have all shared this loss might become the basis for cosmopolitan solidarity across groups; thus a distinctive experiential affect—melancholia—authenticates the theory.[18] Lastly, Patchen Markell has sought to challenge the notion that affect can only be made safe for democracy through rigorously civic forms of nationalism by drawing out the ways in which Habermas recognizes—if he does not fully elaborate—the extent to which a strongly felt resistance to identity helps to thwart ideologies of national unity. Markell notes that Habermas in his political writings characterizes large-scale demonstrations of solidarity with the victims of hate crimes against Turkish immigrants in Germany as salutary acts of disidentification from the state: the demonstrators "refused the claim of the state to be a true or an adequate instantiation of the will of the German people."[19] For Markell the key moment here is the refusal of identification as a single homogeneous will.

I contend that one does not need to rescue Habermas by imagining that an authenticating affect must revise, interrupt, or thwart proceduralism. It is interesting to think, again, of demonstrations against the invasion of Iraq, where affect and solidarity are produced with regard not only to an alienation from a posited national will and identity (Markell's emphasis), but also, for many protesters, as indeed for many members of the polled citizenry, a *commitment to procedures*: only multilateral action, and only in compliance with international law. As with the example of overcoming ethnic nationalism, this example emphasizes that a commitment to proceduralism is always a historical experience. What frequently goes by the name of the thin—the procedural, the universal, the abstract—is not the evacuation of history, but an achievement within it, not a draining of affect, but a felt aspiration.

---

[17] Seyla Benhabib, *Critique, Norm, and Utopia: A Study of the Foundations of Critical Theory* (New York: Columbia University Press, 1986), 316–53, and *Situating the Self: Gender, Community and Postmodernism in Contemporary Ethics* (New York: Routledge, 1992), 148–77.

[18] Max Penksy, "Cosmopolitanism and the Solidarity Problem: Habermas on National and Cultural Identities," *Constellations* 7, no. 1 (2000): 64–79.

[19] Patchen Markell, "Making Affect Safe for Democracy? On 'Constitutional Patriotism,'" *Political Theory* 28, no. 1 (2000): 57.

The final aspect of proceduralism that I want to consider is the way in which argument functions as a key practice within it, as the preeminent form of deliberative democracy and as a key moment before some of the decisive moments of deliberative closure (e.g., vote taking, consensus, compromise). Argument actually becomes, in a certain way, the key collective ethos of proceduralism. But what does it mean to conceive of argument as ethos?

For Habermas, what crucially sets Rawls's proceduralism in a different direction than his is their divergent ways of reconciling an aspiration to Kantian universalization (aiming at what is good for all) with the contemporary fact of social and ideological pluralism. Rawls responds to pluralism by imposing a common perspective on all, an "original position" enforcing informational constraints that effectively neutralize difference (the famous "veil of ignorance"). In contrast, Habermas invests his hope in a discourse ethics that privileges an enlargement of perspective brought about precisely through argumentation. As he puts it, "Discourse ethics, by contrast [with Rawls], views the moral point of view as embodied in an intersubjective praxis of argumentation which enjoins those involved to an idealizing enlargement of their interpretive perspectives."[20] Asserted here is an integral link between the ongoing aspiration to transcend one's current horizon and the social practice of argumentation. Indeed, for Habermas, argument, which we might gloss as reflective communicative action, is both a privileged form of ethicopolitical practice and the very condition for the possibility of justifying proceduralism: "Because there are no 'ultimate' sources of evidence or 'definitive' kinds of arguments in practical questions, we must have recourse to the process of argumentation as our 'procedure' if we are to explain how it is possible for us to raise and vindicate validity claims that 'transcend' the present context."[21]

Linked to this is also Habermas's strong sense that argument keeps the democratic project fundamentally open and incomplete, a desideratum that he believes Rawls's theory precludes insofar as it emphasizes the act of constitution making as a founding moment.[22] In his own understanding of decision making within proceduralism, Habermas requires that participants in democratic decision-making processes be self-reflective, and this self-reflectiveness involves awareness of clashing value systems

---

[20] Jürgen Habermas, "Reconciliation Through the Public Use of Reason," in *The Inclusion of the Other*, 57.

[21] Habermas, "Reply to Symposium Participants," 408.

[22] "The act of founding the democratic constitution cannot be repeated under the institutional conditions of an already constituted just society, and the process of realizing the system of basic rights cannot be assured on an ongoing basis. It is not possible for citizens to experience this process as open and incomplete, as the shifting historical circumstances demand." Habermas, "Reconciliation Through the Public Use of Reason," 69.

and the possibility of persistent disagreements. What Habermas asks participants to understand as they are forced to come to decisions within these sublunary conditions, is that they regard such decisions as interim results of an ongoing discussion seeking the "one right answer" to a practical-political problem but interrupted by institutional pressures for a decision. The use of the regulative ideal of the "one right answer" has prompted sharp critiques based on an assumption that Habermas is introducing a form of authoritian reason. But the "one right answer" functions in precisely the way that the horizon of the universal or the pressure of aiming for the right over the good does: it simply enjoins participants to continue the argument, to respond with the rigorous refusal to imagine that one has actually come up with the one right answer. It is an ideal that allows the process of argument to prevail over any given perspective. In this conception, argument as ethos would always trump identity as ethos.

The question of how dialogue under conditions of pluralism might ideally be conceived has led to alternate theories that define themselves against Habermasian proceduralism, which is seen as ethnocentrically invested in rationality and consensus. It is important, in my view, to acknowledge how fundamental to these alternate views remains the attempt to define ethos against argument, which amounts to refusing the idea of argument as ethos. As in the case of the Foucault/Habermas "debate," and in certain articulations of the new cosmopolitanism, ethos in these alternate models is elevated above argument, most visibly as a critique of reason and abstract universalism, but also, I shall argue, as a model of difference that poses problems for democratic politics and particularly for the fate of debate within it. In the Rawlsian model of overlapping consensus (where people with fundamentally different conceptions of the good agree on political principles but for different reasons) and in models of accommodation that have been proffered in objection to what are seen as the deficiencies of the consensus models, there is an expectation of fundamental, nonnegotiable disagreement among parties who nonetheless have an investment in cohabiting within a pluralistic democratic state.

One of the more thoughtful critiques of Habermasian proceduralism along accommodationist lines is that of Thomas McCarthy, who argues that Habermas's emphases on rational acceptance and a cooperative search for truth intended to gain the assent of a universal audience are not themselves the proper informing ideals of a discourse proceduralism enacted under the "conditions of posttraditional pluralism and individualism."[23] McCarthy argues that Habermas wants to prevent any skepticism about

---

[23] Thomas McCarthy, "Legitimacy and Diversity: Dialectical Reflections on Analytic Distinctions," in Rosenfeld and Arato, eds., *Habermas on Law and Democracy*, 139. Further page number references will be cited parenthetically in the text.

the possibility of ethicopolitical consensus from undercutting the orientation to reasoned agreement on which he bases his conception of legitimacy. For McCarthy, by contrast, participants need to recognize the possibility of *reasoned disagreements* and then use this recognition to devise democratic procedures that will enable and enhance coexistence. McCarthy therefore suggests that Habermas's organizing presuppositions, which favor procedures meant to promote consensus and negotiated compromise, might be foreclosing the possibility of devising a different order of proceduralism that would aim to promote not agreement but rather mutual accommodation. He concludes, tantalizingly: "it would be an important and interesting task to explore the logic of the ethical-political dialogue that could produce such mutual accommodation and to elaborate its differences from the logics both of truth-oriented discourse and of strategic, self-interested bargaining" (151).

In his reply to McCarthy's critique, Habermas refuses the concept of mutual accommodation that McCarthy introduces. He entirely cedes the point that we must expect disagreement—an ideal of argument presupposes this—and that this awareness should form part of reflective participation in democratic debate. He then maps out three positions on dialogue under conditions of pluralism, rejecting the first two and endorsing the third. The first position holds that it is impossible to escape clashing horizons; when they encounter one another, the only possibility for overcoming their differences is the assimilation of one to the other. The second position, which is Rawls's, envisions an overlapping consensus (parties accept a consensus result for different reasons).[24] And the third position promotes the progressive expansion of horizons: beyond the limit of their respective self-interpretations and world views, the different parties refer to a presumptively shared moral point of view that, under the symmetrical conditions of discourse and mutual learning, requires an ever broader decentering of perspectives. What Habermas insists upon is the necessity that people accept regulating procedures elaborated with the goal of coexistence *for the same reasons*. As he concludes, "We can agree to the mutual toleration of forms of life and worldviews that represent existential challenges for each other only if we have a basis of shared beliefs for 'agreeing to disagree.' "[25]

In the case of McCarthy, whose position is closer to Rawls's, the elaboration of those virtues that would best express a goal of accommodation—

---

[24] Rawls's central example in *Political Liberalism* is a case where inhabitants of a liberal political state are drawn from three groups: subscribers to comprehensive liberalism of the type espoused by J. S. Mill; religious believers whose idea of toleration, while emanating from religious doctrine, supports their views of liberal democracy; and ad hoc pluralists without a discernible comprehensive doctrine of their own.

[25] Habermas, "Reply to Symposium Participants," 402.

tolerance, respect—are elevated above any principle of shared reasons. This creates a situation in which ethos, in the sense of an avowed form of ethical life, is somehow allowed to cushion the participants against argumentative challenges, a condition that Habermas is persistently concerned to disallow. In its most pronounced form, such an approach risks collapsing argument into identity: here the ineluctable fact of difference—whether radically conceived or more traditionally pluralist—becomes the overriding reason for reasoned disagreement. But of course the position that McCarthy advances need not be taken so far: read another way, there is a potential similarity between McCarthy's position and the new cosmopolitanism, insofar as both locate a virtue in refusing the insistence on explicit justification and rational agreement that we find in Habermas. The logic of accommodation implies a willingness not to argue out every last detail, but rather to exercise the tact that consists in recognizing that we may differ. Nonetheless, it is important to recognize that accommodation here operates as an attitude informing democratic practices that otherwise still need to be based on procedures for ensuring open debate and equitable forms of representation. These procedures can be refined and debated themselves, but never suspended completely. Ethos in this view does not replace or eclipse procedure, just as cosmopolitanism has the potential to refine universalism through tact and phronesis, without disavowing its fundamental universalistic principles.

By way of closing, I want to address objections that have been raised against the privileging of argument and debate as an ethicopolitical ideal. It has been claimed that such an ideal is too narrow in its conception of how political commitments find expression, and unable to comprehend nonrational forms of solidarity or aesthetic political practices (theatrical display, performativity, ironic critique). I argued in chapter 1 for a democratic model of politics that could acknowledge a wide range of forms of expression as possessing theoretical and political significance: in this sense I have no quarrel with those critics of Habermas who seek to emphasize affective or aesthetic modes. And I have suggested elsewhere in this volume, most particularly in the essay on pragmatism, that liberalism should remain open to a plurality of characterological and expressive modes, rather than seek to elevate a specific temperament or persona.

I would argue, however, that the accommodation of plural modes of expression still requires procedural elaboration if it is to have any political meaning or effectiveness, as McCarthy's own critique makes clear. In order to affect institutionalized deliberative procedures, nonrational forms of political expression require some form of translation into terms that can impact decision making and policy. While dramatic displays of protest that rely on theatrical tactics and visceral power cannot entirely be explained in rational terms, and can be recognized to have a force on their own terms, in order to affect policy they have to be translated into claims recognizable within existing political institutions. We do not remain inarticulate about the visceral if it effectively affects our political views and our social interactions.

A second critique that has been leveled against the argument model of politics focuses on the forces that mitigate against rational argumentative ideals. Gerald F. Gaus has argued specifically against the principle of sincerity presupposed in models of deliberative democracy.[26] His central claim is that sincerity will be more likely to produce disagreement than consensus, which always requires some fudging and bending, and which fares better under conditions of incomplete honesty. Ultimately we rely on the procedures of democracy as a kind of umpire: at some point we take a vote, not because we have been readied and steadied by exhaustive political debate, but because we need a way to adjudicate difference. Argument, Gaus contends, is a philosophical ideal, not a political one. Moreover, it cannot be seen to function empirically in the ways that certain political theorists would want. Gaus cites research on the heuristics employed in argument, which tend not so much toward some ideal of exhaustive consideration of information and viewpoints but more toward shortcuts: preeminently, vividness of example and available information. There is a desire for economy and also for closure. This, along with the studies that show that reasonable people often adhere to unreasonable beliefs even in the light of new information, makes the idea of exhaustive reasonable debate, for Gaus, impractical. It will tend to produce impasses of disagreement, no more.

From an empirical standpoint, Gaus's observations certainly make a good deal of sense: there are myriad ways in which rational argument is thwarted or truncated in political argument, and many practices of persuasion and achieved consensus rely precisely upon conditions of insincerity and adjudication. But this type of criticism is itself weak when it imagines it has delivered a fatal blow to theories that rely on an ideal of argument. First, it overstates the case against rational argument when it imagines that a pragmatic and almost cynical attitude prevails in the political arena, while idealism remains the dream of philosophers. Both philosophers and politicians in the democratic tradition have long argued in service of the kind of procedural ideals and universal principles that Habermas elaborates—and debate animated by these principles is readily identified even if it does not achieve pure forms or animate all

---

[26] Gerald F. Gaus, "Reason, Justification, and Consensus: Why Democracy Can't Have It All," in James Bohman and William Rehg, eds., *Deliberative Democracy: Essays on Reason and Politics* (Cambridge, Mass.: MIT Press, 1997), 205–42.

instances of discourse. In discussing the relation between philosophy and citizenship, and the need for philosophy to avoid either an apologetic relation to the status quo or a paternalistic role, Habermas insists upon the very close connection between the impartial standpoint of philosophy and the stance of social critique: "insofar as it draws on procedural properties of practical reason, [philosophy] can find *confirmation* in a perspective that it encounters in society itself: by the moral point of view from which modern societies are criticized by their own social movements."[27]

Moreover, what Habermas elsewhere refers to as "the process of argumentation" is a regulative idea, not an empirical reality, and communicative action oriented toward understanding relies upon presuppositions that are continuous with that idea. It is true that Habermas does not typically acknowledge the many ways in which actors can be irrational, but such an acknowledgment, along with the acknowledgments he does make about the ways in which speech situations fail to approximate the ideal, need not be fatal to the project. Second, and perhaps more tellingly, the very critique advanced by Gaus itself relies on the very ideal he intends to debunk. It is only possible to identify the many ways in which rational argument falls short if one is actually measuring against some standards of rational completeness.

Let me conclude by trying to summarize what I take to be the value of affirming argument as ethos, rather than privileging ethos in any of its other various guises—authentic ethical life, charismatic critique, or accommodating tact. While I understand the motivation behind McCarthy's critique of Habermas, his sense that we may need to expect disagreement more than aim for agreement, I think the Habermasian principle of "an intersubjective praxis of argumentation" more closely achieves the ideals of universalization and respect that undergird the democratic project. Simply accepting the views of others because they are asserted to be fundamentally linked to their nonnegotiable conceptions of the good or to their given cultural identity—accepting a merely overlapping consensus, or insisting on accommodation of ways and customs that may seem to jar with liberal democratic practice—seems to me precisely to fail in according the forms of respect that the model seems to claim for itself.[28]

I am not arguing that identity issues should be excluded from consideration, but simply that they should not be permitted to stand inviolable or uncontestable. Argument with those from whom we differ is a form

[27] Habermas, " 'Reasonable' versus 'True,' " 98.

[28] Another prime example of the accommodationist approach is James Tully, *Strange Multiplicity: Constitutionalism in an Age of Diversity* (Cambridge: Cambridge University Press, 1995).

of respect and it implies an aspiration to universalism. Committed to the possibility of agreement as well as the conditions of pluralism, it does not attempt to tame or stabilize disagreement: it is capable of reasoned disagreement, but it is perhaps more fundamentally characterized by a *dissatisfied* recognition of disagreement. To take a current example, the debate over the banning of the *hajib* (Muslim headscarf) and other religious symbols in schools in France has created a certain dialogical demand whose benefits outweigh, it seems to me, a situation in which clarification and articulation of self-reflective pluralism are simply avoided in the name of passive toleration. This is not to imply that this particular issue cannot be resolved in favor of toleration. What the French debate importantly demands is that citizens of a pluralist state go beyond peremptory appeals to cultural identity and clarify their understanding of what it means to live together under conditions of pluralism with the collective responsibility of providing education consonant with the secular principles of the state. This demand extends not only to Muslims and Jews, but also to the historically dominant Catholic population, whose own partial universalism is revealed in the attempt to include only "large crosses" in the ban. In this situation, there is a need to negotiate between differing forms of affiliation, as well as between political principle and cultural identity. The process of argument is what enables the very act of pluralist self-clarification to occur, and the society in question must cultivate an ethos of argument if it is to meet the ongoing challenges of its political (re)constitution.

When argument can itself be recognized as an ethos, disagreement remains live, not merely the nonnegotiable emanation of a pregiven cultural identity or holistic ethos. To put this in yet another way, tolerance and respect are not utterly coterminous, as the accommodationist position would have us believe. Indeed, if we collapse these terms, we are left in a situation where the tradition of sincerity—conceived of in its broadest terms as allied with critique and the promotion of political integrity—remains impotent in the face of peremptory appeals to authenticity. Proceduralism is itself a dialectical overcoming of the sincerity/authenticity problematic, but, unlike in Trilling, its polemical relation to received opinion is not in the service of nature, fate, or the unconscious, but rather in the service of an aspiration toward universalism.

Index